BURYING THE DEAD

AN ARCHAEOLOGICAL HISTORY OF BURIAL GROUNDS, GRAVEYARDS AND CEMETERIES

BURYING THE DEAD

AN ARCHAEOLOGICAL HISTORY OF BURIAL GROUNDS, GRAVEYARDS AND CEMETERIES

LORRAINE EVANS

PEN & SWORD HISTORY

AN IMPRINT OF PEN & SWORD BOOKS LTD.
YORKSHIRE - PHILADELPHIA

First published in Great Britain in 2020 by
Pen & Sword History
An imprint of
Pen & Sword Books Ltd
Yorkshire - Philadelphia

Copyright © 2020 Lorraine Evans

ISBN 978 1 52670 667 6

The right of Lorraine Evans to be identified as Author of this work has been asserted by her in accordance with the Copyright, Designs and Patents Act 1988.

A CIP catalogue record for this book is available from the British Library.

All rights reserved. No part of this book may be reproduced or transmitted in any form or by any means, electronic or mechanical including photocopying, recording or by any information storage and retrieval system, without permission from the Publisher in writing.

Printed and bound in England
By TJ Books Ltd.

Pen & Sword Books Ltd incorporates the Imprints of Pen & Sword Archaeology, Atlas, Aviation, Battleground, Discovery, Family History, History, Maritime, Military, Naval, Politics, Railways, Select, Transport, True Crime, Fiction, Frontline Books, Leo Cooper, Praetorian Press, Seaforth Publishing, Wharncliffe and White Owl.

For a complete list of Pen & Sword titles please contact
PEN & SWORD BOOKS LIMITED
47 Church Street, Barnsley, South Yorkshire, S70 2AS, England
E-mail: enquiries@pen-and-sword.co.uk
Website: www.pen-and-sword.co.uk

Or

PEN AND SWORD BOOKS
1950 Lawrence Rd, Havertown, PA 19083, USA
E-mail: uspen-and-sword@casematepublishers.com
Website: www.penandswordbooks.com

The one thing no man can judge you on is your effort. Your effort is one hundred per cent between you and you.

Ray Lewis – Baltimore Ravens Hall of Famer

Contents

Author's Note viii
Acknowledgments ix
Introduction x

1 The Pagan Way 1
2 Piety and Power 21
3 The Deviant Ones 41
4 They Died in Heaps 62
5 A Watery Grave 84
6 Boneyards of Steel 100
7 The Return of the Cemetery 113
8 Lest We Forget 133
9 Thinking Outside the Box 150

Appendix 1: The Burial Acts 169
Appendix 2: Graveyard Symbolism 172
Notes and References 176
Select Bibliography 195

Author's Note

All writings of a historical nature are clearly reliant on some form of chronological framework. Thereupon it was agreed that the timeframe for *Burying the Dead* would commence with the fall of the Roman Empire up to the present day. As one can imagine, with a vast timespan and finite word count, it has been impossible to discuss certain subject matters in depth. Because of this I have set up an accompanying website, whereby topics included in the book, or otherwise, can be expanded upon in much greater detail. I would also like to add that every effort has been made to contact all relevant copyright holders, to whom I am eternally grateful. However, at the end of the day I am only human, and if an error or omission has been made, I apologise most profusely.

Lorraine Evans
Orkney 2019

Burying the Dead can be followed at www.buryingthedead.com
Lorraine Evans can be followed at www.lorraineevans.com

Acknowledgments

I would like to express my gratitude to the following people for their invaluable support and assistance; to my publishers Pen and Sword, in particular to my commissioning editor Jonathan Wright, as well as Aileen Pringle and Laura Hirst for their patience and understanding during difficult times; to my copy editor extraordinare Kate Bohdanowicz for her advice, diligence and unwavering good nature; my GP Shona Forth who never gave up the fight, even when the odds looked bleak; to Gary Parsons for his unwavering friendship; to the Skye posse Pere Valfago, Aida Cristobal, Malcolm Browning and Amy Gregory for the coffee, laughs, good times and the inevitable 'have you finished writing that book yet?'; to both the Hendry and Baird families for their kindness and hospitality; Professor Adam Jones; Dr Alison Klevnäs; Michael Weatherhead at CADW; Professor Howard Williams; Brookwood Cemetery; Cromarty Museum; Cheri Horkman at Random Currents; the staff at Doxdirect; the staff at Storage Inverness; Suzie Lennox for invaluable advice; Dr George Simkiss; pacoulmag; Michel Wurtz; Kasper and Ali at Struy House; John Critchley; Lynn Kaczenski at the Natural History and Heritage Command US; Rob Hebblethwaite; Dr Jennifer Crangle; Katie at Memorial Reefs International; The Skull Society and John MacPherson. I would also like to extend my appreciation to those on certain social media platforms who have offered their support and knowledge unquestioningly.

Introduction

I have always had a fascination with the dead. Those who know me well would probably call it an obsession. Two defining moments from my childhood have shaped this fixation. The first was coming face-to-face with the golden mask of Tutankhamun, the ancient Egyptian pharaoh, while on a school trip to the British Museum. Call it my 'Indiana Jones' moment, but from that day forward I knew I wanted to be an archaeologist. The second happened a little closer to home and took place in South Ealing Cemetery in west London. Established in 1861, by the Ealing and Old Brentford Burial Board, both my grandfather and aunt are buried behind its walls and every weekend my grandmother, who had lived opposite the cemetery since the end of the Second World War, would take my brother and I into the cemetery to tend my grandfather's grave. I remember these visits vividly. I remember collecting water in an old, rusty tin watering can, while watching squirrels sprint from one side of the avenue to the other. I remember the large horse chestnut tree near the chapel, where my brother and I used to collect its fallen fruit in preparation for the autumnal conker season. I also remember the fear and trepidation I used to feel each time we visited my aunt's gravesite. For unlike my grandfather, who was buried in a bright, airy, expanse of tendered lawn, my aunt was interred in the old Victorian section of the cemetery, located adjacent to the boundary wall. It was a grim place; dark, dank and downright scary for a 9-year-old. Whenever we visited her grave, which was not often, I always had a feeling we were being watched. Surprising as it may sound, it was in these rare moments that my interest for burial grounds was born.

The meanings attached to death vary from one society to another, as does the disposal of the dead, which tells us much about how

Introduction

people perceived themselves and their world. Each community had a geographical space designated to cater for the deceased. Some of these spaces were deliberately located in relation to topographical features in the landscape, whereas others, as argued by archaeologist Professor Michael Parker Pearson, are invested with cosmological, social and/or political significance. Thousands of sites have been excavated over the centuries, which in turn has yielded tens of thousands of graves, and funerary artefacts, that provide a rich seam of archaeological evidence for the enthusiastic academic researcher. With the addition of an adventurous backstory, and a savvy social media campaign, the appeal of such mortuary evidence is often magnified as details of new discoveries swiftly enter the public domain. Considering the ruinous state of many burial grounds and cemeteries throughout the world, raising public awareness via a web-based platform must be applauded. In spite of the fact that such platforms are open to exploitation by nighthawkers, unscrupulous individuals who steal artefacts from protected archaeological sites, under the cover of darkness. In summary, cemetery archaeology not only provides an important source for social historians but, in many instances, for the committed lay person it provides a welcome distraction from an otherwise mundane world.

So how and where did our ancestors bury their dead? What has changed and what traditions have remained the same? After studying a wide range of pagan burial sites, together with the conversion to Christian practices, I took the decision to veer away from the more traditional chronological path and instead chose to explore those areas which may not be immediately apparent to the reader, such as mass graves, commemorative cemeteries, underwater sites and those of a non-organic nature, to name but a few. Within this framework I was able to uncover some compelling archetypes, such as a prostitutes' burial ground in London, a pirates' graveyard in the middle of the Indian Ocean, a Spanish burial cave full of mummies and a well-known American racing driver who is still perplexed by the cemetery of old NASCAR (National Association for Stock Car Auto Racing) vehicles that adorn his property. Oh, and not forgetting a shout out to the Gunfight at the O.K. Corral. Graveyard symbolism is also briefly addressed, complete with a guide of definitions. The final chapter is primarily concerned with the issues surrounding the current worldwide burial crisis and what alternatives are on offer.

Finally, a few words with regards to terminology. Expressions such as burial ground, cemetery, graveyard etc. are often interchangeable, yet there are subtle differences worth noting. A burial ground is just as it states, a site used primarily for interment and it can take on many guises, be it in a field, a cave, up a tree or even in water. Such sites usually have a sacred element attached to them, but they are not traditionally associated with regular religious worship. Naturally, there are exceptions to the rule, one example being the graveyards/churchyards found in the Highlands of Scotland that are often referred to as burial grounds. Graveyards and churchyards are almost always associated with a church, are located in the church environs and are places where the community congregate regularly for prayers. Cemeteries, on the other hand, are not defined as sites of religious worship and are for interment only. Having said that, archaeologists have uncovered many a post-hole in pagan Anglo-Saxon cemeteries, which they suggest could indicate a temple-like structure. Similarly, the Victorian garden cemeteries of the nineteenth century always have a church/chapel sited within the landscape, although it is important to stress that these were used for funerary services only. Likewise, Islamic cemeteries often have a mosque attached, but many were constructed after the site had been utilised for the purposes of burial. It is perhaps ironic that the word cemetery comes from the French word *cimetière*, which unhelpfully translates as 'graveyard'. I much prefer its original definition, believed to derive from the Greek *koimeterion*, meaning 'a sleeping place'. In each representative case the appropriate nomenclature has been assigned.

1

The Pagan Way

In September AD 476, the last Roman Emperor of the West, Romulus Augustulus, was deposed by a German warlord named Odoacer, a former officer in the Roman Army. His success was the culmination of a series of mitigating factors, such as a failing economy, imperial incompetence, a decrease in agricultural production, wide-scale corruption and attacks from Barbarian tribes, to name but a few. Although his origins are unclear, historian Edward Gibbons states that he was king of the Torcilingi, it is generally accepted that his ascension to power marked the end of the Roman Empire in western Europe.[1] The centralised super state that had ruled for approximately 500 years had been vanquished, replaced by dozens of independent kingdoms. Understandably this is a massive oversimplification of a complicated series of events, but for the purposes of our investigation it is important to note that with the implementation of new social structures there came a new kind of funerary provision, a breed of formalised cemetery that would have a profound effect on the European landscape. In Britain it heralded a series of dramatic transformations, with the immigration of various Anglo-Saxon groups from Northern Europe disseminating new ideologies and mortuary practices across much of lowland Britain.

The study of Anglo-Saxon burial practices is a good place to commence our inquiry. Not only is there considerable diversity in the archaeological record, but the surviving textual and material evidence attests to the evolution from pagan to early medieval Christian rites, where the use of field cemeteries is systematically replaced by churchyard interment. In truth, the archaeology of early Anglo-Saxon England is dominated by the cemetery evidence with around 1,200 individual sites and fifty or so large field cemeteries having been securely identified so far. It is generally accepted that the study of early cemeteries began in 1653, when workers near St Brice's Church, Tournai, Belgium, uncovered the treasure-laden fifth-century royal burial of King Childeric. However, the earliest record of an Anglo-Saxon excavation dates to the twelfth century, when several monks are reported to have dug up the burial mounds at Redbourne, Hertfordshire, in search of the bones of St Amphibalus.[2] The first antiquarian record is attributed to Thomas Browne who, in the seventeenth century, published a pamphlet entitled *Hydriotaphia Urne-Buriall*, which documented a number of early medieval graves at Walsingham in Norfolk.[3] Between 1759 and 1773 barrow-digger Bryan Faussett excavated a number of cemeteries in Kent, uncovering around 750 graves in the process. He mistakenly attributed them to Roman Britain.[4] James Douglas, who excavated a number of sites between 1779 and 1793, including those at Chatham Lines and Greenwich Park, is often regarded as the first excavator to correctly identify his findings as Anglo-Saxon.[5] From the mid-nineteenth century, cemeteries, burial mounds and funerary sculpture would make interesting reading in local newspapers and journals, culminating with a new zeal of exploration in the twentieth century that lead to such wonderful discoveries as the high-status cemetery site at Sutton Hoo near Woodbridge in Suffolk.[6] Due to these people's efforts, the discerning scholar now has a vast database of funerary evidence available to hand.

Cremation and inhumation were both practised by the early Anglo-Saxons, the latter appearing first, sometime in the middle of the fifth century, with each typically accompanied by grave goods, such as weaponry, food and jewellery. There are many examples of mixed-rite cemeteries throughout this period, each co-existing harmoniously with the other, such as Portway, in Andover, Hampshire and Mucking and Great Chesterford in Essex. Cemetery II at Mucking, which dates from the fifth to the early seventh century, is one of the largest and most complete Anglo-Saxon cemeteries yet excavated, totalling 282 inhumations and 463 cremations.[7] The use and size of cremation-only cemeteries varied tremendously depending on where they were located. Cemeteries in certain areas of eastern England were at least twice the size of those where inhumation was the only or the predominant burial rite. It is estimated that two of the largest known cremation cemeteries, Spong Hill in Norfolk and Loveden Hill in Lincolnshire, may have contained up to 3,000 cremations.[8] If you consider that the cremation rite only lasted for approximately 200 years, the size of these cemeteries is truly extraordinary.

Inhumations are found throughout southern and eastern England and vary widely in design, with burials exhibiting either a cluster, row or linear pattern of arrangement.[9] Individual graves could be irregular, square or circular in shape; some were flat whereas others had scooped floors. Some burials resembled just a hollow in the ground, such as those at Horton Kirby in Kent, where a number of the corpses had to be bent/moulded into a specific position in order to fit into the tiny grave space.[10] Body positioning varied, with supine (placed on the back), the most common, but others have been found buried prone (on the front) or on their sides. Although the majority of graves were designed for a single inhumation, multiple burials during this period are not unknown. Evidence of possible mortuary markers has been detected in a few cemeteries in the guise of post-holes and slots, such as the one uncovered at Sewerby, East Yorkshire, where archaeologists found a layer of chalk covering three separate burials in association with at least one post-hole.[11] Circular and rectangular ditches are sometimes located within the cemetery and appear to demarcate the burial space.[12]

Anglo-Saxon graves also display an assortment of orientations, although south-north and west-east appears to be most common. Why this is so is not known. There are numerous ethnographic examples of grave orientation being related to a place of mythical origin, or to other forms of cosmological principles.[13] Some have argued a Christian influence whereas the local topography, including other ancient structures, could also be a factor.[14] The reuse of monuments from earlier periods appears to be commonplace, with Roman and prehistoric structures providing a focus for Anglo-Saxon cemeteries and burial groups. For example, archaeologist Professor Richard Bradley has argued that the positioning and alignment of timber halls and burial sites at Yeavering and Millfield in Northumberland sought deliberately to reuse long-abandoned prehistoric monuments.[15] Indeed many cemeteries exhibit remarkable continuity over time, an excellent example is Wasperton in Warwickshire, which originally began life as a Romano-British burial site dating to the third century. Towards the end of the fifth century Anglian cremations can easily be identified and were deposited within a specific fenced area inside the cemetery boundary. A few decades later the burial rite changed to furnished inhumation, with grave goods identifying individuals from the East Anglia region and later from Wessex. In the sixth century, rich persons of Anglo-Saxon heritage were buried in purpose-built barrow mounds, with one particular individual, of obvious high status, interred in an already existing Bronze Age barrow. The use of barrow mounds was the final mortuary practice to be adopted and effectively closed the cemetery.[16]

According to Professor Howard Williams, Bronze Age round barrows are by far the favoured choice for reuse by the early Anglo-Saxons, constituting sixty-one per cent of all known cases.[17] Other favoured monuments include Neolithic megaliths, earthen long barrows, Iron Age square barrows, prehistoric henges, stone circles, monoliths, linear earthworks, hillforts, ringworks and well, any ancient enclosure they took a liking to. Such a proclivity appears to date back to the fifth century, where Anglo-Saxon grave reuse has been uncovered in a number of large pre-existing cemeteries, such as Saxton Road, Abingdon, Oxfordshire[18] and Bishopstone in Sussex.[19] At some cemetery sites this included a few isolated graves and/or small burial groups deliberately placed at the highest point of an ancient monument.[20] At others the entire Anglo-Saxon cemetery appears to have been carefully secreted in between adjacent monumental structures. Existing prehistoric and Roman structures were also used to denote the cemetery boundary, such as the Bronze Age ringwork at Springfield Lyons in Essex and the Roman signal station at Thornham, Norfolk.[21] The entire reuse practice appears to have reached a crescendo in the seventh century among 'final phase' cemeteries, a term often used to describe cemeteries that exhibit some form of Christian influence, such as those at Marina Drive, Dunstable in Bedfordshire and Snells Corner, Horndean in Hampshire.[22]

Why the Anglo-Saxons chose to use the burial landscapes of their predecessors in this manner is not fully understood, but it has been suggested it was central to the construction of identity and social structure. In *Death and Memory in Early Medieval Britain*, Williams argues that 'the choice to reuse sites is likely to have been a deliberate appropriation of an unknown past, imbuing the monument with new meanings that served to create connections to an invented ancestral past, and perhaps also to stake claims for the future.'[23] Taking this into consideration, maybe Anglo-Saxon cemeteries were not simply viewed by the community as just a collection of graves, but also as places of power in the landscape, where the living, the dead, the ancestors (real or invented), and the past were communicated.[24] On a more practical level the adoption of barrow mounds – artificial high places in the landscape – makes perfect strategic sense. Here smaller elite groups could direct the rest of the society for whatever purpose necessary. Such cemeteries, therefore, rendered a political influence within its territory. A perfect demonstration of this policy can be found in the mound cemeteries of fifth-century Japan, where numerous 300-metre-long monumental keyhole-shaped hills, called *kofan*, emerged during the formation of the powerful Yamato state. The Yamato dynasty is attributed with the unification of the southern provinces under a single ruling emperor, the ancestors of today's Imperial family. The Mozu tombs of Sakai City, which once numbered 100, are particularly significant – the mound tomb of Emperor Nintoku being the largest in existence (821 metres) – as they act as a form of political centralisation, thereby legitimising the Imperial family's right to rule.[25] It has been suggested that the construction of barrow mounds by the wealthy social elite in Anglo-Saxon England served a similar purpose. At the world-renowned burial ground of Sutton Hoo, a small seventh-century cemetery, designated number two, was erected on a separate site away from other burials. In use for barely sixty years, it became monumental in size and form, and housed a variety of elaborate interments, such as a horse burial, a chamber burial, a bed burial and the world-famous treasure-laden ship burial. It has been inferred, by some, that the construction of this new elite cemetery was in direct response to the politically charged atmosphere prevalent at that time and was important for declaring monarchical control. It also coincided with the arrival of Christianity, leaving others to suggest that mound-building was an act of 'asserted independence and a statement of defiance in the face of perceived Christian provocation', which threatened to undermine the kingdom's relations with its natural allies across the North Sea.[26]

Akin to the Anglo-Saxon elite cemeteries in southern England is the site of Gamla Uppsala, one of the most sacred places in Scandinavia. Located in south-eastern Sweden, it once comprised a pagan temple, renowned throughout Northern Europe, a number of palatial buildings and a vast cemetery complex with 2,000-3,000 barrow mounds. Only 300 mounds remain visible to the naked eye today as the vast majority have been ploughed over by successive farming activity. Of the surviving examples, three appear to have special significance. Measuring between twenty-nine and thirty-two feet in height, folklore has attributed them to the gods Odin, Freyr and Thor, while traditional sources state they belong to the kings of the Yngling dynasty – the term 'Yngling' is tellingly derived from the fertility god Freyr.[27] According to the *Ynglinga Saga*, written by Icelandic poet and historian Snorri Sturlurson in 1225, the kings Aun, Egil and Adils are buried somewhere within the Uppsala necropolis.[28]

Dating to the fifth and sixth century, the three supposed Royal Mounds have been labelled Eastern Mound, Middle Mound and Western Mound, with only two out of the three fully explored so far. The first to be excavated was the Eastern Mound, in 1846, under the direction of the Custodian of National Antiquities Bror Emil Hildebrand. Reaching nine metres in height and seventy-five by fifty-five metres in width, at its base there had been deposited a burial urn believed to contain the burnt remains of a woman and a young boy, the latter around 10 to 14 years of age. Analysis of the burnt material also revealed the presence of high-status goods including at least three dogs, a hunting hawk, bone from bear claws, a tiny bone in the shape of a duck, a bone comb, some gaming pieces and remains of glass beakers.[29] The Western Mound, also under the direction of Hildebrand, was opened in 1874, measures around ten metres in height and sixty-seven metres by fifty-one metres in width and is often referred to as a 'princely burial'. The original excavation report documents the presence of a man and a woman, but a fresh look at the evidence in 1999 confirmed the mound actually contained just one man, possibly a prince or a warrior based upon the accompanying grave goods, which included part of a sword mount, two dogs, a goshawk, ivory gaming pieces, gold fittings and the remains of two glass beakers.[30] The Middle Mound has never been fully investigated and the burial inside, if there is one, remains intact. Moreover, in 1973, on ground located to the west of Old Uppsala Church, thought by many to sit upon the foundations of the original pagan temple, four boat graves, one horse grave and five cremation burials were uncovered. One of the boat graves contained the remains of an elderly woman dressed in the finest silk, probably from China, with a pendant depicting Freya, the goddess of fertility, placed around her neck.[31] If any further proof of the site's importance was necessary, in November 2018 two further boat graves were unexpectedly found by archaeologists during an excavation at the old vicarage. Discovered beneath a cellar and a well, one of the graves was remarkably intact and included the remains of a man, a dog and a horse.[32]

Boat and/or ship graves had special significance to the people of Northern Europe, as is demonstrated by the following two examples, namely the iconic pre-Viking Scandinavian grave cemeteries of Vendel and Valsgärde, located to the north of Uppsala. Dating to AD 550-800, and the site of a much larger pre-Christian burial ground, Vendel was the first to be excavated, in 1881, and subsequently gave its name to the archaeological period. A total of fourteen boat burials were unearthed but regrettably all had succumbed to the activities of tomb robbers. The first burial, Vendel 1, was found by accident by workmen digging a foundation trench for the local church. It was later discovered that the workmen, believing they had stumbled across a gold hoard, had indiscriminately hacked their way through the site, using picks and crowbars, destroying much of the grave and most of the grave goods within, including a helmet and at least three glass vessels. 'A visiting smith then took up the sword and took a swing with it, "to test the steel" breaking it into pieces,' quoted lead archaeologist Hjalmar Stolpe.[33] In the spring of 1882, Stolpe returned to the site and found a further ten boat graves, predominantly sited around the wall of the church. No more discoveries were made until 1893, when gravediggers excavating the new part of the churchyard found some clinker rivets. They subsequently ransacked the area, and in doing so destroyed a helmet, a shield, three swords, and a glass vessel.[34] This particular grave is known as Vendel XII and appears to have been one of the few burials untouched by ancient grave robbers, only for it to be destroyed upon discovery. In an effort to locate any remaining burials, and prevent further destruction, Stolpe dug a number of exploratory trenches, unearthing Vendel XIV. A boat-shaped patch of richer grass near the sites main road also revealed Vendel XIII, which was probably intact until the building of a nearby road damaged it beyond all recognition.[35]

In his archaeological summing up, Stolpe recorded that each burial was in a poor state of preservation, the wooden sides of each boat had rotted away and their rivets were loose in the soil: 'The stern of the boat was completely rifled, so that the clinker nails lay spread here and there in the fill.'[36] Few human remains were found suggesting that the original grave robbers were able to focus their efforts on the spot where the body lay. Animal offerings, including horses, dogs, cattle, swine and sheep, were fully disarticulated, while metallic grave goods were left broken in the disturbed fills. Archaeologists now believe that the reopening of the boat graves probably took place during the thirteenth century, before or during the construction of the nearby church, as there is evidence of widespread reworking of monuments at this time, with special significance accorded to interred human remains.[37]

In direct comparison to its neighbour, the cemetery at Valsgärde was strategically sited on a group of small hills, alongside the Fyris River, a major traffic artery for long-distance travel to continental Europe. First excavated in the 1920s, by archaeologists from Uppsala University, and then again in the 1950s, not only did the site house a significant number of boat burials but also the remains of chamber tombs, cists and sixty-two cremations, which were contemporary with the boat interments. The boat burials, numbering fifteen, were initially found in 1928, half a century later than those at Vendel, when a local farmer came across a large horse skull, complete with gilded bridle, while tending his crops. Thirteen out of the fifteen burials had been strategically placed in a continual line, at various distances apart, while the remaining three boat burials, numbers five, six and seven, were located on the other side of a thoroughfare that is believed to have once passed through the cemetery environs. Each boat was constructed from either oak or pine and measured between eight to twelve metres in length. Five of them date from the Vendel period – the first burial taking place at the beginning of the seventh century – with the remaining ten dating from the Viking period. Archaeologists believe the boats would probably have been functional throughout their lifetime, used as a mode of transport to traverse the surroundings streams or lakes.[38] Dragged up onto dry land, as the burial took place, they were then covered with soil. Each housed a number of high-status grave goods including highly decorated weapons and gaming pieces, together with the remains of animals, but again little human skeletal material. In Boat Grave 1 a few pieces of a tibia were found, Boat Grave 4 the remains of a tooth, Boat Grave 6 a femur and Boat Grave 13 a small metatarsal.[39]

Boat burials are not exclusive to Sweden and can be found throughout Northern Europe during the latter part of the first millennium, such as

The Pagan Way

the astonishingly well-preserved Viking ship from Oseberg, Norway. Excavated in 1904, it contained the remains of two women along with a wide variety of high-status grave goods. Gokstad, also in Norway, has another fine example, as does Ladby in Denmark. A boat grave containing a man with high-status weapons, together with a young child, was unearthed in Kaldárhöfði, Iceland in 1946, while in 2008 the remains of a ship burial were uncovered in Salme, Estonia, which contained the skeletal remains of seven men.[40] Two individual boat burials, each dating to the Viking period, have been found in Scotland. The first is the Scar boat burial from Sandy, Orkney, discovered by a farmer in 1985, which contained a rich array of grave goods as well as the remains of three individuals, a man of around 30, an older woman of approximately 70 and a child of around 10. The second Scottish boat grave was found in 2011, in Swordle Bay, located to the north of the Ardnamurchan Peninsula, on Scotland's west coast. Thought to date to the tenth century, it contained atypical warrior accoutrements, including the remnants of a sword, axe, a shield and a drinking horn mount.[41] Comparable high-status examples in England include the sixth-century, fourteen-metre boat burial unearthed at Snape Anglo-Saxon Cemetery, Suffolk, in 1862, by local landowner Septimus Davidson, and the world-renowned Sutton Hoo ship burial, which also dates to the Anglo-Saxon period, that was found in the Royal Burial Ground at Sutton Hoo, Suffolk. Historians believe the cemetery once belonged to the Wuffingas, the royal dynasty of East Anglia.[42] There are approximately eighteen burial mounds at Sutton Hoo, all dating to the seventh century. Most were opened and robbed during antiquity, including the so-named Mound Two that previously housed a large boat burial. The most famous burial of them all is King's Mound One, which once contained a huge twenty-seven-metre ship burial. Remaining hidden for millennia, its existence was not uncovered until 1939, when local archaeologist Basil Brown was invited to excavate the site by landowner, Mrs Edith Pretty. Originally made of oak, little remained of the ship as its wooden foundations had been destroyed by the acidic nature of the sand. Only a 'ghost' imprint in the soil could be ascertained. Yet in its centre, Brown found an untouched burial chamber housing one of the greatest treasure hoards ever discovered, including the gold and *cloisonné* regalia of a warrior king, weapons, silver feasting equipment, exquisite items of jewellery and endless riches to accompany the king on his final journey.⁴³ The treasure is now on display in the British Museum.

As the ruling elite of Northern Europe were being laid to rest in their elaborate burial mounds, thousands of miles away in the Americas, on the Yucatan Peninsula, comparable high-status individuals were being interred in equally spectacular chambers and tombs. Stretching for over 181,000 square kilometres, the Yucatan Peninsula, in south-eastern Mexico, separates the Caribbean Sea from the Gulf of Mexico, and was once home to the indigenous Mayan civilisation, their dominance extending into what is now present day Guatemala and Honduras.⁴⁴ The area is proliferated with archaeological sites, including such gems as Chichen Itza, Tulum and Uxmal, but it is the mid to late Classic Period, AD 450-900, regarded by many as the golden age of the Mayan empire, which is of particular interest. With the Mayan population reaching its zenith, it was the age of lavish tombs, pyramid structures and rare necropolises.

As with other major civilisations, the burial practices of the Maya were varied and evolved considerably over time; the earliest period is characterised by simple burials in a hole in the ground, the skeleton laid to rest in a traditional flexed position. Cremation was not introduced until a later date.⁴⁵ The chosen burial site was usually oriented to provide access to 'Xibalba', the Mayan otherworld, where the graves would face either north or west, in the direction of the heavens.⁴⁶ Some ritualised burial grounds have also been found located in caves, or cenotes, the designated entrances to the Underworld, such as Sac Actun in Quintana Roo, and the remarkable Actun Tunichil Muknal cave system, located in the jungles of Belize, which was found to house the remains of children all depicting signs of ritual sacrifice. Discovered in 1989, and dating from AD 700-900, the skeletal remains vary in age, with the youngest victim believed to be around 1-year-old. Almost all were killed by blunt force trauma to the head. One victim, the 'Crystal Maiden', was an 18-year-old female who appeared to have experienced a particularly gruesome end. Both her skull and vertebrae were crushed into pieces, while the rest of her calcite-covered remains were deposited in the far reaches of the cave.⁴⁷

Large scale cemeteries are not prolific, but the odd one does exist, such as Jaina Island, located just over eighty kilometres north of the city of Campeche. Here, a small limestone outcrop called 'Hail na', meaning 'house of water', served as an elite Maya burial ground comprising over 20,000 graves. Around 1,000 graves have been excavated so far, each one containing a single skeleton buried with one, sometimes two, brightly coloured clay figurines, either placed upon their chests or gripped in their hands.[48] The majority of the population, including some high-status officials, were generally buried under or adjacent to the family residence, in what are often termed 'household burial shrines', and were often sited on the east side of residential plazas.[49] In the case of the officials, they would normally be laid to rest inside a stone sarcophagus housed within a specially constructed burial vault. Royal figures have also been found buried in this manner. For example, in the northern rainforests of Guatemala, in 2007, archaeologists digging under the royal palace site at El Perú-Waka found a burial of what they believe to be a Mayan king. This vast city complex had been hidden for years, enveloped by centuries of dense vegetation, and was only rediscovered by chance in the 1960s when a group of petroleum workers stumbled across the ruins while surveying the area. The burial itself contained the remains of a well-built man adorned with gold, jewels and a red-painted jade mask, depicting him as the 'Maize God', his forehead inscribed with symbolic lettering. Other artefacts included several ceramic vessels and a crocodile pendant. No inscriptions were found inside the tomb to identify the remains but the co-director of the excavation, David Freidel, Professor of Anthropology at Washington University, St Louis, believes the remains could belong to King Te' Chan Aka, a known dynastic ruler.[50]

Another feature of this period was the utilisation of pyramid structures, exclusively reserved for the Mayan ruling elite, as found at the temple site of Palenque in southern Mexico. Described as 'vast, mysterious and enchanting', a number of spectacular funerary pyramids dominate the ritual landscape, the largest being the Temple of Inscriptions, which was only uncovered 200 years ago. Archaeologists believe it was constructed sometime between AD 683-702, and when it was fully excavated in the 1950s, the intact skeleton of King K'inich Janaab Pakal, a Mayan King of great repute who ruled the city-state of Palenque for over seventy years, was found. Buried inside an elaborately decorated sarcophagus, he was wearing a delicate death mask crafted from the finest jade, surrounded by goods and offerings, including sacrificial humans, to sustain him in the next life. Adjacent to the Temple of Inscriptions is a smaller pyramid, labelled Temple XIII, which was first excavated in 1994 by Arnoldo González Cruz, the archaeological director of Palenque, and his team. Having dug a tunnel into the heart of the pyramid, they found three separate chambers, the first two were empty, whereas the third, and largest, was sealed by a wall. After painstakingly removing the wall, block by block, they found two sets of human remains lying beside a large stone sarcophagus; one was of an adolescent male, approximately 11 years of age, the other an adult female in her thirties. Both demonstrated evidence of sacrificial ritual. Inside the sarcophagus were the remains of an old woman, between 50 to 60 years of age, covered in red cinnabar powder, earning her the epithet the 'Red Queen'. She had been interred with a great many riches, including necklaces, wristlets and earrings made from jade, pearls and other precious stones, and her skull was crowned with a diadem constructed of flat circular jade beads. Deposited in her chest area were more flat jade beads, four obsidian blades and a tiny limestone figurine inside a seashell. Broken pieces of malachite, which would have once formed her death mask, lay around her upper torso. Who this woman was remains a mystery, albeit she had to have been of exceptionally high status to be buried next to Pakal. DNA testing on her remains discounted a familial relationship, so the latest thinking is that she was probably Pakal's wife.[51]

Staying in the Americas, in 1999, during routine maintenance work beneath an old shanty town in Lima, Peru, workmen stumbled across an Inca necropolis containing over 2,200 mummies. Hidden for over 600 years, a team of Peruvian and American archaeologists were hastily put together to excavate the cemetery before scavengers and grave robbers could plunder the site. Unable to dig directly under the houses, the archaeologists were frustratingly confined to the streets and open spaces surrounding the burial ground. Nevertheless, they successfully excavated more than 1,200 'funerary bundles', in essence where a mummified body and possessions are carefully wrapped together before being buried. This number included rare high-ranking burials called *'cabezas falsas'*, or 'false-head' bundles, where a protuberance at the apex of the mummy wrapping is filled with cotton to resemble a human head. Only one such false-head Incan funerary bundle had ever been found before. Some of the excavated mummies were still wearing their distinctive Incan feathered headdresses, whereas one remarkable find, nicknamed the 'Cotton King', was wrapped in 300 pounds of raw cotton, together with the mummified remains of a baby. In addition, approximately seventy funerary items were buried with him, including food, pottery, animal skins and corn to make a fermented drink known as chicha. Almost half the mummies unearthed were of children.[52]

The art of mummification was not the sole preserve of the ancient Egyptians, as many believe, but was practised by a variety of pagan cultures, each putting their own mark on this unique funerary practice. The arid coastline of South America, stretching from Peru in the north to Chile in the south, gave rise to some of the world's earliest examples of deliberate mummification; for instance the Chinchorro people began to mummify their dead some 2,000 years before the ancient Egyptians. Successive civilisations have followed suit. In 1925, archaeologists Julio Tello and Toriba Xesspe discovered Huaca Malèna, an ancient burial ground of the Wari culture, a civilisation that once flourished in the Andes between the seventh and twelfth century. Located around ninety-seven kilometres south of Lima, the remains of 300 mummies were unearthed, each carefully wrapped in woven fabric.[53] The Nazca culture, another Peruvian people, often mummified their dead before placing them in mud-brick tombs. Unfortunately, their most famous burial ground, Chauchilla Cemetery, like many other ancient sites in South America, fell foul to the activities of grave robbers. A concerted effort by the Peruvian Government, however, has now restored Chauchilla to its former glory, or thereabouts, with many of the disinterred human remains returned to their tombs. Dating to the height of the Nazca culture, around AD 450-800, the Chauchilla mummies are in a remarkable state of preservation, with many still retaining their hair and skin. A unique collection of rare mummified heads has also been found on site, each with a series of holes drilled into the back of the skull. Archaeologists are still perplexed as to what said practice represents.[54]

In the northern Philippines, along the mountain slopes of Kabayan, the indigenous people known as the Ibaloi also mummified their dead before placing them inside wooden coffins and depositing them in vast burial caves. One cave named Timbac is thought to contain the remains of over 200 tribal members. Sometimes referred to as 'Fire Mummies', due to the unique method of using fire to 'smoke' the corpse, the Kabayan Mummy Caves, together with other mummies found in neighbouring caves in Benguit, comprise some of the most endangered burial grounds in the world.[55] The majority of the burials date from 1200-1500 and the use of mummification appears to have ceased when the Spanish colonised the islands in the sixteenth century. Although local communities had known of their existence for years, it wasn't until the twentieth century, when logging activity intensified in the forests north of Manila, that outside workers came across the ancient burial caves full of coffins, and skulls. With little security or protection, many of the mummies were subsequently stolen or vandalised, such as Apo Annu, an important tribal leader whose mummy was stolen by a visiting Filipino pastor in the early 1900s. Missing for decades, his remains finally turned up in 1984 when an antiquities collector donated them to the National Museum. He was later returned to his ancestral home, Nabalicong Village, where he was reinterred in the burial cave from whence he was taken. In 1998, the World Monuments Fund placed the burial caves on their Monuments Watch list, securing funding from American Express for their conservation and the creation of a comprehensive management plan. It is believed that since 1999 around eighty mummies have gone missing from the caves. Today, the remains are protected by both the government and the Ibaloi tribe, and the whereabouts of many of the mummy caves remain a closely guarded secret.[56]

Among the thousands of archaeological discoveries throughout Europe during the twentieth century the Guanche mummies, found in burial caves and crags on the island of Tenerife, have to rate as one of the most compelling. Originating from the Berber tribes of North Africa, the Guanches were the indigenous inhabitants of the Canary Islands, who are believed to have migrated to the archipelago in around 1,000 BC. Their existence was first documented by Spanish explorers in the fourteenth century, who conveniently noted that the general population was predominantly buried in simple sandy graves, whereas the elite were mummified and laid to rest in secluded caves.[57] Tragically, the Guanche civilisation was all but destroyed in the fifteenth century when invading Spanish conquistadors plundered the islands. Those that survived the slaughter were shipped off to Spain to spend the rest of their lives in servitude. Those that remained were forced to abandon their traditional lifestyle for ever.[58]

The Pagan Way

Like the Ibaloi tribe, the Guanche mummy caves have undergone systematic grave robbing for centuries. For instance, when a Guanche necropolis was excavated in 1933, in the district of San Miguel de Abona in southern Tenerife, archaeologists discovered the entire cemetery had been looted. Called Uchova, it is estimated that it once contained the burials of sixty to seventy-four mummies. Many of the known mortuary caves are believed to have contained up to 1,000 mummies at any one time, but only twenty complete mummies remain throughout the island chain, the majority of which are housed in the Museum of Nature and Mankind in Santa Cruz, Tenerife.[59] One of the most famous is the Guanche Mummy of Madrid, a man in his early thirties, who died sometime between the eleventh and twelfth century AD. His mummified remains were stolen from a burial cave in Barranco de Herques, south of Tenerife, by persons unknown, before being gifted to King Charles III of Spain sometime in the eighteenth century. Languishing in the royal library for a number of years the mummy is now on display at Spain's National Archaeological Museum in Madrid.[60]

Recently, in 2018, two local spider hunters, Sergio Marrero and Domingo Garcia, came across the mummified remains of two Guanche infants while exploring a cave near the town of Guía de Isora in western Tenerife. Initial tests found that one child, carefully wrapped in animal skin, was in an excellent state of preservation, with both soft tissue and organs intact, while only skeletal fragments from the other had survived. Dr Conrado Rodriguez-Maffiotte, Director of the Canarian Institute of Bioanthropology, believes the cave, which sits some 1,390 metres above sea level, was once a Guanche burial ground dating back to the fifteenth or sixteenth century. 'I have never seen a ritual burial of two babies together,' he said excitedly. It is the first Guanche mummy cave to be found on the island since 1969.[61]

Burial within caves was a common phenomenon during European prehistory – albeit its popularity wavered – and human remains within cave sediments have often been found during excavations. One of the oldest was discovered in 1823, by the geologist and palaeontologist William Buckland, inside Paviland Cave on the Gower Peninsula, South Wales. Mistakenly dubbed the 'Red Lady of Paviland', as the skeletal remains had been dusted with red ochre, recent analysis has revealed it to be the remains of a young man, dating to c. 35,000 BC.[62] Recently the remains of a Pictish man, possibly of royal birth, were found deposited in a Rosemarkie cave on the Black Isle, Scotland. Discovered in 2016, by a team of archaeologists from the Rosemarkie Caves Project, the skeleton was found in a cross-legged position with a number of stones weighing down his limbs. Evidence showed he had suffered a brutal death, with the skull displaying severe cranial and facial injuries.[63] Another extraordinary example is Cloghermore Cave in County Kerry, Ireland, where pagan-style interment continued up to the ninth century, when the use of the cave for burial purposes was taken over by the Vikings.[64]

In some parts of the world the funerary custom is still practised, or its proclivity is remembered by those currently living. One such place is Hawaii, USA, where generations of family members would traditionally be buried inside a cave alongside their ancestors; the cave was believed to be the residence of their spirit. Highly ritualised in nature, the burial process would commence immediately after death, when the bones and organs would be carefully removed and preserved in salt. The upper part of the body would then be lifted, with the face bent towards the knees in a standardised foetal position shape, and fastened with cord. It was then wrapped in a coarse mat before being interred inside the cave. Archaeologists excavating in 1961 wrote: 'The skull rests on a pillow and white cotton cloth is wrapped around the pelvis, ribs and near the skull. Brown gala fragments lie near the feet.' Later burials, those found closest to the cave entrance, were buried in an extended pose, possibly caused by the influence of Christian missionaries, who arrived on the islands in the nineteenth century.[65] One missionary from England, Reverend William Ellis, wrote in his diary in 1825:

> Sometimes the inhabitants of a village deposited their dead in one large cavern, but in general each family had a distinct sepulchral cave. Inside their artificial grave were either simple pits dug into the earth, or large enclosures. One of the latter, which we saw at Keahou, was a space surrounded by high stone walls, appearing much like an ancient temple. We proposed to several natives of the village to accompany us on a visit to it, and give us an outline of its history, but they appeared startled

at the thought, said it was a Sahi (evil place), filled with dead bodies, and objected so strongly to our approaching it.[66]

Hawaiian chiefs, their families and other social elites had their own secret burial caves, away from the general population, the location of which was closely guarded by a family retainer or 'kahu'. These were hidden by stone wall emplacements, to resemble the surrounding cliff, but they did little good. When the authorities began to document and catalogue the caves, they discovered to their dismay that most of them had already been ransacked and looted.[67] It is a practice that continues to this day. In 2004, it was reported that artefacts and human remains that had been reinterred in Kanupa Cave, Kohala – a burial cave for lesser chiefs – at the end of 2003, had begun to appear for sale on the black market. According to those who had attended the night-time reburial, after the bones and artefacts had been placed inside the lower levels of the cave system, a number of large boulders had been placed over the entrance to protect it from grave robbers. However, less than a year later the stones had been removed and the entrance to the cave lay wide open.[68] Similarly, during the summer of 2004, repatriated items from the Joseph Emerson collection, including items from the Captain Cook expedition and a rare palaoa – a hook-shaped ornament hanging on a necklace of human hair – were offered to private collectors. These objects had originally been found by Emerson in Kanupa Cave. The sale of such objects is illegal under state and federal laws, including the 1990 Native American Graves Protection and Repatriation Act. When questioned by federal agents, working with the US Department of the Interior, the collectors said that the dealer who approached them was supposedly acting as a 'fence' for others and told them that he had obtained the items from 'a local Hawaiian guy who said he found them in a cave.' Investigations are continuing into this worrying trend.[69]

Lying to the east of Borneo is the island of Sulawesi, one of the four largest Sunda Islands of Indonesia and the eleventh largest island in the world. To the south of the island is the mountainous region of Tana Toraja, home to the Toraja people, meaning 'people of the uplands', an indigenous ethnic group renowned for their elaborate funerary rites, including burial within sacred cave sites. The Toraja believe they are descended from the stars, whereas the ground they inhabit equates to the Earth Mother. It was she who gave life to the land and, because of this, the Toraja believe that burial into the soil is a sacrilegious act, dishonouring her name. Many, therefore, bury their dead away from the ground in hollowed-out caves, usually in the face of a cliff, sometimes as much as thirty metres high. Those of high-ranking status would be buried furthest up the cliff face, while those from the lesser ranks would be buried in caves lower down. Inside the caves the majority of the remains are left out in the open, the skeletons exposed for all to see, and an effigy called a 'tau tau' is sometimes placed at the cave entrance to guard the spirit of the dead. Some corpses are buried in coffins, which are hung from the cave entrance, or the cliff walls, where they remain in situ until the rope holding them in place snaps or the coffin finally disintegrates, scattering the bones across the floor below. One burial cave at Londa, in the Sanggalangi district, has now become a worldwide tourist attraction. Around 1,000 metres deep in places, the cave houses an assortment of bones and skulls, some over 400 years old, together with artefacts buried with the deceased. For around ten dollars, visitors can hire a local tribesman to guide them through the jungle vegetation to the base of the cave.[70]

Dug into the steep isolated hills of Upper Mustang in northern Nepal, alongside the Kali Gandaki River, lies a series of over 10,000 man-made funerary caves. Mustang was formerly known as the Kingdom of Lo, before it was annexed by Nepal at the end of the eighteenth century, with Upper Mustang a restricted demilitarised area until 1992. For this reason it is only in the last few decades that archaeologists have been able to explore these remote caves and their investigations have uncovered a wealth of artefacts, including priceless Buddhist paintings and manuscripts, dating to the twelfth, and fourteenth centuries, as well as silk fabrics and bronze jewellery.[71] In 2010, a team of archaeologists and climbers, led by seven-time Everest mountaineer Pete Athans, discovered the remains of twenty-seven individuals in two large caves near Samdzong. Dating to between the third and eighth century, the remains included men, women, children, as well as livestock, and fragments of wood found beside each body indicated that some form of bed structure may have housed the bones at one time or another. Upon cleaning and analysing each bone, team bioarchaeologist Jacqueline Eng found cut marks, indicative of a defleshing practice commonly found in sky burials. This type of burial is indigenous to many Himalayan people, especially those with a Tibetan heritage, and is still practised in Mustang today.[72]

The act of defleshing a corpse before burial is referred to as excarnation and was once widely practised throughout the world. In its simplest form, a corpse would be left where it fell, allowing nature to take its course. For instance, anthropologists have discovered that throughout Africa, leaving the dead in the bush to be consumed by carnivorous wildlife was once a common method of disposal. But where scavenging animals were scarce, the use of specific localised communal 'dumping sites' was adopted. In East Africa, it was the chosen funerary method practised by Bantu and non-Bantu speakers alike. The Sangu people of Tanzania, the indigenous inhabitants of the Usangu Plains, north of Lake Malawi, would often toss their dead into chosen 'burial' ravines, which naturally horrified the German missionaries when they arrived in the nation's capital, Usangu, in 1895. Excarnation here slowly faded as Christianity took hold, yet contemporary linguistics does retain evidence of said practice, for example the phrase *'kitaga umunu'*, meaning 'to throw away a person', has been retained in the Sangu language as a polite euphemism for burial. Furthermore, north east of Utengule Usangu, the once designated tribal disposal site of Pitago, translated as 'the place for throwing away', has now become the town cemetery.[73]

Natural excarnation was also used by many Native American tribes, such as the Choctaws from Carolina, where the deceased would be laid out on a raised platform, or scaffold, some six metres high, until the flesh had become putrid and could be easily removed from the bone. Once carefully defleshed, the bones were then buried in a specialised bone house.[74] Another form was the Zoroastrian dakhma, or 'tower of silence', which is a circular, raised structure upon which the dead were exposed to carrion birds, predominantly vultures. Within the Iranian tradition, these towers were built atop hills or low mountains in desert locations, away from centres of population, until the practice was outlawed in the 1970s.[75] The Parsi community in India – Zoroastrians who fled Persia (Iran) in the seventh century – still strive to continue the tradition. Although their efforts have been severely hampered in recent times by the rapid urbanisation of Indian cities – their small squat towers now surrounded by modern high rises – together with the total decimation of India's vulture population (by 2008 approximately 99.9 per cent of the birds had been wiped out by government sanctioned diclofenac poisoning).[76] The most well-known form of excarnation is the aforementioned Himalaya sky burial, a mortuary custom practised by those who live on the high mountain slopes of Tibet, as well as ethnic people in Mongolia, such as the Tumed, and those from the Kingdom of Bhutan. First recorded in the twelfth century, a sky burial usually commences at dawn, when the body is transported to a specialist charnel ground, which can range from a simple flat rock to an elaborate temple setting, such as the Drigung Til Monastery, located on a mountain ridge around 120 kilometres north east of Lhasa, Tibet. The monastery is reputed to have the best sky burial ceremony facilitation currently available.[77] At the charnel ground, cuts are administered to the corpse, making it easier for vultures and other scavengers to gain access to the flesh and internal organs. When only the bones remain they are pounded into smaller pieces and made into a paste, which is then fed back to the waiting carrion birds.[78] Sky burials were once banned in Tibet, by the Chinese Government, but their resurgence in recent years has descended into nothing more than a ghoulish tourist attraction. At a sky burial site near Sertar in Sichuan, the Chinese authorities have even constructed an accompanying 'Temple of Death' in order to attract and entertain the growing number of Chinese tourists visiting the area.[79]

2

Piety and Power

The impact of monotheistic religions, in particular Christianity, on pagan mortuary practices would be profound, with the work of missionaries especially influential. From early medieval accounts, we hear how large swathes of the population were often converted from their pagan ways by such charismatic individuals, usually supported by the performance of a miracle, or two, to convince the heathen throng of the power of Christ. We thus read of St Columba, an Irish abbot and missionary, and his attempts to convert the Pictish kingdom of King Bridei, near Inverness, by utilising the word of God to banish a ferocious water beast, the supposed Loch Ness Monster, to the depths of the River Ness. Whereas in his desire to supplant the ancient druidic religion of Ireland, witnesses describe how St Patrick 'threw a druid into the air with the power of God and crushed his skull against a rock, and then summoned an earthquake to kill the rest.'[1] Nonetheless, not all missionaries were successful in their aims. Many kingdoms would not convert unless their monarch led the way and examples from Anglo-Saxon England and Frankia show how various kings were forced to implement legislation to outlaw pagan practices and reward those who converted to Christianity.[2]

The change from pagan to Christian burial was not immediate or absolute but more of an evolutionary process, and there are numerous burial grounds that demonstrate this transition. One of the best examples can be seen in Denmark, at the Royal Danish necropolis of Jelling, located at the heart of the Jutland Peninsula. Here lie some of the most important monuments from the Viking Age, including two royal burial mounds, a large stone ship, two free-standing rune stones and a medieval Christian church, currently believed to sit on the foundations of an earlier church built during the 960s by King Harald Bluetooth. The first excavations of the site were carried out as early as 1704, later resumed in 1861 by King

Frederik VII and J. J. A. Worsaae. Since 1941, several excavation teams have explored the burial mounds, culminating with the establishment in 2009 of the National Museum Jelling Project, a joint effort by the National Museum and the universities of Aarhus and Copenhagen. The Vejle Museum continues to excavate the monuments and the surrounding area, combining new discoveries with a re-evaluation of the previous archaeological research.[3]

The two flat-topped barrow mounds, measuring seventy metres in diameter by up to eleven metres in height, are built from stacked layers of turf and are almost identical in shape and size and construction. The North Mound is presumed to be the original interment site of King Gorm and was constructed in the winter of AD 958/59 over an impressive oak-timbered burial chamber. The South Mound was built over a similar light timber framework, but contained no burial chamber inside. Dendrochronology dates for the South Mound indicate that it was not completed before AD 970. Beneath the mounds archaeologists found the remnants of an enormous stone ship, measuring some 354 metres in length, the longest uncovered to date, with the North Mound at its centre. Analysis of lichen found covering the stones suggests the ship probably stood in the open for twenty to thirty years before being covered by the burial mounds.[4] However, it is the two rune stones that stand proudly in front of the church that bear testament to the evolution of the site. The smaller of the two stones bears no ornament, just an inscription that states: 'King Gorm made this memorial to his wife Thyri, glory [or adornment] of Denmark.' It is unclear precisely what memorial the inscription is referring to. The larger of the two runic stones is the famous Jelling Stone of Harald Bluetooth and it is located exactly midway between the two burial mounds. Adorned with an interlaced Nordic dragon the accompanying inscription reads: 'King Harald bade this monument be made in memory of Gorm his father and Thyra his mother, that Harald who won for himself all Denmark and Norway and made the Danes Christians.'[5] It should be noted that King Harald's claim of converting the Danish pagans to Christians has recently been called into question by archaeologists excavating underneath Ribe Cathedral. Here they discovered a series of Christian graves dating from the eighth century, whereas it is known that King Harald did not convert to Christianity until around AD 965.[6] This evidence suggests that the Christianisation of the Danes had been an ongoing process long before the emergence of the Jelling royal dynasty. Despite this, the southwest face of the Jelling rune stone does have the earliest depiction of Christ in Scandinavia. Adjacent to the royal burial mounds is the simple whitewashed Jelling Church, believed to lie on the site of at least three earlier wooden churches, all of which were destroyed by fire. It is said that after his conversion to Christianity King Harald removed the body of his father, King Gorm, from the North Mound and reburied him inside the church.[7]

At times, it was entirely possible for Christian practices to have existed alongside pagan ones. In Lithuania, the last European country to convert to Christianity, there are many surviving church reports that bemoan the inappropriate burial customs practised by the 'New Christians,' while the two nineteenth-century cemeteries in Vilnius, namely Rasos and Bernardine, demonstrate both mixed pagan and Christian cultural codes in burial rite and spatial provision.[8] The Spirit Box Cemetery of Eklutna, located approximately forty kilometres outside of Anchorage, Alaska, is a more recent example. Housing the descendants of the Dana'ina tribe, the cemetery uniquely exhibits a combination of Russian Orthodox tradition with native Athabascans Indian practices. Before the arrival of missionaries in the 1830s it was customary for the Athabascans to cremate their dead. But as the indigenous customs gradually began to blend with Christian ideals, the Athabascans dispensed with conventional cremation and began to bury their dead in the graveyard surrounding St Nicholas Russian Orthodox Church, a practice still continued to this day. Each inhumation is commemorated by a colourful tiny dollhouse-like structure, called a 'spirit house', atop which is positioned a three-bar Russian Orthodox cross. Unlike contemporary funerary monuments, none of the houses are maintained, as the Athabascans believe that what is taken from the Earth must be allowed to return, so the spirit houses are left to rot and decay.[9] Similar mortuary houses, albeit full-scale, were also common among the Toraja people of Indonesia, until the arrival of Dutch missionaries that is, when the dead houses were obliged to display a Christian cross.[10] Such dual observances are not restricted to Christianity. For example, in the ancient kingdom of Ghana, under some Muslim rulers, traditional religious, cultural and funerary practices continued to persist, with Islamic followers obliged to adapt to these pagan systems.[11]

Burying the Dead

Unsurprisingly some of the earliest Christian-only burial grounds are to be found in a monastic setting. One of the oldest in the world is St Catherine's Monastery in Egypt, located on the Sinai Peninsula. Officially known as the Sacred Monastery of the God-Trodden Mount Sinai, it was constructed between AD 548-565, by the orders of Emperor Justinian I, on the traditional site of the burning bush of Moses. Burial provision here is unique. As the area is considered too rocky for a permanent grave, let alone for the establishment of a permanent cemetery, upon death each monk is initially buried in the ground for a few years, to allow for decomposition to take hold, before his bones are dug up and interred in what is commonly referred to as a charnel house, more of which shall be discussed shortly.[12] In Britain, around the time that St Catherine's Monastery was being constructed, approximately three kilometres south west of the Llŷn Peninsula, North Wales, on the mysterious Bardsey Island, Einon, the King of Llŷn, invited the monk St Cadfan to establish a religious community. Together they constructed St Mary's Abbey, which flourished until 1537 when it was destroyed by Henry VIII in his Act for the Dissolution of the Lesser Monasteries. Once home to around 2,500 monks, many are believed to have been buried on the island, hence why it is often referred to as the 'island of 20,000 saints'.[13] In 1012, the *Brut y Tywysogion* chronicle makes reference to the death of Larddur, a monk of Bardsey, while the historian Gerald of Wales states:

> Either because of its pure air which comes across the sea from Ireland or through some miracle occasioned by the merits of the holy men who live there the island has this peculiarity that no one dies there except in extreme old age, for disease is almost unheard of. In fact, no one dies there at all unless he is very old indeed. The bodies of a vast number of holy men are buried there, or so they say, among them that of Daniel, bishop of Bangor.

In the chapel graveyard, an inscription reads: 'Respect the remains of 20,000 saints buried near this spot.' In 1995, the Bardsey Trust was given permission to excavate the site and, under the direction of archaeologist Christopher Arnold, they uncovered twenty-five medieval graves located near the modern-day chapel. One of the bodies was found with a tenth-century coin inserted into its mouth.[14] Further airborne scanning of the site was carried out in February 2017, the results of which are still being analysed.[15]

One of the most sacred sites in Christian Britain lies just off the west coast of Scotland, on the Hebridean island of Iona. Founded in AD 563 by St Columba and his Irish followers, Iona Abbey quickly established itself as the heart of Christianity in Scotland, and by the seventh century had become the centre of a monastic network stretching across Scotland, Ireland and northern England. It was a place of pilgrimage for over 1,400 years, and was established as a royal burial ground from the ninth to the eleventh century. Sadly, nothing exists of the original abbey, but a short walk from its initial location, down the appropriately named 'Street of the Dead', you will arrive at the burial ground of Rèilig Odhrain. It is reputed to hold the bones of at least sixty kings; an inventory dating to 1549 records that forty-eight Scottish kings, eight Norwegian kings and four Irish kings are buried here, yet regrettably none of their funerary monuments have survived.[16] Instead there are a number of beautifully carved medieval grave slabs, which were removed from the turf in order to protect them from the elements. Initially relocated to the adjacent chapel of St Oran, and to the abbey's cloister, the most spectacular examples, depicting effigies of warriors and probable clan chiefs, are now on display in Iona Abbey Museum. A number of older grave slabs still remain in the cemetery, lying alongside more modern burials.

The archaeological history of Iona is somewhat chaotic with numerous parties having a voice. The site was initially owned by the dukes of Argyll and in 2000 was placed into the care of the state; the National Trust for Scotland owns most of the island; Historic Environment Scotland manages the scheduled monuments; the Iona Cathedral Trust owns the buildings; the Iona Community occupy the buildings; while the local community continually use the graveyard and the cathedral. Early antiquarian investigations, such as those carried out by the Iona Club in 1834, were only limited to clearance work, either to stabilise the ruins or to search for burial monuments. Additional renovations by the Duke of Argyll and the Iona Cathedral Trust, at the turn of the 1900s, were associated with the rebuilding of the cathedral structure, with further remodelling of the monastic structures completed in the 1960s by the Iona Community. Although important structural features were preserved by this work, there was no systematic recording of any subsurface features, especially in the surrounding burial ground. The first serious excavations were undertaken between 1956 and 1963, directed by Charles Thomas, who opened up more than 100 trenches across the site. These were privately funded by the Russell Trust and the results were never published. In 1979 the National Trust for Scotland carried out a full geophysical survey in the fields surrounding the abbey, as did others within the scheduled areas, revealing a series of previously unknown enclosures. Large scale digs were continually undertaken throughout the late 1970s and early 1980s, with a targeted excavation carried out by Dr Ewan Campbell from the University of Glasgow and Cathy MacIver from AOC Archaeology between 13 May and 3 June 2017. Focusing on the previous work of Charles Thomas, the full results are yet to be published, but an interim report entitled *Excavations at Iona Abbey 2017, Data Structure Report* is available via the University of Glasgow website.[17]

Church Burial

The roots of church burial are often difficult to address, although tradition states that in the seventh century St Cuthbert was granted permission by the Pope to establish graveyards around holy places, to remind the living of their mortality.[18] In Britain, from as early as AD 680 a royal burial inside a church was probably commonplace, commencing with the Kentish Royal House in Canterbury, with historical evidence attesting to further royal burials at Repton Minster, AD 660–670, and Gloucester Minster, AD 679.[19] A minster is a church established during Anglo-Saxon times. By the end of the eighth century a fair proportion of the high-status laity were also interred inside a minster, in stone mausolea, as Guy Halsall observed, in 'an expensively constructed above ground chamber', effectively a barrow in stone.[20] Nevertheless, burials in or adjacent to barrow mounds continued, including the deposition of grave goods. A similar trait can be seen in Welsh churchyards, which are often oval or round in shape due to early Christians burying their dead inside or adjacent to Bronze Age round barrows. It appears that distinctions of faith did not necessarily produce distinctions of death at this time.

Radiocarbon evidence from minster sites such as Canterbury, Ripon, Jarrow, Waltham in Essex, and Winchester (Wessex) place the origin of minster cemeteries around AD 720, but it is almost impossible to determine whether those buried inside were individuals from religious communities or not.[21] Regarding burial in English churchyards, the historian John Burgess states: 'The practice was confirmed as established by AD 752 with about thirty feet round the church being set aside for that purpose.' In nearby Frankia, in AD 786 and then again in AD 810-13, Charlemagne prohibited the use of earlier non-Christian cemeteries,[22] while in Scotland large tracts of land were granted to both Saxon and Norman nobles, by Alexander I and David I, for the construction of new chapels and churches. These would be maintained by the nobility for the use of themselves and their tenants, and served by priests appointed by the lord as patron.[23]

After AD 900, a churchyard consecration rite slowly began to develop with parish burials for individuals becoming mandatory. The elite generally favoured burial within a religious house, and a right to such a burial was a recognised return for their benefactions. Burial inside a parish church was usually reserved for members of locally important families. Some medieval bishops even made it a formal requirement.[24] The burial location reflected the particular status of the deceased; the most popular place of interment was beneath the high altar, the sepulchre of Christ, followed by burial in and around the chancel, which was usually reserved for parish priests and those from the highest secular authorities. The ordinary parishioner would be buried in the churchyard, usually uncoffined.[25] Even when a coffin had been used in transporting the corpse, it would not necessarily be interred with it. Burial indoors naturally demanded some care in the enclosing of the corpse. High-status burials primarily used a stone sarcophagus, either carved from a single block of fairly soft stone, such as sandstone or limestone, or constructed from slabs. The sarcophagus was usually placed just below the floor level, although sometimes it was built into a monument above ground. In either case, secure sealing was essential, with the lid thoroughly mortared in place. A survey of wills from the diocese of Salisbury reveals that before 1399, sixty-five per cent anticipated burial in the churchyard, while in the fifteenth century sixty-one per cent asked for burial within the church.[26]

There has been suggestion that churchyards exhibited some form of internal organisation; a few sites have been found to contain clusters of same sex individuals, presumably members of religious orders. Other sites have unearthed groupings of individuals exhibiting disease or skeletal trauma, whereas archaeologists have found that some churchyards appear to have designated restricted areas accessed by those, for example, who did not engage in manual labour.[27] In Goltho, Lincolnshire the most noticeable feature was the clustering of children's graves around the walls of the church, while a similar pattern of behaviour was also observed at Cherry Hinton in Cambridgeshire and Tanners Row in Yorkshire. As Duncan Sayer points out in *Christian Burial Practices in Early Middle Ages: Rethinking the Anglo-Saxon Funerary Sphere*, early Christian communities in England considered churchyards to be significant places for the burial of children, up to fifty-one per cent in churchyards compared to twenty-five per cent in field cemeteries.[28] Why this is so is unclear, albeit the burial of unbaptised children on the north side of the churchyard is a tradition that continued to at least the nineteenth century in some places.[29]

Church Monuments

Church monuments are varied in design and can range from a simple commemorative plaque to a large, elaborate structure, or mural monument, often depicting heraldic symbols or an effigy of the deceased person, sometimes shown with other family members. The monument is usually placed immediately above or close to the burial vault or grave. The first monuments were predominantly coffin-shaped stone coverings, sometimes incised with a cross. The raised hogback is an early example of this form. Found exclusively in areas settled by the Vikings, such as Scotland, northern Britain, Cumbria and Yorkshire, the bow-sided shape of the hogback is thought to represent the shape of a classic Viking house. Govan Old Church, now part of the city of Glasgow, has a remarkable collection of hogbacks currently on public display. Commemorative imagery first appeared in the thirteenth century, initially in horizontal low relief, gradually replaced by full high-relief effigies, usually recumbent, shown in prayer or dressed in full warrior garb complete with sword. At the feet of the effigy there often sat a form of stylised animal, usually a lion for men, representing valour and nobility, or a dog for women, characterising loyalty.[30] Some effigies were raised on tomb-style chests, referred to as tomb chests, altar tombs or table tombs, and they were highly decorated with foliage, heraldry or architectural detailing, such as small figures of weepers. By the end of the thirteenth century these often had architectural canopies.

Characteristic of the fifteenth century are the wonderfully carved cadaver monuments, a unique church monument depicting either a life-size skeleton or a decomposing body riddled with worms. A representation, or reminder, of the infallibility of life, they were popular throughout Europe during this period, especially among the nobility. In the Basilica of Saint-Denis near Paris, the double tombs of French kings Louis XII, Francis I and Henry II are shown, with their respective queens, first as living effigies and then as naked cadavers.[31] Many such monuments survive in English cathedrals and parish churches. The earliest example, in Lincoln Cathedral, dates to 1431 and is dedicated to Bishop Richard Fleming, who founded Lincoln College, Oxford. There is also the well-known cadaver of Henry Chichele, Archbishop of Canterbury, which dates to 1443, that can be seen in Canterbury Cathedral, whereas Winchester Cathedral has two examples.[32] Eleven known examples survive in Ireland. The best, currently in Triskel Christchurch, Cork, dating to 1554, depicts a cadaver form inscribed upon a limestone slab and is dedicated to a Thomas Ronan and his wife.[33] Notable examples in Scotland include the seventeenth-century wall mural in St Nicholas Kirkyard, Aberdeen and the pink sandstone representation currently on display in Kirkmichael Burial Ground, Resolis. Cadaver monuments are also found in many Italian churches, such as those of Cardinal Alain de Coëtivy in Santa Prassede, Ludovico Cardinal d'Albret at Santa Maria in Aracoeli and the very fine depiction on the tomb of Pope Innocent III, in Saint Peter's Basilica in Rome, sculpted by Giovanni Pisano.[34] Cadaver imagery has also been found on incised slabs, wall murals and monumental brasses, often referred to as 'shroud brasses', of which many survive in England.[35]

The devastation caused by Henry VIII's Dissolution of the Monasteries, 1536-1541, and the subsequent Reformation was considerable, and one can only guess at just how many intramural memorials were destroyed during this period. Even royalty was not immune. In the old Greyfriars

Church, London, there was once buried Margaret, second wife of Edward I; Isabella, widow of Edward II; Joan Makepeace, wife of David Bruce, King of Scotland; the hearts of Edward II and Queen Eleanor, the wife of Henry III; together with the bodies of four duchesses, four countesses, one duke, twenty-eight barons and thirty-five knights. In 1545, ten of the finest royal tombs and 140 gravestones of persons of note were destroyed and sold by Sir Martin Bowes, Lord Mayor of London, for fifty pounds.[36] As an aside, a similar fate befell the French monarchy in July 1793 when, in honour of the first anniversary of the French Republic, the authorities ordered the destruction of all royal tombs, the majority of which were located in the royal necropolis inside the basilica of Saint-Denis, near Paris. Coffins were emptied, the remains were dumped in a number of mass trenches, metallic monuments were melted down and tombs were broken up. In 1817, when the Bourbon monarchy was restored, all that survived intact were the lower portions of three corpses.[37] After the Reformation burial inside a church was banned, and every man and woman now had the right to be buried in their own plot of land inside the churchyard. It would be many years before the rest of Europe followed suit; in France the practice wasn't abolished until 1776; in Sardinia in 1777 and in Austria in 1783.[38] In the centuries that followed, the empty voids left behind in churches slowly began to fill with monuments once more, the difference being that the adoption of specific mortuary expressions now filtered through into the surrounding graveyard, in the guise of grave markers. During the sixteenth century, these were highly influenced by Renaissance forms, such as wreaths, obelisks, allegorical figures and skulls, with further forms adopting a more classical approach as marble became freely available. During the seventeenth and eighteenth centuries funerary exposition added symbolic carvings to its repertoire, which consisted of both mortality symbols and emblems of trade (see Appendix 2), followed by Greek and Gothic revivals that dominated the Victorian era. By the end of the nineteenth century, large-scale funerary monuments were no longer fashionable.

Many smaller medieval churches and chapels, together with their assigned burial grounds did not survive the Reformation, and have since vanished. Against all the odds a gem or two can still be found, as demonstrated by the following case study. I have chosen two neighbouring sites, Newhall Point Cemetery and Kirkmichael Burial

Ground, both located in the rural hamlet of Balblair, on the Black Isle, Scotland. The former is a rare low-status burial ground dating from at least the eleventh century, while Kirkmichael has on display some of the finest monumental grave markers to be found in Scotland. It is also a rare example of a rural working burial ground, still utilised by the surrounding hamlets and villages today, with more than 500 years of continuous use. Both sites have special significance to me personally, as not only did I once reside but a ten-minute walk away, they also played a significant part in my recuperation from a serious health issue. I was extremely privileged to have sat on the working committee of the Kirkmichael Trust for a short time. Its aim was to raise funds for the restoration and maintenance of both the church and the surrounding burial ground, which after almost twenty years it finally achieved.

The cemetery at Newhall Point, overlooking the Cromarty Firth, is thought to be the site of a pre-Reformation chapel, although no historical records have so far been found alluding to this. Likewise, no archaeological remains of its existence have been unearthed to date, although substantial worked stones have been found in adjacent properties, suggesting they are possibly from the original chapel building. A rectangular masoned stone, possibly a cross base, was uncovered in an adjacent garden. The site itself currently lies directly under a neighbour's house and surrounding garden, and it is quite common for him to unearth skeletal remains when turning over his flower beds. Any bones that do surface, of which there have been many, he carefully reburies in another part of the garden. It cannot be a coincidence that his vegetable plot is one of the most productive in the neighbourhood. In 1985, prior to the construction of the family house, and with the burial site under threat, the local authority initiated a rescue excavation. Funded by Historic Scotland, the dig, which took place at very short notice, unearthed a circular-shaped cemetery some twenty metres in diameter, that was partly enclosed by a ditch. Three trenches were opened, in which archaeologists found a number of extended skeletons, in east/west and north/south orientations, all were in a poor condition and many were designated by crude sandstone uprights. The majority of graves had been cut into the natural beach sand and no artefacts were found in any of the three excavated areas. Thirty-eight graves were identified, containing twenty-four adults and fourteen infants, and carbon dating revealed the date of interment ranged from the beginning of the tenth century to the end of the eleventh century, suggesting that the cemetery may have been in use for at least a couple of hundred years.[39] The cemetery is now a scheduled ancient monument. In the summer of 2015, my neighbour invited me to dig an exploratory trench on her land, as she believed the cemetery limits encroached over the recognised boundary. After years of incapacity, resulting in many failed opportunities, I naturally jumped at the chance of getting my hands dirty once more. I remember it being an exceedingly hot afternoon, a rarity in the Highlands, so the decision was taken to limit the excavation to two one-metre test pits placed well outside the designated scheduled area. Alas, to everyone's disappointment, no evidence of the cemetery was found that day; total finds equated to one rusty beer bottle top and three irate woodlice! Not my finest hour, archaeologically speaking, but it did confirm my suspicions that the cemetery probably extended westwards onto neighbouring properties.

It appears that for reasons unknown, Newhall Point Cemetery was abandoned and the community moved their burial provision to a new location, Kirkmichael, a ten-minute walk along the coastline. Considering the compacted nature of the site, with little room for expansion, space may have been the overriding factor behind the decision. Located on the shores of Udale Bay, Kirkmichael is also a pre-Reformation parish church, which was altered for use as a protestant kirk, and then later reused as a mausoleum. The building is a scheduled ancient monument as well as a listed building, while the graveyard wall also has listed building status. Adjacent to today's building, to the west, lies evidence of an earlier church site, a rough rubble wall with a round arch tomb recess, possibly sixteenth century in origin. The base of its west gable wall is still evident beneath the turf. The earliest documentary reference to Kirkmichael, dating to 1429, refers to is as a church that supported a canon of the nearby Fortrose Cathedral, although this does not mean it was used by local parishioners or that the surrounding burial ground was in existence at this time. In preparation for future restoration of the kirk, in 2013 a series of test pits were dug by Highland Archaeology Services. All were excavated by hand to a depth of just under a metre. Two were excavated in the opposing corners of the nave, the larger part of the kirk, and two in the adjacent chancel. The two sections of the church were used as burial aisles for high-ranking members of local families; the 'chancel' is the mausoleum of the powerful Urquhart family of Braelangwell and the Gordons and Shaw-Mackenzies of Newhall, while the 'nave', is the private burial place for the Gunn Munros of Poyntzfield. Test pits 1 and 2, in the nave, revealed sandy mixed deposits containing fragments of shell and disarticulated human remains. Test pit 2 also revealed the remnants of a coffin and we agreed on site it was probably that of a young child. None of the findings were surprising to those of us who knew the kirk well. After all, I had been finding bits of human bones scattered about the kirk floor for years. The test pits dug in the chancel revealed layers of disturbed material together with a variety of rodent remains. The principal archaeological works commenced in the nave, otherwise known as Trench 1, on 17 October 2016 and continued until 7 November 2016. A significant amount of debris from the recent roof collapse, as well as organic material and lime, were uncovered together with six caches of human bone. The caches occur at various levels, suggesting that they were deposited at different times and consisted of long bones and skull fragments. It would later transpire that none of the remains found equated to one single individual. No finds were found in relation to the bones, but coffin handles, nails and shroud pins were uncovered in the grave layers.[40]

Some of the more remarkable finds came from the surrounding burial ground. I was most familiar with this particular area. It had become part of my daily rehabilitation, whereby I would hobble the ten minutes down the road to the entrance gates, spend time among the dead, and then hobble back home. On good days, I would stay and investigate further, measuring, recording and photographing the grave markers, many of which would form part of my first photographic exhibition in Cromarty Museum in 2016. The burial ground is split into two distinct areas. To the east is the kirk building and the older grave memorials, including a fine pink sandstone mausoleum complete with skull and crossbones, whereas the western side is the current burying ground. In close proximity to the kirk are a number of high-status grave slabs, complete with symbols of mortality, together with a rare cavalry cross grave marker, the design of which is the emblem for the Kirkmichael Trust. In January 2017, a number of trenches were dug across the site, Trench 5 being the largest. Measuring approximately fifty metres in length and one-and-a-half metres wide, fourteen stone burial monuments were uncovered from the topsoil. They included a magnificent early seventeenth-century grave slab, measuring nearly two metres long, inscribed with a claymore type sword and accompanying inscription; a sandstone slab bearing unusual wigged skull and crossbones and an early eighteenth century elaborately carved stone depicting a relief stag's head, the emblem of the clan MacKenzie. Yet another previously unknown slab bearing a rare claymore sword was unearthed in Trench 9. Dating to 1630, it measured well over two metres in length and was inscribed with the Urquhart name. Lying adjacent to this was yet another Urquhart stone slab with decorative carvings and what appeared to be an hourglass figure, an atypical symbol of mortality. Many of these wonderful medieval grave markers now adorn the inside of the church, which has since become a heritage centre.[41]

It may surprise some of you to learn that the humble graveyard/churchyard was not the calm, serene place of quiet contemplation it is today. During the Middle Ages the churchyard was a multi-purpose space for the use of the community – it was a pasture, a market place, builders' yard and sports field. Many were used to host fairs and markets, such as the St Boniface Fair in and around Fortrose Cathedral on the Black Isle. A surviving stone, in the centre of today's churchyard, enabled traders to tether their horses. A similar example can be seen in the grounds of Dornoch Cathedral in Sutherland, where a large slab of stone, known as the Plaiden Ell, is sited among the existing grave markers. The stone was once used by traders as an official measure when buying or selling cloth. Local records state that the market continued here until at least the nineteenth century. Grazing rights were an important source of income for the church as they allowed a clergyman to augment his paltry earnings. This long-established practice still continues in many rural areas, such as Cil Chrisiod on the Isle of Skye, where I have experienced many a personal battle with sheep when attempting to photograph and record the gravestones, while at St Chad's Saddleworth, sheep have recently been allowed to graze the churchyard, to keep the vegetation under control.[42] These are two of many such examples. Furthermore, in Wales many nineteenth-century church engravings depict cattle grazing within the churchyard boundaries, indicating the custom prevailed until late Victorian times.[43]

Evidence of the noble art of beekeeping can be found in many religious establishments, in the shape of bee boles – alcoves where straw or wicker beehives called skeps, from the Anglo-Saxon word 'skeppa' meaning 'basket' were housed.[44] Examples include Lindisfarne Abbey, famous for its mead production; Titchfield Abbey, Hampshire, where four separate alcoves were located along the boundary wall (they have long since been bricked up); Pluscarden Abbey near Elgin, where the monks still use skep hives today to capture swarms and finally Llantrithyd Place and gardens in Glamorgan, Wales, where four bee boles, dating to the sixteenth century, have been found in a stone wall just below the churchyard.[45] But perhaps the strangest activity of them all has to be the 'wappenshaw', a Scottish word for the display of weapons. In 1457, an Act of Scottish Parliament decreed that in every parish, a wappenshaw had to be held four times a year in the local churchyard, together with provision for regular weekly arrow practice, which would take place on a Sunday. Betty Willsher, in her book *Understanding Scottish Graveyards*, notes that impressions in the stonework, where bowmen once sharpened their arrowheads, can still be seen in the church tower in Crail Churchyard, Fife.[46]

Followers of other religious denominations were excluded from parish churchyards, and thus had their own designated burial grounds. The Jewish community has always traditionally buried their dead aside from others and two examples worthy of mention include the Old Jewish Cemetery in Prague, Czech Republic, one of the oldest surviving Jewish burial grounds in the world. Founded in the early half of the fifteenth century, and comprising around 12,000 gravestones, the site expanded several times over its course, to meet the growing needs of the Jewish community. Even still, many corpses were buried one on top of the other, in graves some ten feet deep. The final burial took place in 1787.[47] The second site is Beth Haim Cemetery on the Caribbean island of Curacao, which houses the remains of those Jews who fled Spain and Portugal to escape the wrath of the Inquisition. Dating to 1659, around 5,000 elaborately carved gravestones still survive in situ, although many have been significantly damaged in recent years by pollution from surrounding oil terminals.[48] The first Jewish cemetery in post-Expulsion England was opened in Mile End, London, in 1657, by the Sephardim. Earlier Jewish cemeteries, especially from the medieval period, have long since vanished. This was followed by Ashkenazi burial grounds in Alderney Road in 1696, and at Hoxton and Hackney in the eighteenth century.[49] In the second half of the eighteenth century, regional Jewish congregations also began to establish their own cemeteries. By 1800 there were some twenty Jewish cemeteries outside London, such as the delightful Jewish cemetery in Leskinnick Terrace, Penzance, Cornwall, where a number of beautifully incised slate gravestones, the oldest dating to 1791, are preserved. By 1840, the number of provincial cemeteries had almost doubled.[50]

Burial grounds of Christians who did not belong to the Church of England – such individuals were called Nonconformists or Dissenters – began to appear in the 1650s. The enchanting Bunhill Fields in Islington, London is an early example. Once the site of a charnel depository, hence the name 'Bone Hill,' and later a plague pit, from the seventeenth to the nineteenth century it became the primary burial ground for London's Nonconformists; the nineteenth-century poet, Robert Southey, once described it as 'the Campo Santo [Holy Field] of the Dissenters'.[51] Many influential people of the day are buried within its grounds, including preacher and pamphleteer Richard Price, the mother of John Wesley, the founder of the Methodist movement, John Bunyan, author of the famous allegorical novel *The Pilgrim's Progress*, Daniel Defoe, author of *Robinson Crusoe* and *Moll Flanders* and artist and poet William Blake.[52] A separate burial ground for Quakers, another Christian movement, was opened close to Bunhill Fields in 1661, but sadly most of it was destroyed by bombing during the Second World War. The Quakers, also known as the Religious Society of Friends, originated in Lancashire during the mid-seventeenth century, but quickly spread throughout the nation via the preaching of its founder George Fox. Forbidden by the established Church to use local graveyards, their only option was to purchase unconsecrated land from anyone who was willing to sell, and formalise their own burial sites. Quaker burial grounds are unlike any other, as they are the legal property of the Meetings, that is the Quaker community. They reject all forms of self-display, with 'Friends' reminded to avoid the 'vain and empty' custom of using grave furniture. As a consequence, hundreds of burials in those early gravesites remain unmarked to this day. The use of a headstone did not materialise until much later, in the early to mid-nineteenth century in most cases. When a headstone was used it had to abide to the Quaker testimony of simplicity, whereby only the name, the deceased's age and the date of death were inscribed.[53] Naturally, the odd discrepancy does crop up from time to time. At the Pales, the oldest

Quaker burial ground in Wales, a common addition to the headstone of a farmer was the name of the farm.[54]

A Secondary Burial Ground

Below the streets of Spitalfields in London, there exists a remarkable remnant of its medieval past, a fourteenth-century bone store or charnel house. Discovered in 1999 by the Museum of London Archaeological Service, the store has subsequently been preserved and incorporated into the heart of a multi-million-pound office and retail development with the charnel on display under a series of glass panels built into the modern-day flooring. Measuring some thirteen metres by seven metres, the Spitalfields' charnel house first began life as a vaulted crypt of the then Priory of St Mary's Spital, and for over 200 years this cavernous space was a secondary repository for disinterred human bones. Just how many bodies were placed within its confines is unknown. The charnel fell into disuse when the priory was forced to close under the Dissolution of the Monasteries and the chapel was later demolished after the Great Fire of London in 1666, but Jane Sidell, Inspector of Ancient Monuments at Historic England believes the figure could be in the hundreds.[55]

Charnel chapels are 'a type of medieval religious structure located within the confines of the cemetery of all kinds of ecclesiastical complexes, including abbeys, cathedrals, monasteries and parish churches.'[56] Their primary function was to house disinterred human bones and the term 'charnel' derives from the French *charnier*, meaning 'flesh'. There are two types: free-standing, two-storey buildings and those built below churches. Both consist of a semi-subterranean vault or chamber for the purpose of housing displaced bones from surrounding graveyards.[57] Archaeologists from the University of Sheffield have identified up to sixty potential charnel chapel sites in the UK, but only two survive in situ. One is Hythe Charnel House in St Leonard's Church, Hythe, Kent, which made the headlines in 2018 when a skull was stolen from its store. The earliest reference dates back to 1678 when Samuel Jeake, the town clerk of Rye, described 'an orderly pile of dead men's bones' in the charnel house on the north side of the church. The charnel currently consists of 1,021 skulls, stacked on a series of wooden shelves in four arched bays, adjacent to which is another stack of bones and skulls measuring approximately two metres in height. Recent studies have estimated that the remains are likely to represent around 2,000 individuals.[58] The other example is Rothwell Charnel Chapel, sited beneath Rothwell Parish Church in Northamptonshire. In existence from the late thirteenth to the early fifteenth century, this small charnel chamber is stuffed full of human bones and skulls, the latter, once again, neatly arranged in rows on wooden shelves. It is believed the remains comprise over 2,500 individuals who lived and died between the thirteenth and nineteenth century. Stemming from the doctoral research of Dr Jennifer Crangle, the site is currently being investigated by the Rothwell Charnel Chapel Project.[59]

Comparative structures were also common throughout medieval Europe and are known by a variety of names, such as charnel chapels, charnel houses, ossuaries, bone houses or bone chapels. Sedlec Ossuary, in the Czech Republic, is probably one of the best known and is located beneath the Cemetery Church of All Saints in Sedlec, a small suburb of Kutná Hora. Known locally as 'The Bone Church', it is thought to contain the skeletons of 40,000 to 70,000 people, whose remains have, in many cases, been artistically arranged to form decorative pieces, which include four enormous bell-shaped bone mounds that occupy the corners of the chapel, a huge bone chandelier composed of almost every bone in the human body, two large bone chalices, four baroque bone candelabras, six enormous bone pyramids, two bone monstrances, a vessel used to display the Eucharistic host, various skull candle holders and a vault decorated with a garland of skulls.[60] Another chapel of bones lies directly beneath St Peter and Paul's Church in Melník, also in the Czech Republic. Originally intended as a royal burial ground for ladies of the Bohemian Court, some 15,000 corpses from the surrounding cemeteries were dug up, cleaned and placed into the chapel crypt. Declared a health risk in 1780, the crypt was bricked up, and thus disappeared from the local conscience for over 230 years. It wasn't until 1910, when Czech anthropologist Jindrich Matiegka reopened the entrance to the crypt, that the thousands of human bones, stacked up in mounds around the perimeter walls, became public knowledge once more. Matiegka took it upon himself to arrange the skeletal remains into a series of religious-themed designs, including a large cross of bones, decorated with palm fronds, and a heart shape made from skulls. He also built a tunnel of bones to represent the resurrection of Christ with the largest structure, comprising approximately 10,000 skeletons, adorning the entrance to the crypt.[61]

Other notable examples in Europe include the stunning Skull Chapel, or Kaplica Czaszek, located in the village of Czermna, Poland. From 1776 until 1804 the local priest, Vaclav Tomasek, together with his gravedigger accomplice, dug up the remnants of thousands of corpses once buried in local mass graves, cleaned the bones and reburied them in the chapel. Over 21,000 skeletons were deposited in the crypt, and the skulls from another 3,000 individuals were set aside to decorate the chapel walls and ceiling. Upon his death, the skull of Tomasek was placed neatly upon the altar, above which were placed two carvings of angels, one with a Latin inscription that reads 'Arise from the Dead.'[62] In Italy, the church of Santa Maria della Concezione of the Capuchins has become one of the major attractions in Rome. It was built by Pope Urban, in honour of his brother Cardinal Antonio Barberini, a friar in the Capuchin order. Here, rather than bury the remains of the dead, the monks decorated the walls of the church crypt with their bones. Some 4,000 Capuchin friars, who died between 1528 and 1870, currently adorn the crypt. The ossuary contains a section for skulls, a crypt of leg bones and a separate room for pelvises. One complete skeleton is enclosed in an oval of bones holding a scythe and scales, also made from bones. Other Capuchin monks were mummified, dressed in their daily clothes and hung from the walls and ceilings. An accompanying plaque reads: 'What we are now, we once were, what we are now, you shall be.'[63]

The name Hallstatt in Austria is synonymous with some of the earliest known European Iron Age warrior cultures. This fact often overlooks another feature of historical importance, for behind its Catholic Church, sited in a chapel basement, there is a small building called the Beinhaus, or bone house, inside which are numerous shelves of neatly deposited skulls, numbering over 1,200 in total. Thought to date to the seventeenth century, each skull is accompanied by a record of its birth, death and marriage. Of the 1,200 skulls, some 700 are painted with various symbols, such as a Maltese cross. If a skull belonged to a woman, garlands of flowers and roses were traditionally painted upon its head and if the deceased was a man it would be a wreath of oak or ivy. Buried underneath the shelves are the larger bones, such as the femurs and tibias. The last interment took place in 1995, it was the skull of a local woman who died twelve years earlier, her dying wish was to be placed inside the Beinhaus.[64] Finally, there are the Capela dos Ossos, or Bone Chapels of Portugal, which come in all shapes and sizes. Some of the smallest can be found in communities spanning the beaches of the Algarve, such as the Alcantarilha Bone Chapel, on top of the hill overlooking the sea. Built upon the site of an old cemetery, there are over 5,000 bones and skulls displayed on the walls and ceiling of this local small church.[65] The largest and most stunning example is found in the city of Evora, approximately 140 kilometres from the capital Lisbon. Constructed in the late sixteenth century by monks from the local monastery, it houses the remains from two overflowing Franciscan cemeteries. Around 5,000 skeletons are believed to have been used to decorate the chapel's walls and pillars, with the bones of three Franciscan monks specifically deposited in a small white coffin by the altar. Above the chapel entrance is inscribed '*Nos ossos que aqui estamos, pelos vossos esperamos,*' meaning 'We bones, are here, waiting for yours.'[66]

3

The Deviant Ones

Throughout Europe there exist certain burial grounds in which the proper funerary rites were denied to certain members of the community. In archaeological terms, such burials are often referred to as 'deviant', a term first coined by archaeologist Helen Geake, and they are characterised by the following:

> [A] scarcity or complete lack of grave-goods and by an unusual way of positioning both the grave and the body within the grave. Individual grave-cuts may be absent, with all the bodies placed within one enormous trench. The graves may be disposed around a barrow. Bodies may be found decapitated or with the neck broken, or in a variety of other positions indicating that some sort of ritual abuse or mutilation was carried out before or just after death.[1]

One such example is the deserted medieval village of Wharram Percy, perched on the side of a remote and beautiful valley in the Yorkshire Wolds, which in 2017 hit the headlines when reports began to circulate regarding rather strange phenomena that had been uncovered on site. For scientists, working in collaboration with Historic England and the University of Southampton, had discovered that a number of the surviving skeletons had undergone some form of deliberate mutilation. Many of the limbs had been broken, heads had been severed from bodies, one had even been hacked using some form of sharp instrument, probably a sword or axe, and in a final act of nullification, each corpse had been thrown into a fire to burn.[2] Astonishingly, all this desecration was carried out shortly *after* death. What could possibly account for such bizarre behaviour?

Medieval folk had an abiding fear of the unrestful dead, a belief that corpses could reanimate and become revenants, i.e. the walking dead, in the short period between death and decomposition. To prevent such a travesty, the community as a whole would often take preventative measures to keep a corpse from becoming reanimated. In Geoffrey of Burton's *Life and Miracles of St Modwenna*, an account of two revenants causing havoc in a town in Derbyshire, we read how the villagers exhumed the troublesome duo, cut off their heads, tore out their hearts and threw them onto a fire.[3] In the ancient minster town of Southwell, Nottinghamshire, in 1959, archaeologist Charles Daniels uncovered a male skeleton, dating from AD 550-700, which had metal spikes driven through its shoulders, heart and ankles.[4] In the Balkans, during the fifteenth and sixteenth centuries, people were nailing corpses to the ground, to prevent them from rising. Whereas in eighteenth-century New England, during a devastating tuberculosis epidemic, relatives began exhuming the bodies of deceased family members to check for 'unnatural signs' such as fresh blood in the heart, which was usually taken as a gesture that the corpse was somehow responsible for the continuation of the disease. If blood was found in the heart, or in other organs, it was cut from the body and burned to ashes. This New England folk remedy was given the name 'vampirism'.[5] Because of such affiliation, the term revenant has now become closely linked to that of Nosferatu, or the vampire, especially throughout Eastern European countries, the recognised heartland of vampire mythology. It is perhaps not surprising, therefore, that many deviant burials unearthed in these areas, from the early medieval period onwards, have been interpreted as the remains of vampires.

Vampire burials are often identified in the archaeological record by specific features, such as the mutilation of the corpse, with particular reference to the hands, feet or mouth, together with the deposition of associative grave goods, such as poppy seeds, whose narcotic effect would render the corpse in a continual sleep-like state. Although rare, some also include the deposition of a sharp instrument, especially in the Slavic tradition where it was believed a sickle or scythe would destroy the physical body when the vampire attempted to rise from the grave. The meticulous placement of such objects, particularly over the neck and abdomen, was necessary to prevent this from happening. Examples of this practice can be found in the cemetery site of Drawsko, a rural community in north-west Poland, excavated by the Slavia Field School in Mortuary Archaeology. Dating from the seventeenth to eighteenth century, out of approximately 333 well-preserved skeletons, six exhibited vampirism tendencies, including one adult male, three adult females, one adolescent girl, and one skeleton sex unknown. Five of the graves contained a sickle, placed around the neck area, one female body was discovered with a sickle across her pelvis, a rock on her neck and a coin in her mouth and, according to media reports, the remains of the adult male even had his teeth or 'fangs' removed! This corpse also exhibited a puncture wound to his leg, where it is believed he had been staked in order to prevent his body from rising. Interestingly, approximately a third of the remaining burials unearthed at Drawsko contained grave goods relating to the protection from evil.[6]

To date some fifty vampire burials have been found in Polish burial sites. Archaeologists recently found three such bodies, dating to the thirteenth century, on the outskirts of Gorzyca, one female and two males, each exhibiting prominent holes in the spine where a stake had been driven through the heart. The knees of the female had been forcefully broken before burial and she had also been buried face down, her head pinned to the grave with heavy stones, while one of the male skeletons had been decapitated and dismembered.[7] A similar decapitated body was unearthed in Zamkowa. Likewise in rural Bulgaria, more than 100 designated vampire burials have been uncovered, the most recent find being two skeletons buried near the former monastery of Sozopol by the Black Sea; both were found with iron spikes rammed through their bodies.[8] In the Czech Republic town of Celakovice, about thirty kilometres north of Prague, archaeologists excavating its eleventh-century burial ground discovered fourteen graves where a metal spike had either been driven through the body or heavy boulders had been placed upon the corpse.[9] Moreover, the recent discovery of a late medieval skeleton in Lazzaretto Nuovo, Venice – an elderly woman with a brick forcibly inserted into her mouth – has been determined by archaeologists, Emilio Nuzzolese and Matteo Borrini, as being the 'first vampire burial of its type to be archaeologically attested in the field.' In fairness, this claim has been somewhat disputed by other archaeologists who assert the remains and their context resemble more that of a witch. As a consequence, said individual has now been labelled a 'vampire-witch' by the media.[10]

Staking, the inversion of the burial position, post-mortem mutilation and destruction of the corpse in a pyre are well attested in both the written and archaeological records. This does not mean, however, that such incidences are evidence of solely vampirism, or that the belief in this particular phenomenon was all-pervasive. As we have seen in the last example, some of these burials may represent another category of miscreants. Like their vampire counterparts, a number of proposed witch graves have also been unearthed in Europe in recent years, the occupants buried in a similar prone (face down) position, their bodies mutilated and/or pinned down, often by a heavy stone. In the summer of 2011, during an excavation of a graveyard near Lucca, Tuscany, a team of Italian archaeologists found the simple, shallow grave of a previously known witch. She had no coffin or burial shroud to speak of, which would have been the norm, and the skeletal evidence indicated that at least seven nails had been driven through her jawbone. Furthermore, the discovery of thirteen nails scattered around her body suggests that her clothing had also been pinned down, securing her firmly to her grave. A few years earlier, another witch had been unearthed in the same graveyard in a similar manner, this time a large boulder had been strategically placed over her grave.[11] Again in Italy, in 2014, at the complex of San Calocero in Albenga, archaeologists working for the Vatican's Pontifical Institute of Christian Archaeology found the skeleton of an adolescent girl buried face down in her grave, leading to widespread media coverage describing her as a 'witch girl'.[12] Italian archaeologist Alfonso Forgione was quoted as saying: 'This indicates to me that it was an attempt to make sure these women did not rise from the dead and unnerve the locals who were no doubt convinced they were witches with evil powers.'[13]

Similar practices have been found in burial grounds here in the UK. In 2006, while on a photographic assignment at Portmahomack Burial Ground in Scotland, the curator relayed the tale of a local witch who would rise from her grave at night, climb over the churchyard wall and attempt to secrete herself quietly among the gravestones. Three times she attempted said feat and three times the locals discovered her whereabouts, dug her body back up and returned it to her original burial site. In the last instance, the exasperated villagers buried her face down and placed a large boulder over the grave to prevent her from escaping. A similar example can be found in England, in St Anne's Churchyard,

Woodplumpton, Lancashire, where a local witch, Meg Shelton, would do likewise, until the villagers buried her head first, placing a large stone on top of the grave to prevent any further night-time excursions. The stone remains to this day, accompanied by a small plaque informing visitors that the Witch of Woodplumpton lies buried beneath their feet.[14] Other examples include a grave from Haverhill, Suffolk, and two from the cemetery at St Peter's in Leicester, each displaying the practice of using heavy bricks to weigh down the corpse. Some have argued that securing the body face down in the grave may be connected to the belief that if the soul exits the body through the mouth, lying the corpse face down would prevent this from happening. Others suggest it may have protected the living from the 'evil eye', thus preventing a haunting from beyond the grave. Perhaps there was some penitential element attached, as suggested by Professor Dawn Hadley, after all it was common for religious followers to prostrate themselves, face down, before God when asking for forgiveness. Could a deviant prone burial have a similar purpose, helping the soul of the dead in the interim period between death and final judgment? It may be why a fair proportion of deviant individuals have, surprisingly, been found in consecrated ground.[15]

If asked, most people's impression of a miscreant would probably be that of a rather dubious character, of low moral standing, who had no doubt fallen foul of the law at one time or another. In many ways, they would be correct. Due to the nature of their business, members of the criminal fraternity have always been deemed outcasts, inhabiting the murky fringes of civilised society. Thieves, highwaymen, pirates, they all have a rather romantic quality when viewed from afar, but in reality, nothing could be further from the truth. Even in today's society criminal elements are feared and, dare I say, admired in equal measure, even in death, as demonstrated by the Gangster Graveyard, in Yekaterinburg, Russia, a cemetery renowned for its gangland tradition of flamboyant tombstones, where the deceased proudly display their cars, money, guns and all the trappings of a gangster lifestyle. Similarly, in Jardines Del Humaya graveyard, Mexico, the elaborate mausoleums of dead drug cartel members rival any monumental sculpture that can be found in the cemeteries of London, Paris or Rome. Whereas today a term in prison is often considered a 'badge of honour', in the past transgressors were dealt with rather more harshly.

Criminals who were put to death in Anglo-Saxon England were often interred in separate burial grounds known as execution cemeteries, or 'cwealmstow', which literally means a death or killing place. Archaeological evidence of such sites is relatively scarce but where potential execution victims have been found, evidence indicates that the surrounding burial ground had been in continual use for a significant period of time, such as the execution cemetery at Walkington Wood, Yorkshire, which archaeologists believe was in use for around four centuries, AD 640-1030.[16] The definitive study of execution sites was carried out in 2009 by Dr Andrew Reynolds of University College London, who proposes that there are twenty-seven known examples in England based on the following criteria: they are usually sited in visible locations, near boundaries, route ways or prehistoric earthworks, such as barrow mounds; the bodies often display evidence of decapitation – the skull was often buried beside or between the legs, limbs were tightly bound; multiple interment or burial in a prone (face down) position; many are buried in shallow graves, some with unorthodox orientation. Unfortunately, the majority of these twenty-seven sites were originally excavated during the nineteenth or early twentieth century and are thus characterised by less than adequate excavation reports compared to today's standards. Dating is also an issue because of the almost complete absence of grave goods. Despite this, out of the 343 skeletal remains found buried in definite Anglo-Saxon execution cemeteries so far, seventy-three displayed evidence of being bound, while sixty-two were decapitated.[17]

Few historical records mention decapitation as a means of judicial punishment. It appears to have only been utilised for the most serious of transgressions, for example a cup-bearer to King Æthelstan was beheaded for treason, while a man who took four sheaves of wheat from the royal grain store, without permission from the royal steward, was also sentenced to be beheaded, he was later saved by the intervention of St Swithun.[18] According to Alyxandra Mattison of Sheffield University, there appear to be nine well-dated late Anglo-Saxon execution sites at which decapitated individuals were buried: Bran Ditch and Chesterton Lane (Cambridgeshire), Guildown (Surrey), Meon Hill, Old Dairy Cottage and Stockbridge Down (Hampshire), Staines (Middlesex), Sutton Hoo (Suffolk), and Walkington Wold (Yorkshire).[19] The latter is unusual in that it is the only northern example of an Anglo-Saxon execution cemetery currently in existence and thus sits alone. Excavated by J. E. Bartlett and R. W. Mackey, between 1967 and 1969, on behalf of the East Riding Archaeological Society, Walkington Wold was initially thought to have been Roman in date. It was only when the material was later reanalysed and radiocarbon dated that the cemetery was recognised to be Anglo-Saxon. Consisting entirely of young to adult males, from 18 to 45 years of age, of the twelve skeletons unearthed, only two were intact, the rest were buried without their heads. Moreover, ten disarticulated skulls were found buried randomly on site, although it is impossible to determine if any of these skulls belong to the decapitated corpses. Three of the skulls were found with their mandibulae and/or several of the cervical vertebrae still attached to the head, suggesting they must have been buried in situ before the soft tissue holding them together had fully decomposed. The remaining skulls did not exhibit any associative mandibulae or vertebrae, leading archaeologists to put forward the theory that they were possibly displayed on stakes, a practice well documented in Anglo-Saxon written sources.[20]

Two of the burials from Walkington Wold, namely Skeleton 7 and Skull 8, are particularly unique as the osteological evidence indicates possible frontal decapitation, an unusual way of removing the head. Skeleton 7 was that of a young adult male, 20 to 35 years of age, who had two narrow cut marks running parallel to each other on the front of the first and second thoracic vertebra. The depth of the cuts indicates that the removal of the head was attempted from the front, using a thin blade of some sort rather than an axe. Skull 8, also a young male, 18 to 25 years old, showed similar cut marks on the upper neck region, namely the third and fourth cervical vertebrae, again delivered from the frontal region.[21] Sixteen individuals unearthed at Bran Ditch were also decapitated, with six missing their skulls. One skull each was absent from burials at Old Dairy, Stockbridge Down and Sutton Hoo.[22] Several sites in Ireland exhibit similar characteristics, such as Knoxspark Burial Ground in County Sligo, which had nine burials without skulls, sixteen skull-only burials and a decapitated sub adult with the skull included in the grave.[23] While at Portway, Andover, archaeologists from Cotswold Archaeology believe they may have uncovered one of the largest execution site assemblages to date. Located only 500 metres away from two already identified Anglo-Saxon cemeteries, in 2006 ninety-five graves were excavated, which contained the remains of an estimated 124 individuals, all young men. Many had been buried in a prone position, seven of the graves contained multiple bodies and twenty-three had been decapitated, the skull either missing or placed between the legs or feet. Surprisingly, around sixty per cent of the burials were not Saxon at all, but early Norman in date, 1066-1154.[24]

Decapitation with a sword, or axe, is not an easy process and the evidence shows that a small number of those beheaded did not experience a swift or painless death, it took at least five attempts to sever the head from the body of one poor soul from the Chesterton Lane cemetery and at least three attempts on another skeleton from Old Dairy Cottage. Inhumation 5 from Chesterton Lane and Skulls 2 and 5 from Walkington Wold also exhibited chop marks on the cranium, whereas Skeleton 7 from Meon Hill and Skeleton 575 from Old Dairy Cottage both exhibited cuts on the clavicle, areas that would have been hit if the victim was struggling at the time of execution.[25] Other oddities worthy of mention include the relatively low proportion of women present, only sixty have been identified from sixteen sites. It is believed that women probably received a different punishment from men.[26] Two graves at Stockbridge Down included a decapitated dog and a sheep skull respectively, while four newborn lambs were placed across the knees of an individual interred at Old Dairy Cottage. The remains of a young headless ewe were also found lying across the leg bone of a skeleton from Portway, Andover, while another body from the same cemetery had a sheep's skull and lower mandible buried with the deceased. Why the remains of animals were interred with the executed remains a mystery, although Andrew Reynolds suggests that the Stockbridge Down dog might be evidence of a conviction for coursing.[27] There is also good evidence to show that many of the execution victims were tied or bound in some manner, no doubt to prevent escape before punishment was administered. These include individuals from Chesterton Lane and Guildown, where fifteen skeletons were found buried in a supine position (on their back) with their hands behind their backs, and Stockbridge Down, where two individuals were found buried in an identical manner, together with one prone burial where the hands were found located underneath the front of the pelvis.[28] Twenty-seven of those interred at Portway also displayed evidence of having their hands or feet bound.[29]

Before the eighteenth century, imprisonment was rarely used as a punishment and was primarily used for those awaiting trial. Prisons were rather make-do in nature, and could comprise anything from a simple room in a public basement to an underground chamber in a castle. It wasn't until after this date that a more formalised penal institution began to emerge. In the UK, we find myriad establishments, including a local gaol, a lock up, debtor's prison, convict prison and a bridewell, which is a house of correction for women and children. During the research process, I found an enormous amount of historical documentation relating to prisons in general, but information regarding prison burial grounds was somewhat harder to come by. Many penal institutions no longer exist, for example the largely forgotten British Columbia Penitentiary Cemetery in Canada was only recently found by the construction of a new housing development and to date forty-eight gravestones have been uncovered.[30] Whereas the prison burial ground on Spike Island, County Cork, Ireland, originally a Napoleonic fortress, was purposely entombed under tonnes of earth during the 1860s. Records show that over 1,000 convicts were buried here by the time the prison closed in 1883, with most dying in the first decade of its opening. The Spike Island Project, directed by Dr Barra Ó Donnabháin of University College, Cork, is currently investigating the site.[31] That is not to say it has been impossible to find out any relevant information. For instance, the cemetery at St Margaret Fyebriggate in Combusto, Norwich has been interpreted by archaeologists as a burial ground for fourteenth to sixteenth-century criminals, possibly housing those who were hanged on the gallows just outside the gates of the city of Norwich.[32] Likewise, in 2002, excavations by Oxford Archaeology inside the precinct of Oxford Castle uncovered sixty-two burials dating from the sixteenth to the nineteenth century. Oxford Castle served as the county prison for much of the post-medieval period and public hangings were routinely carried out at the gallows in front of the prison.[33]

Until its abolishment in 1965, the death penalty in the UK was still very much on the statute books, with more than 200 felonies punishable by death, including the less serious crimes of forgery, burglary and highway robbery. From 1900 until 1964 it is believed that around 800 men and women were executed by hanging, with over ninety-eight per cent of the remains buried within the prison confines – protocol dictated that all the remains of executed prisoners belonged to the British Government.[34] Before 1900 it is almost impossible to trace where the executed were laid to rest as many of the official records have been lost or destroyed. A significant number of the condemned also had their sentences commuted to 'transportation to the colonies,' whereby they were forcibly removed to the Americas or Australia for a term of 'indentured servitude' i.e. forced labour. Unable to return home, many were never heard of again. The British Government's recent proclivity for selling off state-owned prisons to private property developers has aided the search. Oxford Prison, for instance, is now a boutique hotel, yet during the hotel's construction the remains of seventy-six inmates were found buried within the old prison grounds.[35] In 2003, the planned closure and redevelopment of Gloucester Prison hit a snag when it was discovered that there could be up to 122 executed criminals buried in unmarked graves underneath the prison. Public executions took place at the gate lodge until the middle of the nineteenth century and 'tradition was prisoners were always buried within the prison'. The Ministry of Justice later conceded that it was aware of seventeen burials dating to between 1874 and 1939.[36] Similarly, in 2017, plans to build homes on the site of the old Dorchester Prison sparked uproar when it was discovered that the remains of former executed inmates would not be exhumed from the prison burial ground before building works commenced.[37]

After contacting the Ministry of Justice to enquire about the number of prison burial grounds on record, I drew a blank. The National Archives in Kew, a wonderful resource, was also surprisingly vague. Nevertheless, a bit of old-fashioned concerted research has proved fruitful. So, here goes. All that remains of London's famed Newgate Prison is a grim-looking passage way linking the old jail to the Old Bailey courts. This area was once the burial ground for executed prisoners, many of whom are still interred under the flagstones in lime-encased coffins. A few bodies have been reburied in the City of London Cemetery, complete with accompanying gravestones.[38] Those who were executed at Wandsworth Prison were buried in unmarked graves within the prison grounds. Alas, the cemetery is no longer visible as it has long since been paved over and there is nothing left to indicate that over 100 prisoners are still buried there.[39] Pentonville Prison at North Wall Gate, Islington has a cemetery of unmarked graves on a well-kept lawn, including those of

Dr Crippen, who was executed at Pentonville for murdering his wife, and serial killer John Reginald Galloway Christie, who murdered all of his female victims at 10 Rillington Place.[40] Executed prisoners in Holloway Prison, London, which became the first and only all-female jail in 1903, were originally buried in unmarked graves behind the prison walls, but have since been moved to cemeteries all over England, a large number of bodies have been reburied in Brookwood Cemetery, Surrey.[41] Bodmin Jail, Cornwall, had two sites for inmate burials, one sited behind the coal-storage shed, the other in an old exercise yard on the western side of the jail. When the jail was redeveloped in the late 1800s, a number of human remains were exhumed and reinterred on the hill behind it.[42] Archaeological excavation of York Castle car park in 1998 unearthed the skeletal remains of five individuals in unmarked graves, thought to be executed prisoners. The car park was once the site of York Castle's County Gaol.[43] Strangeways Prison, now known as HM Prison Manchester, had its own gallows and executed prisoners were buried in unmarked graves in a small cemetery on the grounds. During rebuilding work after the infamous 1990 prison riots, the cemetery was demolished and the remains of sixty to 100 prisoners, including those of the famous Manchester Martyrs, were exhumed, cremated and reinterred in two communal plots at Blackley Cemetery in Manchester.[44] The Crumlin Road Gaol in Northern Ireland, also known as HM Prison Belfast, is the only Victorian era prison of its kind remaining on the island. Seventeen inmates were executed here, their bodies were buried inside the prison in unconsecrated ground and the graves were marked with only their initials and year of execution on the prison walls.[45] The remains of condemned men in Barlinnie Prison, Glasgow, were originally buried in a series of unmarked graves behind the prison walls. During renovation work in 1997, the remains of executed prisoners were exhumed and reburied in various cemeteries throughout Scotland.[46]

During the 1800s, large numbers of prisoners were also housed in huge ships commonly referred to as hulks. In Portsmouth, England, between 1796 and 1814, there were over twenty-four gigantic floating prisons, moored along the harbour wall, each housing around 7,000 inmates. What happened to these prisoners upon their death is little known as there are virtually no surviving records. Many, it is believed, were transported to the colonies. It is also possible that some were dispensed with overboard.[47]

However, if you speak to anyone local to the area they will point you in the direction of Rat Island, a tidal island located in the harbour between Portsmouth and Gosport, where they say the dead from the hulks were once buried. Dismissed as mere rumours, for over 200 years Rat Island held onto its secrets. That is until 2014, when, after a series of winter storms had battered the Portsmouth area, a member of the public, out walking their dog on Rat Island, stumbled across a number of skeletal body parts poking out from the sand and duly notified the authorities. The Ministry of Defence, which owns the island, organised an investigation and in May 2017 a team of archaeologists, together with veteran soldiers from Operation Nightingale, a military initiative that uses archaeology as a means of aiding the recovery of injured service personnel, began a four-day excavation. Working meticulously along the shoreline, at low tide, the group carefully excavated a number of bodies from the sandbanks, together with any grave goods. It appeared the majority of individuals had been interred in coffins, as many of the iron and copper nails were still in situ. Once exhumed, the remains were sent to Cranfield Forensic Institute for further analysis. Initial results indicated that all the remains belonged to one specific group, young men of around 18 to 21 years of age – there were no women or children present – implying they could indeed have been prisoners from the hulks.[48] In March 2019 a combined team of archaeologists, military police, and Operation Nightingale personnel returned to the island to recover any further finds that might have been exposed in the two-year interim period. Not only did they determine that the cemetery was much larger than previously thought, with many burials cutting through earlier graves, they also uncovered the remains from at least a further eleven individuals.[49]

Keeping with the nautical theme, there are certain people whose criminal activities occupy a similar water-like environment. I am referring to pirates of course. I probably get more enquiries regarding the subject of pirates than any other. Not pertaining to their maritime exploits, I hasten to add, but rather to the skull and crossbones symbolism, etched into gravestones, that can be found in cemeteries all over the world. Recalling a similar design on the de facto pirate flag, the so-called Jolly Roger, people are convinced they have stumbled across a pirate burial ground. This is not the case. The skull and crossbones motif is, in fact, a visual representation of the term *'Memento mori,'* the Latin for 'Remember you must die', and has no affiliation with pirates. I am afraid there is no such thing as a pirate graveyard. Or is there?

On the small island of île Sainte-Marie, just over six kilometres off the coast of eastern Madagascar, sits the world's only proclaimed Pirates Graveyard. A recently discovered map, dating to 1733, refers to it simply as 'the island of pirates'. Today it is one of Madagascar's most popular tourist destinations, but during the seventeenth and eighteenth centuries, its inlets and secluded bays provided the perfect base for pirate ships to make anchor. It was during this particular period that colonial warships from the likes of Britain, Spain and France were relentlessly patrolling the Caribbean seas in order to protect their commercial interests, and for the pirates, well, their traditional hunting ground had become too dangerous. The lawless island of île Sainte-Marie, with its proximity to the lucrative East India trade routes, where no European power held dominion, was an attractive alternative.[50] For over a century the island became a land base for approximately 1,000 pirates and included such legends as Adam Baldridge, one of île Saint-Marie's founders who reportedly lived a luxurious and extravagant life on the island, which included a harem of indigenous women. In 1697, he was forced to flee to the American colonies after the local tribe's folk discovered that he had sold a group of natives as slaves.[51] William Kidd, the notorious Scottish privateer was also a resident, as was Abraham Samuel, the king of the pirates, also known as Tolinar Rex and Thomas Tew, who established a privateer route known as the Pirate Round.[52] Many of the pirates married local women, raised families and remained on île Sainte-Marie long after their pirating days were over. Upon death, an unspecified number were buried in a hilltop cemetery, namely the Pirates Graveyard, overlooking the sea. Abandoned for centuries, the graveyard does still exist, albeit overgrown with vegetation. Approximately thirty tombstones are still visible. Some say William Kidd is buried here, in a large black tomb, sitting upright as punishment for his wicked deeds. In fact, Kidd, who came from Greenock in Scotland, was imprisoned in Newgate Prison, London, before being found guilty of piracy on the high seas. He was hanged on the 23 May 1701 at Execution Dock in Wapping. His ship, *Adventure Galley*, was discovered in 2000, moored near the île Sainte-Marie, while his treasure, now lost, is rumoured to be buried somewhere in the surrounding waters.[53]

Burying the Dead

A challenger to île Sainte-Marie's claim of the only pirate graveyard may soon be forthcoming. In March 2018, it was announced that archaeologists had discovered 'America's largest pirate mass burial site' on the shores of Cape Cod, Massachusetts. The newly found burial ground is believed to contain the remains of over 100 individuals, who were washed ashore when their pirate ship, *Whydah Gally*, sank during a heavy storm in April 1717. Archaeologists also believe they have found the grave of its captain, Black Sam Bellamy, often referred to as the 'prince of pirates,' due to his fair nature and avoidance of gratuitous violence. Born in Devon, England his swashbuckling exploits would make him the richest pirate in the world. Bar the skeletal remains, an unusually designed pistol was deposited in the grave which, remarkably, matches historical records pertaining to Bellamy's actual weapon. 'The pistol had some unique features and symbols and it was presented to him in a very decorative silk ribbon. It's completely consistent with Bellamy's pistol,' quoted team member Professor Timothy Palmbach, Chair of Forensic Sciences at the University of New Haven. At present the exact location of the burial ground is being kept secret, but it is thought to lie in a secluded area in the outer cape region of Cape Cod. Casey Sherman, the excavation leader, said that among the discoveries they had made so far included a number of burial hills and vaults, together with solid dating evidence, such as seventeenth-century pottery and cutlery. Once the excavations are complete, he hopes the site can become a memorial graveyard.[54]

Sufferers of disease and deformity were often considered dangerous and powerful in equal measure, and were hence regarded as aberrant. Leper cemeteries are a good example of how the ostracism of such misfortunates occurred not only in life, but also in death. Leprosy is a highly infectious disease, which has been around since ancient times, and is renowned for its disfiguring skin sores, stunted appendages and mutilated facial features. Those who became afflicted often faced widespread persecution from the rest of society. In England, the Canon De Leprosis of 1179 declared that lepers could not live among the healthy. A few years later, in 1200, they were banned from the streets of London entirely.[55] Whereas in 1321, King of France, Philip V, ordered the nationwide burning of lepers on the basis they had conspired with Jews and Muslims to poison the wells and destroy Christianity.[56] From the eleventh to the fourteen century there is an unprecedented rise in the foundation of leper hospitals throughout Western Europe. In England, there are at least 320 known institutions, all established between 1066 and 1536; many were small in size, having an average of only ten beds. To date around 800 burials from the accompanying hospital cemeteries have been unearthed and almost half were recovered from a single archaeological excavation at St James and St Mary Magdalene in Chichester – 330 skeletons were excavated in 1986/7 and a further forty-four burials were excavated in 1993. Other examples include St Margaret's Hospital, High Wycombe, Buckinghamshire. Founded by 1229, around fifty to sixty bodies were exhumed from the cemetery in 1883, and a further twelve adult burials were uncovered during roadworks in 1986. St Nicholas' Hospital, Lewes, was founded as a leper house in 1264-5 and in 1994, excavations at the site recovered 102 burials. St Mary Magdalen's Hospital, Brook Street, Colchester, was founded for leprous males in the early twelfth century. Excavations here in 1989 uncovered twelve burials relating to the leper hospital, which were sealed by the cemetery of a later church, while excavations of the medieval cemetery of St Leonard's Leper Hospital, Midland Road, Peterborough in 2014 unearthed a total of 131 inhumations.[57]

In other parts of the world lepers were not fortunate enough to spend their final days in a designated hospital setting. In fact, many were forcibly removed from their families and exiled on some remote, godforsaken corner of the planet. In 1863, many Hawaiian natives, who had already succumbed to a number of foreign diseases brought in by visiting merchant ships, began suffering from a new ailment referred to locally as 'mai pake'. It was later diagnosed as 'the genuine Oriental leprosy'. To prevent it spreading across the island chain, King Kamehameha V issued an Act to Prevent the Spread of Leprosy, whereby those infected were rounded up and relocated to an isolated peninsula on the island of Molokai. The leper colony they established was called Kalaupapa. During its formative years the state made no provision of food or healthcare for the community, and those children born to leper patients were seized from their mothers and given away to adoptive families. This would have a devastating effect on traditional tribal communities. Thousands are thought to have died within the colony and the vast majority are buried within twenty documented cemeteries dotted across the Kalaupapa peninsula. Fewer than 1,300 gravestones are visible today, the rest remain unmarked. Limited archaeological surveys estimate the number of burials to be somewhere in the range of 2,000-5,000 individuals.[58]

In 1904 a similar fate befell residents of Greece, when those suffering from leprosy were forcibly removed from their communities to the remote islet of Spinalonga. Any property or monetary assets the lepers owned were seized by the Greek Government, their citizenship rights were forfeited and upon its closure, in 1957, the Greek authorities tried to destroy all knowledge of the colony's existence by burning the files. At its peak, the colony comprised nearly 400 inhabitants; the dead are apparently buried in the small cemetery of the Church of St George.[59] Similarly, the famed correctional facility of Robben Island near Cape Town, South Africa, was once a leper colony when the country was under British rule. In 1843, the Colonial Secretary, John Montagu, believed Robben Island's geographical isolation would be an ideal location for diseased misfortunates. As it offered a certain degree of autonomy, many lepers chose to leave their old colony at Hemel-en-Aarde, Caledon and transfer to the new, up-to-date facility on Robben Island. They were given an inordinate amount of freedom and could even travel back and forth to the mainland if they wished. This all came to an end after the Leprosy Repression Act was introduced in 1892. Before this date an average of twenty-five lepers a year were admitted to Robben Island, but in 1892 that number rose to 338, with a further 250 people forcibly admitted in 1893. Upon death, many of the lepers were buried in a large cemetery located to the north of the Church of the Good Shepherd and the male leprosarium, the latter was demolished due to fear of the disease spreading, and it is believed the cemetery could contain the remains of thousands of individuals. The majority of the graves are unmarked and the few that are not have a simple shallow shale grave marker with no discernible inscription. Outside this area, to the south, there lies just one grave, while to the west and north, there are further rows of graves lying under a forest of Australian myrtle and wattle trees. Archaeologists believe the cemetery possibly extends to the site of the maximum security prison, where human bones were unearthed during the digging of foundation trenches in the 1960s and also when a tennis court was constructed in A-Section in the 1970s.[60]

The Deviant Ones

Along Redcross Way, a quiet back street in Southwark, London, there exists a large empty plot of land otherwise known as Crossbones Graveyard. During medieval times this particular area was the city's primary red light district – prostitution here dates back to the Roman era – and Crossbones Graveyard became the final resting place for the thousands of prostitutes who lived, worked and died in the area. Southwark, at this time, was not controlled by the Crown, but by the Bishop of Winchester, who was responsible for the licensing and taxation of the borough's prostitutes. As such, the women were often referred to as 'Winchester Geese'. In the 1598 Survey of London, written by Tudor historian John Stow, it states:

> I have heard of ancient men, of good credit, report, that these single women were forbidden the rites of the church, so long as they continued that sinful life, and were excluded from Christian burial, if they were not reconciled before their death. And therefore, there was a plot of ground called the Single Woman's churchyard, appointed for them far from the parish church.

By the seventeenth century the brothels of Southwark had all but gone, as had the prostitutes. Crossbones now began to receive the remains of the poor and destitute from the parish of St Saviour's, which was regarded as one of the worst slums in London, together with those who had been denied a Christian burial. A surviving parish letter from 1832 notes that the ground was 'so very full of coffins that it is necessary to bury within two feet of the surface', while one commentator states that it was 'completely overcharged with the dead'. Following public concerns regarding hygiene and safety, in 1853 the decision was taken to close the graveyard. A few years' later the parish of St Saviour's decided that the abandoned graveyard would be the ideal location to build a new school. They were wrong and, in 1908, the school was forced to close its doors as 'many bones were seen sticking out of the ground'.[61]

Over the next eighty years the graveyard was all but forgotten, the site was neglected and soon became overgrown with vegetation. It wasn't until the early 1990s that Crossbones entered the public consciousness once more, when the land was acquired by Transport for

London for their underground expansion plans. As is mandatory for all major construction projects, especially in London, an archaeological excavation was required before any work could commence. In 1992, archaeologists from the Museum of London were given six weeks to excavate the graveyard. What they uncovered was a site compacted with human remains, with numerous multiple burials deposited one on top of the other. A total of 148 graves were unearthed, all dating from the nineteenth century, with 66.2 per cent of the bodies children 5 years or younger. In the limited timeframe they were given, the archaeologists estimated they had touched upon only one per cent of the graveyard, had not yet reached the medieval layers, and concluded that when Crossbones was finally abandoned it contained thousands, perhaps tens of thousands of bodies.[62] Although not open to the public today, Crossbones has become a place of pilgrimage for many. Its large rusting gates are now permanently decorated with a wide range of trinkets, beads and feathers to commemorate those buried inside. In 2006, the graveyard was officially recognised with the addition of a plaque honouring 'The Outcast Dead' and the opening of the Crossbones Memorial Garden. Since then, around the time of Halloween, a play is performed in memory to those who lie, in peace, within the graveyard site.[63]

The discovery of the remains of so many young children at Crossbones naturally evokes a pitying response, but that has not always been the case. According to Michael MacDonald's book *Sleepless Souls: Suicide in Early Modern England*, unbaptised infants were often considered among the most dangerous of all the dead. That such beliefs existed is exemplified by a passage from Burchard of Worms' *Corrector*: 'When any child has died without baptism they take the corpse of the little one and place it in some secret place and transfix it with a stake ... lest it rise up and injure many.'[64] In a similar manner, in the fifth century St Augustine of Hippo proclaimed that the souls of unbaptised infants were condemned to Hell because of the original sin, and shall thus remain for all eternity in an unholy void, commonly known as *limbo infantus*.[65] To prevent either from occurring, many stillborn infants were often baptised by midwives, a practice ratified in Lateran IV, where it was determined that anyone could administer the sacrament of baptism should the need arise.[66] Some were secretly buried in consecrated ground, within a churchyard environment, usually under the cover of darkness, as seen in the churchyard of Hereford Cathedral, which in 1398 was forced to construct an enclosure wall to prevent such clandestine burials.[67]

It is hard to believe that the dead body of any baby would be deemed deviant, yet in Ireland there exists a unique type of burial ground called a cillín, which was primarily used for unbaptised babies and infants, although the skeletal remains of children as old as 6 have been unearthed at a site in Caherlehillan, County Kerry. Unofficial in nature, graves found within such burial locations are usually of a simple affair, often surrounded by a few stones to designate their outline or marked by a tiny flagstone. According to tradition, the burial of an infant would take place at night with only the men in attendance. 'Other family members were not encouraged to recognize the birth of the child or to accompany it on its final journey,' said Flan Kelly, a local farmer, when speaking to the *Irish Examiner*. Comparable social outcasts such as suicides, the mentally infirm, those with physical deformities and excommunicates have also, on rare occasions, been found buried inside a cillín enclosure. For example, an 1842 newspaper report from County Down refers to the body of a suicide victim interred within one, while the remains of adult burials have been unearthed lying next to those of children in an excavated cillín at Aughinish Castle, County Limerick. Emer Dennehy, an archaeologist working with Transport Infrastructure Ireland, explains that mothers and babies who died in childbirth were often buried together. 'In some cases, it's recorded that the baby would be buried between the mother's legs in what were known as "tandem burials",' she said. 'And if the mother died without being "churched" (a blessing given to mothers after recovery from childbirth) then she could be buried in the cillín as well.' The majority of cillíní are to be found in rural areas, many on sites that previously had a sacred element attached to them, such as holy wells, ancient earthworks or abandoned graveyards. In Caherlehillan, cillín graves were found clustered around the cross-slabs and corner-post shrine of an early ecclesiastical enclosure. In fact, fifty-one per cent of cillín burial grounds found in County Kerry were sited within the confines of a pre-existing archaeological monument. The last official study, in 2013, found there were approximately 1,440 known children's burial grounds throughout Ireland, including 500 sites listed in County Galway and 250 sites in County Kerry.[68]

Before we bid a fond farewell to the deviant ones, no investigation into the subject matter can exclude, in my humble opinion, the following site. In fact, when I began mulling over chapter titles in my head and came up with the deviant tag, two examples immediately sprang to mind – Anglo-Saxon execution cemeteries and Boot Hill. The latter is a graveyard of immense historical and cultural importance, whose infamy spread throughout the Wild West during the late nineteenth century. It became a stalwart of the American cowboy movie genre and is frequently depicted in Hollywood films, such as the epic *Gunfight at the O. K. Corral* (1957), *Tombstone* (1993) and *Wyatt Earp* (1994), to name but a few. Located in Tombstone, Arizona, over the succeeding decades Boot Hill has become somewhat of an icon within cinematography studies, with many believing the graveyard was a figment of some Hollywood scriptwriter's imagination. It is not. Boot Hill really does exist.

The city of Tombstone was founded in 1877 by Ed Schieffelin, a mining prospector who struck it lucky when he stumbled across a rich deposit of silver. Word quickly spread about the find and soon an assortment of misfits, including fellow prospectors, cowboys, pioneer folk and businessmen, flocked to the area in order to make their fortune. In a few short years, alongside San Francisco and St Louis, Tombstone was the fastest growing city in America, and thus required its own cemetery.[69] Established in 1878, the chosen site was originally called the Old City Cemetery, but by 1929 people were referring to it as Boot Hill, so named because the majority of men buried there 'died with their boots on'. It is a small graveyard, with perhaps 250 burials at most, the vast majority of which are murderers, thieves, cattle rustlers and prostitutes. They include the popular madam Dutch Annie, 'Queen of the Red Light District' and China Mary, the boss of the Chinese neighbourhood, who was buried in the cemetery in 1906. The perpetrators of the Bisbee massacre, Dan 'Big Dan' Dowd, Omer W. 'Red' Sample, James 'Tex' Howard, William E. 'Billy' Delaney and Daniel 'York' Kelly, who were all hanged on 28 March 1884, are interred in its grounds, as is Marshal Fred White, who was killed by Curly Bill Brocius on 30 October 1880. But undoubtedly its most famous residents are cowboys Tom McLaury, Frank McLaury and Billy Clanton, who were killed in the legendary gun battle at the O.K. Corral on 26 October 1881, by Wyatt Earp, his brothers, and the notorious gambler and gunslinger Doc Holliday. It is generally regarded as the most famous shootout in the history of the American Wild West.[70]

Like many prospector towns that had gone before, by the early 1930s Boot Hill had ceased to exist in all but name. Tombstone's boom years had long gone; records show that in the mid-1880s the population was around the 7,500 mark, but by the late 1930s it had dropped to only 150. As a consequence, Boot Hill rapidly fell into decline, with many of the wooden grave markers stolen as souvenirs by passers-by or destroyed in the harsh climate. It wasn't until the 1940s that an enterprising group of residents from Tombstone and Cochise County began the painstaking task of researching burial records, consulting with relatives and older residents and using all means available to identify Boot Hill's occupants and mark their graves accordingly. The task took several years, but slowly the cemetery was restored to its former glory.[71] Today, Boot Hill has become a popular tourist attraction, complete with the obligatory gift shop.

4

They Died in Heaps

'There is nothing more awful than standing on the edge of a mass grave to watch the bodies being dug up and their families looking on, identifying them, saying this is my husband, this is my son,' said Ann Clwyd, UK MP and Special Envoy on Human Rights in Iraq.[1] Sadly, such a nightmarish vision is all too common nowadays. Mass graves, such as the one described, are an exceptional form of funerary practice as they contain multiple interments and usually arise after a large number of people have been killed. They are typically the result of some catastrophic event, such as famine, disease, war or genocide. Further subdivisions can be made, such as a criminal mass grave, which is one defined by the United Nations as a burial site containing three or more victims of execution. Many have been found in pre-existing burial grounds, surrounded by other inhumations, whereas others stand in isolation, their presence often revealed by accident. The sheer scope of the subject matter is exhaustive and, for that reason, I have decided to focus on three main areas, plague, war and genocide. However, to begin with, here are a few additional examples.

During the Great Irish Potato Famine of 1845-1849 it is estimated that one million people died from hunger. Such an excessive number of deaths, in a relatively short period of time, made it impossible for many to receive a proper burial, so thousands now lie, unidentified, in large communal pits in what are often referred to as famine graveyards, such as the ones found at Callan, County Kilkenny or Abbeystrowry Graveyard, Skibbereen in County Cork. A recent find at Kilkenny Union Workhouse, also dating to the potato famine, has special poignancy. Incorporating the remains of over 1,000 individuals, archaeologists found that the majority of those unearthed were young children.[2] Estimates of those who perished during the Great Famine of China, 1958-1961, are even higher, where it is believed that tens of millions of the population starved to death. In the province of Henan, for example, one of the most populous in China, surviving documents state how the corpses of workers would be dragged from the fields and thrown into large open pits, which were conveniently placed alongside field boundaries.[3]

Mass graves are also an effective tool against the spread of disease and infection. During the 1918 Spanish flu pandemic, which claimed an estimated fifty million lives worldwide, there wasn't a corner of the earth that wasn't affected in one way or another. Even remote regions such as Alaska were devastated by the disease. One surviving report describes how a native Alaskan village called Savonoski was in a 'deplorable state' and 'wretched'. A visiting expedition team, from a nearby cannery, discovered that the entire adult population, around sixty-two individuals, had succumbed to the disease, so they hastily buried the corpses in a makeshift communal pit.[4] Many graveyards in the UK are home to cholera pits, such as those that were dug in 1832 to house the victims of a nationwide outbreak. In Scotland, St Maurs-Glencairn Church in Kilmaurs, Ayrshire, has a large cholera pit located in the south-west corner of the churchyard; a cholera pit was once marked by a mound in the Irvine Old Parish Church Cemetery, Ayrshire until the ground was levelled; 420 victims of the disease are also buried under a mound in St Michael's churchyard, Dumfries.[5] In Glasnevin, Dublin, a large cholera pit and memorial are located in the churchyard grounds, whereas in Belfast some 3,000 cholera victims are thought to be buried in a lime-filled mound known as 'Cholera Pit' or 'Plaguey Hill'.[6]

The devastation caused by natural disasters often necessitates the use of mass graves for the disposal of large numbers of corpses as quickly as possible. In 2010, the island of Haiti was all but destroyed by a large earthquake, killing an estimated 250,000 people. With little time for the niceties of formal burial, the authorities simply collected the bodies that were decomposing in the streets and transported them to a series of mass trenches high up in the hills above the nation's capital Port-au-Prince. Measuring around 100 feet in length, at the height of the disaster around 10,000 bodies was being buried in these graves every day. The Haitians were to suffer yet more tragedy in 2016 when Hurricane Matthew decimated the island, killing thousands of people in its path. In response, more mass graves were dug in the hillside to accommodate those who had lost their lives.⁷ Moreover, in 2014, disaster struck the small village of Argo, in north-eastern Afghanistan, when it was hit by a double landslide that came rushing down the mountainside, engulfing the village below. The first mudslide killed everyone in the village, the second buried hundreds of rescuers who had been brought in to look for survivors. In light of the tragedy, a year later, the entire village was declared a mass grave by the Afghan Government.⁸

Mass paupers' graves were once a familiar site in graveyards and cemeteries. Primarily used by the poor and destitute, who were unable to afford a proper burial, or by those who had no family or friends to bury them, surviving examples include Angel Meadow, Manchester, where 40,000 bodies are believed to have been interred, and a recent find in Bristol, dating to the nineteenth century, that contained the corpses of around 3,000 individuals.⁹ Now referred to as public health funerals – the name pauper has been dropped due to social sensitivities – mass graves for the poor are steadily making a comeback. It was reported recently that from 2006 to 2011, around 100,000 pensioners in the UK who died penniless and alone were buried in paupers' graves.¹⁰ In the USA, paupers' graves are sometimes known as potter's field, a biblical term referring to Akeldama, meaning 'field of blood' in Aramaic. Some of New York City's prime real estate areas, such as Madison Square Park, Washington Square Park and Bryant Park, were once potters' fields, as was the southernmost portion of the famous Chicago City Cemetery, now covered by a number of baseball fields. From 1843 to 1871 it is believed that more than 15,000 people, including the remains of 4,000 Confederate soldiers, were buried in one mass pit.¹¹

Plague

In 2012, while excavating sections of the Saint Just i Pastor Basilica in Barcelona, archaeologists stumbled across the remains of 120 plague victims, buried in a mass grave under the sacristy. Post-excavation analysis revealed that the grave dated back to the time of the Black Death, c. 1348, and, significantly, was the first of its kind to have been unearthed in Spain. 'When we began to exhume the remains, it was clear that this was a mass grave from the time of the epidemic,' said Julia Beltrán, the scientific director of the excavation. 'Bones had been very well preserved, and none of them showed any signs of the kind of damage that could have killed somebody. What's more, there were people of both sexes, children, and of all ages. The victims were all buried within a short time frame.' The grave itself measured no more than three-and-a-half metres in width by one-and-a-half metres in depth and initial investigations indicated that up to 400 bodies had originally been interred. Many are thought to have been removed during renovations to the Basilica in the fifteenth century. Although each body had been stripped of its clothing and personal adornments, great care and attention had been given to each burial. All the bodies had been neatly wrapped in a linen shroud and placed gently within the grave structure, which was demarcated with a series of rows. They were then covered in a solution of quicklime dissolved in water in an attempt to stop the disease spreading, as well as mask the smell of rotting remains. Who these individuals were is not known but they were obviously deemed of high status to have been buried in such a prominent location. 'One thing is clear,' said Beltrán, 'plague does not discriminate against social status.'[12]

The use of mass burial trenches is well documented in Europe throughout this period. In 1348, while witnessing the Black Death decimate the city of Florence, the Italian writer and poet Giovanni Boccaccio recorded:

> As consecrated ground there was not in extant sufficient to provide tombs for the vast multitudes of corpses ... if ancient custom were to be observed and a separate resting-place assigned to each, they dug for each graveyard, as soon as it was full, a huge trench in which they laid the corpses as they arrived by the hundreds at a time, piling them up as merchandise was stowed in the hold of a ship, tier upon tier, each covered with a little earth, until the trench would hold no more.[13]

It is generally accepted that the plague first entered Europe via Sicily, in October 1347, carried by Genoese galleys, and rapidly spread from here to the surrounding area. A separate fleet of infected ships from Kaffa reached Genoa and Venice in January 1348. Venice was particularly badly hit and at the height of the pestilence 600 Venetians were reportedly dying a day. Remote burial grounds were designated across the lagoon, well away from the general population, such as the island of S. Marco Boccacalme, which appears to have now vanished beneath the water. Special barges were provided to transport the dead to these new graveyards, where they were buried en masse at least one-and-a-half metres beneath the soil. In recent years, mass plague pits have also been found on the islands of Lazzaretto Nuovo and Lazzaretto Vecchio, the former became a quarantine station during the Black Death for ships arriving from different ports in the Mediterranean.[14]

From Italy, the disease spread rapidly across Europe, entering France at the end of January 1348; one of the diseased galleys expelled from Italy had made its way to the French port of Marseille. From here the plague ravaged French towns and villages, such as Rouen, Normandy, where three-quarters of the population were completely eradicated in only a few short weeks. A new cemetery was built near the Church of Saint-Maclou, with one large mass grave dug to accommodate those who had died from the pestilence. Even as late as June 1349, Philip VI authorised the Mayor of Amiens to open a new cemetery on the grounds that, 'The mortality ... is so marvellously great that people are dying suddenly, as quickly as between one evening and the following morning and often quicker than that.'[15] By the summer of 1348 the plague had crossed the English Channel, entering England via a southern port town. Shocked at the veracity of the disease, William of Dene, a monk of Rochester stated, 'the plague carried off so vast a multitude of people of both sexes that nobody could be found who would bear the corpses to the grave. Men and women carried their own children on their shoulders to the church and threw them into a common pit.' In the town of Winchester, as people were dying in their hundreds, the Church insisted that all corpses must be buried in consecrated ground. The local populace, what was left of them, vehemently disagreed and argued that the bodies of plague victims must be taken outside the city walls and buried in a common pit.[16] The populace won. In September 1348, the pestilence finally hit London. With squalid living conditions and narrow streets overflowing with sewage, the pestilence had found the perfect breeding ground.

Under normal circumstances London would have been able to cope with its regular intake of dead bodies, but the situation it now faced was anything but normal. The capital's existing graveyards were just too small to deal with the crisis, so in 1348 two emergency cemeteries were consecrated. The most recognised is East Smithfield, which was opened by 'one John Corey, a Clergyman, ... in which were buried innumerable Bodies, during the Time of the Pestilence.'[17] Located on the site of today's Royal Mint, between 1986 and 1988 large areas of the cemetery were excavated by archaeologists from the Museum of London, who found that the plague burials clustered in two distinct areas, to the west and east. The western side of the cemetery contained three mass burial trenches, the largest trench measuring sixty-seven metres in length, two metres in width, with a depth of around one-and-a-half metres, and contained the remains of 300 individuals. A separate mass pit was found adjacent to this and housed the bodies of eight adults and children. There were also 250 single inhumations. To the archaeologists' surprise each corpse had been carefully laid to rest, rather than hurriedly thrown into the pits, and some had even been buried in coffins before interment. Moreover, fifty-one children were delicately placed in between the bodies of the adults. The eastern side of the cemetery consisted of just one large burial pit, stretching for an incredible 125 metres, and contained the skeletal remains of 102 individuals, together with ninety single inhumation burials. Archaeologists believe that between forty to fifty per cent of the cemetery still lies in situ, underneath the Royal Mint.[18]

As with any major city that undergoes constant redevelopment, the vast majority of London's ancient pestilence sites have now been built over. For example, Liverpool Street Station sits on the site of an old plague pit, and during the construction of the Piccadilly tube line, where Brompton Road and Knightsbridge meet, a pit containing extensive human remains was found that was so dense it was nigh on impossible to tunnel through. Other examples, as detailed by Catherine Arnold, in her book *Necropolis – London and its Dead*, include cartloads of human remains discovered at Beak Street, Golden Square and Poland Street, Soho, and a large number of human bones buried eight feet underneath the floor of a bookshop in Oxford Street. The most recent find came in March 2013 when engineers working on the Crossrail project uncovered twenty-five skeletons lying in a five-and-a-half-metre wide shaft, alongside pottery dating to the mid-fourteenth century. Samples extracted from the skeletons' teeth revealed the presence of Yersinia pestis bacteria, the strain identifiable with the plague. Surviving documentation does suggest that out of the thousands of Londoners who perished during the Black Death, the majority were buried in a mass grave outside the City limits. As yet its exact location had remained a conundrum, but with this new find archaeologists believe it now lies under Charterhouse Square near the Barbican. Crossrail's lead archaeologist, Jay Carver, said the find finally 'solves a 660-year-old mystery and further excavations will follow to see if – as we expect – we come across a much bigger mass burial trench.'[19]

For the next 300 years variations of the plague repeatedly returned to haunt Europe. Between 1665 and 1666 almost a quarter of London's population perished in what is often termed the Great Plague of London. In Stepney it is said that over 1,000 people were dying a week, and with the churchyard full to bursting point a large pit was dug at the corner of Mile End Road to receive bodies. In the old parish of Aldgate archaeologists have uncovered a large pit near the churchyard, over fifteen metres long and seven metres wide, which contained the skeletal remains of 1,114 bodies. In west London, it is said the Army was drafted in to dig a number of mass trenches in Hyde Park to receive the city's overflow of corpses.[20] In Venice, in 1629, another outbreak of plague saw an estimated 80,000 die within the first seven months. Many of the infected were forcibly transported to the island of Poveglia, where they awaited death.[21] The island is today regarded as one large mass grave, with over fifty per cent of the soil containing human remains. Almost 100 years later, in 1720, the Great Plague of Marseille devastated the city, killing around 100,000 of its residents. In 1998, archaeological excavations carried out across the city, by the Université de la Méditerranée, found a series of mass plague pits containing hundreds of bodies.[22]

War

The use of mass graves during times of conflict is not a new invention and harks back to ancient times. Warfare is a fast-moving enterprise and there is often little time to bury the dead. The spread of disease generated by large numbers of rotting corpses can, therefore, be a real threat and necessitates the quick disposal of bodies. A recent example of this was unearthed in the autumn of 2018, when a mass grave was discovered by workmen in Volgograd, Russia, containing the remains of 1,837 German soldiers killed during the Battle of Stalingrad, (1942-1943). Still wearing their uniforms, and in possession of various conflict paraphernalia, it was immediately apparent to archaeologists that the men had been buried with much haste.[23] Sometimes there is also the need for concealment. Throughout Spain there are over 2,000 known mass graves stemming from the Spanish Civil War, where an estimated 500,000 people died between 1936 and 1939. Approximately 135,000 were also killed after the war ended. Several excavations are currently being conducted by both archaeologists and forensic anthropologists, based upon witness testimony, such as the mass grave unearthed during the summer of 2008 near the town of San Juan del Monte. Here, the skeletal remains of five individuals were found, believed to be those who were kidnapped, tortured and killed after the 1936 military coup.[24] Similarly, in Quang Ngai, Vietnam, a mass grave of ten Vietnamese soldiers was discovered on 28 December 2011. In an attempt to conceal their deaths, personal belongings, including wallets, backpacks, guns, bullets, mirrors, and combs, had been buried with them.[25]

In November 1632, in a small town in central Germany just south west of Leipzig, one of the largest battles of the Thirty Years' War began, namely the Battle of Lützen. The Thirty Years' War is regarded by historians as one of the most brutal conflicts in European history, yet it is surprising that many have little knowledge of its existence. Commencing in 1618, the conflict initially began as a struggle between Catholicism and Protestantism, when the future Holy Roman Emperor and King of Bohemia, Ferdinand II, attempted to impose the Roman Catholic religion upon his realm. Understandably the Protestant nobles of Bohemia and Austria were not too happy at this sudden turn of events and after much remonstration they rose up in rebellion against their king. What followed would have a profound effect on the future geographical layout of Europe, as the countries of Sweden, Denmark, Poland and Russia were all drawn into the melee. Nevertheless, it would be in the towns and villages of Germany, where the majority of the fighting would take place, with Lützen at the heart of the conflict. The battle itself is not renowned for any military significance, more for its sheer brutality. Fought between the Protestant Army of Sweden's King Gustav II Adolf and the Roman Catholic Habsburg Imperial Army, led by General

Albrecht von Wallenstein, around 20,000 soldiers were involved in the slaughter and it is estimated that around 6,000-9,000 of this number perished, the most notable death being King Gustav of Sweden.

In 2006, after a metal detector survey uncovered around 3,000 projectiles and ammunitions in a local field, archaeologists believed they had finally located the exact location of the conflict; until then much of the known battlefield was covered by a nursing home and shopping development. Over a five-year period they embarked upon a painstaking analysis of the site, digging numerous test pits throughout the designated boundary, until in 2011, while excavating an exploratory trench, they found a mass grave. I would like to add that mass graves from this era are not unique. Others have been unearthed in Germany, for example a mass burial ground was found during the construction of a house in Höchstadt, Franconia, in 1985, another was uncovered during gravel dredging in Wittstock, Brandenburg in 2007 – the grave itself was put on display in the Brandenburg State Archaeological Museum – while another mass burial pit was exposed by pipeline engineers in Alerheim, south-west Germany in 2008. Back in Lützen, worried that the find would attract the attention of looters, instead of continuing with the excavation on site, as is the norm, the archaeologists decided to experiment with a somewhat unconventional methodology. With the aid of heavy diggers, cranes, and a large flatbed lorry, the entire mass grave was hoisted out of the ground, in one fifty-five tonne block, and transported back to a laboratory in the city of Halle, where it could be examined more closely. Once there the grave was split into two, with each piece placed inside a protective wooden casing to prevent the soil from disintegrating. A bioarchaeological team from the State Office for Heritage Management and Archaeology, led by Nicole Nicklisch, began their analysis, immediately identifying the presence of forty-seven separate skeletons. Sixteen of them had experienced previous battle-related head injuries, with one man suffering four separate head wounds before he died, while twenty-one exhibited other forms of fractures or broken limbs, specifically in the arms, legs and ribs. Twenty-one also suffered gunshot wounds to the head, a rarity for this time, eleven still had bullets lodged in their skull. The majority of the corpses were buried naked and a few were interred in rows, albeit the majority appear to have been thrown into the pit at random, probably by the local townsfolk who were left to clear up the mess a few days after the battle had finished. 'It can certainly be assumed that the local populations of Lützen did not have a positive attitude towards the fallen soldiers, regardless of any military affiliation,' said Nicklisch. Work is still continuing on each grave section; the team believes that each one could be holding hundreds of bodies.[26]

Somewhat closer to home is Culloden Moor, the site of the last battle to be fought on British soil. Located around eight kilometres east of Inverness, in the Highlands of Scotland, it was here, on 16 April 1746, that Bonnie Prince Charlie's attempts to restore the Stuart dynasty to the British throne came to a disastrous and bloody end. In less than an hour a well-equipped government army, led by Charlie's distant cousin William Duke of Cumberland, defeated the vastly outnumbered and outgunned Jacobite Army, which was predominantly made up of Highlander clansfolk. Records show that some fifty government troops were killed with a further 300 wounded. A much larger number of Jacobites perished – it is estimated around 1,250 – with many dying from their wounds on the battlefield. In the aftermath, a total of 3,470 Jacobites, and their supporters, were taken prisoner, of these 120 were executed, eighty-eight died in prison, 936 were transported to the colonies, while 222 were 'banished'. The fate of almost 700 Jacobites is still unknown.[27]

In June 2000, and again in September 2001, a programme of archaeological fieldwork was carried out on the battlefield site by GUARD, a commercial archaeological service formerly part of Glasgow University. The fieldwork included a ground-penetrating radar survey of the Field of the English, where government troops are presumed to have been buried, and the site of the Jacobite clan graves, the results of which were broadcast in 2002 on the popular BBC2 TV programme *Two Men in a Trench*. The survey was repeated in April 2006 where mounds in the clan cemetery revealed the presence of numerous burial pits hidden underneath. Archaeologists and historians believe the pits contain bodies from some of the following Highland clans: the McDonalds, MacGillivrays, Macleans, the Stewarts of Appin, Maclachans, Camerons, Frasers, Campbells, Mackintoshes and Atholl Highlanders together with a series of mass interments simply entitled 'mixed clans'.[28] Some twelve years later, in April 2018, just before the 272nd anniversary of the battle, news filtered out that another potential mass grave had been discovered on site. According to witness testimony at the time of the conflict, sixteen Jacobite officers, who escaped the battlefield and were found hiding in the dungeon at Culloden House, were shot dead by government troops and buried by the Bargas Tree, an imposing English elm complete with leg and neck irons. The tree no longer exists, nor does a commemorative stone, which was apparently inscribed with the words: 'Here lie soldiers killed by the English at the Battle of Culloden'. What does remain is one small grassy knoll. Having obtained permission to investigate the knoll, in 2018 Lochaber Archaeological Society carried out a geophysical survey of the site and found three large pits hidden directly under the mound. Robert Cairns, Chairman of the Lochaber Archaeological Society said:

> We are very excited about the results. The mound has three distinctive pits in it so obviously it is quite significant. It is not something that you would normally find in a mound. We are planning to put in a small trench later in the year to see if there are any human remains in the largest pit. We are confident we will find human remains.

David McGovern, a member of A Circle of Gentlemen, a Jacobite society founded in 1747, added: 'It looks like we have found the martyrs' graves. History has always said they were buried there but now modern science seems to have confirmed it.'[29]

War can take on many guises. As the eyes of the world have been focused on events in the Middle East in recent years, an equally brutal conflict has been taking place in South America, between rival drug cartels or drug cartels and government parties. Mexico, in particular, has suffered greatly, with many commentators arguing that the country is now just one open mass grave. One of just hundreds of examples came to light in 2010, in an abandoned mine on the outskirts of the city of Taxco, Mexico, when two security watchmen, Juan Viveros and Nabor Baena, heard trucks arriving in the dead of night, followed by a foul smell emanating from one of the mines a few days later. After a closer inspection, they were shocked at what they found. 'It bothered us when we came, because there was a lot of blood,' said Viveros. 'I told Nabor, "Look, where did that blood come from?" He answered, "Who knows, maybe they brought an animal?"' Reporting their concerns to the authorities, a team from the National Civil Protection System searched the mine and found a large recess full of human remains. According to the official reports fifty-five bodies were uncovered, but according to the families, who went to the morgue to identify missing family members, the figure was nearer 120.[30]

Between December 2006 and October 2018, 37,485 people were officially reported missing, presumably murdered by the cartels. The unofficial figure is believed to be considerably higher. A recent investigation by a team of Mexican journalists found that between 2006 and 2016 almost 2,000 clandestine mass graves had been found throughout the country. The remains recovered so far include 2,884 bodies, 324 craniums, 217 bones, 799 bone remnants, and thousands of other body parts that belong to an undetermined number of individuals. Their report also showed that as the drug war escalated, the phenomenon of mass graves reached catastrophic levels. In 2006, only two graves were found, increasing to ten burial pits in five different states in 2007. By 2010 the figure rose to 105 graves in fourteen states; in 2011, it leapt to 375 mass graves throughout twenty states, equivalent to one per day on average. Since 2012, at least 245 burial pits have been found each year.[31]

Eight states refused to release their figures to the investigative team, denying that any mass graves had been found within their jurisdiction. Despite this, the data the team did manage to uncover is truly mindblowing. States with the highest number of exhumed mass graves over eleven years are Veracruz (332), Tamaulipas (280), Guerrero (216), Chihuahua (194), Sinaloa (139), Zacatecas (138), Jalisco (137), Nuevo León (114), Sonora (86), Michoacán (76), and San Luis Potosí (65). Those containing the highest number of corpses included Durango (497 bodies), Chihuahua (391), Tamaulipas (336), Guerrero (325), Veracruz (222), Jalisco (214), Sinaloa (176), Michoacán (132), Nuevo León (119), Sonora (96), and Zacatecas (81). In one area alone, Colinas de Santa Fe, a team of forensic archaeologists found 22,079 separate bone fragments, while in San Fernando, an hour and a half away from the Texas border, 139 mass graves, containing 190 bodies and numerous bone fragments, were recorded over a two-year period. Even the Pacific coast beach resort of Acapulco, made famous by the jet set in the 1950s and 1960s, reported that 108 burial pits had been found over a ten-year period.[32]

Attempts to identify the corpses have not been easy, especially when the remains have been incinerated or dissolved in acid, a favourite method of body disposal among drug cartels. For example, in Coahuila, out of the eighty-seven interment sites excavated, from which 102,717 biological samples were taken, only nineteen people have been positively identified. Moreover, exhumed remains that end up in the federal facilities in Mexico City are not recorded in official state records, so families are unaware if their loved ones have been found or not. This has led to an underreporting of the number of mass graves on an unprecedented scale. Jacobo Dayán, an expert on crimes against humanity, at Colegio de México, said that the investigative reporters have exposed the state's failure in the matter. 'There is no official information about burial pits in the country, nor about the bodies' locations,' he said. 'It's urgent to have a clear record of missing people, and additionally of fragments, remains, and graves to start creating search, exhumation, and identification policies.' While Mercedes Doretti, Director of the Argentine Forensic Anthropology Team, believes that the findings reveal the need to create a 'standardized protocol throughout the country to record graves and remains.' On 1 December 2018, Mexico elected a new president, Andrés Manuel López Obrador, whose number one priority, he said, would be a 'radical transformation of this country's policy to tackle production of illegal drugs.' Bold words indeed, but with the US State Department estimating that Mexican drug cartels control seventy percent of all narcotics flown into the US, plus their annual turnover is somewhere in the range of nineteen billion to twenty-nine billion dollars per year, it is safe to assume that the war on drugs will not be ending any day soon, and mass graves will simply become a statistic.[33]

Genocide

Darfur, Armenia, Wounded Knee, Cambodia, Poland, Iraq, Sri Lanka, East Timor, Burundi, Biafra, Burma, and not forgetting those killed in the Holocaust during the Second World War, have all borne witness to some of the most appalling crimes against humanity imaginable. The term commonly used to describe such atrocities is 'genocide', which consists of the Greek prefix *genos*, meaning 'race' or 'tribe', and the Latin suffix *cide*, meaning 'killing'. The term was first used in 1944 by Polish lawyer, Raphael Lemkin, in the book *Axis Rule in Occupied Europe*, to document the Nazis' barbarity against the Jewish people during the Second World War. Because of the heinous nature of these acts, in 1946 genocide was recognised as a crime under international law by the United Nations General Assembly, and was codified as an independent crime in 1948. Today genocide is legally defined by the following acts committed with intent to destroy, in whole or in part, a national, ethnical, racial or religious group, such as: killing members of the group; causing serious bodily or mental harm to members of the group; deliberately inflicting on the group conditions of life calculated to bring about its physical destruction in whole or in part; imposing measures intended to prevent births within the group; forcibly transferring children of the group to another group.[34]

Iraq

'There is another Iraq, buried under Iraq,' quoted the Kurdistan Mass Graves Commission. 'In essence Iraq is just one mass burial ground.' During the 1980s, under the autocratic rule of its dictator Saddam Hussein, the deserts of Iraq provided the ideal habitat to dispose of those murdered by Saddam's vicious regime. Victims numbered in the thousands, with the majority hailing from predominantly Kurdish towns and villages located in the north of the country. Casualties included over 8,000 Kurds, who were rounded up and executed in 1983, and thousands of innocent women and children who were killed during the 1988 Anfal campaign when the Iraq Government unleashed a cocktail of chemical weapons. The worst incident occurred in Halabja, Kurdistan, around 240 kilometres from Baghdad, where 5,000 Kurdish civilians are believed to have perished during an aerial bombardment of mustard gas and nerve agents, which included napalm, sarin, tabun and VX. Human Rights Watch estimates over 100,000 Kurds disappeared during this period, in a systematic programme of ethnic cleansing. Many would be found later, dumped in a series of mass graves.[35]

In 2003, after the toppling of Saddam's government, the Iraqi authorities estimated that around 500,000 people had gone missing. Yet according to the International Commission on Missing Persons (ICMP) the figure is far higher, at more than one million. 'Saddam Hussein has been one of the most effective dictators in terms of killing people,' said Jonathan McCaskill, head of the ICMP in Iraq. 'He took most of the victims into prison camps, distributed them around the country and then killed them.' That same year, a mass grave containing more than 3,000 bodies was discovered near the farming community of Mahaweel, sixty kilometres south of Baghdad. In 2004, the Iraqi Ministry of Human Rights announced that it had found a further 400 mass graves containing the bodies of around 4,000 Kurdish victims, mostly from the Garmiyan area, east of Kirkuk. This discovery eventually led to the Law of Protection of Mass Graves, passed in 2006, which aimed to provide a legal mechanism in Iraq for locating missing persons and conducting excavations of mass burial sites. In 2011, a further seven mass graves were uncovered, this time in southern Iraq, in the Al Diwaniya province, which also contained the bodies of executed Kurds. Local residents reported that in late 1987 they had witnessed hundreds of bodies arriving on military vehicles during the night, and then being buried in a number of large pits.[36]

The victimisation of Iraqi civilians would not end here. In 2014, Islamic State, otherwise known as Da'esh, ISIL or ISIS, invaded Iraq and subjected its citizens to three years of brutal occupation. For those who did not adhere to its strict fundamentalist ideals – such as the previous government, Muslims of a more moderate persuasion and those with homosexual tendencies – the punishment was death. Christians were a particular target, as were those who hailed from the Yazidi community, an ethnic group indigenous to Iraq, Syria and Turkey. When Islamic State began to encircle Yazidi territory, over 40,000 Yazidis fled to Mount Sinjar, in north-west Iraq, to avoid being slaughtered. Nevertheless, thousands of their men were killed – many were beheaded on the spot – whereas the majority of women and girls were forced into sexual slavery. Those deemed too old or too young were killed instantly. To date, sixty-nine mass graves have been unearthed in the Yazidi homeland of Sinjar.[3]

In November 2018, the United Nations announced that a further 200 mass graves, holding as many as 12,000 bodies, had been found in areas of Iraq once controlled by Islamic State. Most are sited in the four provinces of northern and western Iraq, namely Anbar, Kirkuk, Salahuddin and Nineveh, which includes Mosul, the largest city once controlled by the extremists. Some of the graves are small in nature, holding the remains of only a few people but massive pits, thought to contain the bodies of thousands of individuals, have also been found, such as the Khasfa Sinkhole which is believed to contain the remains of 6,000 people. 'ISIL's horrific crimes in Iraq have left the headlines, but the trauma of the victims' families endures, with thousands of women, men and children still unaccounted for,' said Michelle Bachelet, a United Nations human rights commissioner. So far, the Iraqi authorities have successfully dug twenty-eight of the mass burial sites, with a total of 1,258 bodies exhumed.[38]

Rwanda

In September 2018, I awoke to the news that authorities in Rwanda had found a number of previously unknown mass graves, almost twenty-five years after ethnic bloodshed had briefly engulfed the country. Naphtal Ahishakiye, Executive Secretary of Ibuka, a genocide survivor's organisation, told *The Associated Press* that 5,400 bodies had been exhumed from twenty-six mass graves in the capital's Kicukiro district, all dating back to the 1994 genocide. He said the discovery followed a tip-off from a man who had heard about the graves as a child.[39] A few months earlier, in April 2018, another four mass graves were uncovered in the Gasabo district, near the capital Kigali, when a local woman, who claimed to have witnessed the graves being dug, took the authorities to the location. The graves were found twenty-four metres beneath the ground surface and a number of houses had to be destroyed in order to gain access. Around 200 bodies have been exhumed. Relatives of genocide victims have been scouring the site in search of their loved ones' remains. 'I have information that both my parents were killed and dumped in one of [the] mass graves here,' said Isabelle Uwimana, a survivor of the genocide. 'I came with hope that I can identify the clothes they were wearing when they left.' Between April and September 2018, the Rwandan authorities discovered a staggering forty new mass graves, housing the remains of 62,000 individuals, all dating to the 1994 genocide.[40]

I remember the events in Rwanda as if they were yesterday. Graphic images of butchered bodies decomposing in the streets, together with disturbing scenes of thousands of people fleeing to escape the ongoing slaughter, slowly filtered through to our TV screens during the late spring of 1994. At first the eyes of the world turned away from the atrocities being committed by the militant Hutu Government against the predominantly Tutsi population. After all, few people had even heard of Rwanda, let alone know its whereabouts. Soon it became impossible to ignore. The chain of events appears to be as follows: on 6 April 1994, a plane carrying Rwandan President Juvénal Habyarimana and Burundian President Cyprien Ntaryamira was shot down above Kigali. Both officials were Hutus. Within hours of the crash Hutu extremists, including organised gangs of government soldiers and militias, began to hack their way through the Tutsi population using machetes, clubs or anything they had to hand. Even Hutus of a more moderate persuasion were killed on sight. Those who fled to their local church in search of refuge were subsequently burnt alive. Between April and June 1994, it is believed that one million Rwandans were killed in the space of only 100 days.[41]

The identity of those responsible for the death of President Habyarimana remains a mystery, albeit each side continually points the finger of blame at the other. Any suggestion, however, that the ethnic cleansing was as a direct result of the plane crash is absurd. There is strong evidence to indicate that the Rwandan genocide was at least two years in the planning, long before the plane had fallen from the sky. Furthermore, there is equally strong evidence to show that at least one major Western power, that shall remain nameless, was complicit in the bloodshed that followed. So too was the Catholic Church. But I digress. Naturally much has been written about the matter in the ensuing years and for those of you who would like to read more about the genocide and its aftermath I highly recommend the books, *Conspiracy to Murder, The Rwandan Genocide* by Linda Melvern and *From Genocide to Continental War* by Gérard Prunier.

As soon as a Tutsi/Ugandan coalition defeated the Hutu militia, the majority of the perpetrators fled into the neighbouring Democratic Republic of Congo to avoid retribution, mass graves began to surface in quick succession. In September 1994, peacekeeping troops from Australia uncovered a grave containing 1,400 bodies in the south of the country, while a few days later a further 4,000 bodies were found in a mass grave at Gafunzo, near the border with the Congo.[42] In October 1994, *The New York Times* reported another mass grave of more than

7,000 victims had been discovered at Mabanza, ninety-six kilometres west of Kigali, whereas an estimated 4,000-6,000 people were murdered at Kibuye Catholic Church, when those inside were attacked by armed civilians, police and gendarmes. The burial of these bodies took place in at least four mass graves.[43] Before long, so many mass graves were being unearthed by teams of forensic archaeologists and anthropologists that the Rwandan authorities ran out of chemicals required to treat the bodies, and had to wait for further supplies to arrive from Britain. In the chaotic aftermath, those in power were determined to give those who were killed a decent burial. As such, throughout Rwanda there now exists a number of memorial burial grounds housing the remains of hundreds of thousands of genocide victims, together with exhibits of photographs and personal belongings, such as clothing and shoes, to remind people about the evils that befell the country. Here are just a few examples.

Kigali Genocide Memorial Centre and Burial Ground

A ten-minute drive from the city centre, in Gisozi, this is probably the best known as it is the final resting place of 250,000 genocide victims. Opened in 1999, the centre is managed by Aegis, a UK non-governmental organisation committed to the prevention of genocide, and is renowned for its graphic display of victims' skulls and their personal belongings. The memorial garden contains a series of mass graves – victims were buried here in lots of 100,000 – where survivors and those who lost loved ones can come to 'reconnect'. The centre is a designated open burial ground.

Murambi Genocide Memorial and Burial Ground

Located on the grounds of the former Murambi Technical School, it is the site of one of the worst atrocities. Thousands of Tutsi people were advised to hide in the school on the pretext that French soldiers were coming to protect them. Alas, it was a trap and after gathering in the classrooms the militia stormed the building and slaughtered those inside. The grounds now house several mass graves, with former classrooms exhibiting a number of remains.

Nyamata Genocide Memorial Centre

Located thirty kilometres south of Kigali, Nyamata is sited in the town's former church and commemorates 25,000 genocide victims who were massacred within its walls. Believing the church to be a sanctuary, the local Tutsi population gathered inside and locked the doors. It did not save them. The Hutu militias blasted open the doors, and butchered those inside with machetes. The altar cloth is still stained with blood from several victims, plus the clothes and national ID cards of many of those killed have been left on the church pews. Outside, the mass graves surrounding the church are open to public viewing.

Nyanza Genocide Memorial Site

On the grounds of Kigali's École Technique Officielle, in the Kicukiro district, this particular site is the official memorial ground for the annual genocide anniversary commemorations, which occur every April. The mass grave contains more than 10,000 genocide victims.

Bisesero Genocide Memorial

Located sixty kilometres from Kibuye, it is believed that 40,000 people died here. The memorial tells the story of Tutsi resistance against the Hutu militias in the hills of Bisesero.

Ntarama Genocide Memorial Centre

The site of a former Catholic church, 5,000 Tutsis who sought refuge inside were massacred by Hutu militias. To get to their prey, the Hutus dismantled the building by removing the bricks, one by one.

The Bosnian War – Srebrenica

'You could smell the grave at Cerska long before you could see it,' wrote Elizabeth Neuffer, former European Bureau Chief for *The Boston Globe*.

'The sickly-sweet smell of the bodies came wafting through the trees lining the dirt track up to the grave.' The year is 1999 and in their search for the missing men of Srebrenica, in the Bosnian town of Cerska, investigators with the International Criminal Tribunal for the Former Yugoslavia had uncovered yet another mass grave. With their hands tied behind their backs, and dressed in civilian clothes, it was plain to see that the victims had been shot in the back of the head. The opposing Bosnian Serbian leadership claimed that each had been a fighter, killed in combat. As it would later transpire, nothing could be further from the truth.[44]

In the early 1990s, the Balkan country of Yugoslavia fell apart. Formerly a communist state, the country was initially created after the Second World War, and consisted of a loose federation of Serbs, Croats, Bosnian Muslims, Albanians and Slovenes, all living relatively peacefully together under the leadership of President Tito. But after Tito's death in 1980, tensions began to surface among the various factions, fuelled, in part, by the rhetoric of nationalistic politicians. Following the Slovenian and Croatian secessions from the Socialist Federal Republic of Yugoslavia in 1991, the multi-ethnic Socialist Republic of Bosnia and Herzegovina passed a referendum for independence on 29 February 1992. Although their claim received the official blessing from the European Union, the result was rejected by the political representatives of the Bosnian Serbs, who had boycotted the referendum, with the ultra-nationalist Bosnian Serb leader, Radovan Karadzic, threatening bloodshed if they went ahead. Unperturbed, the Republic of Bosnia and Herzegovina proceeded and officially declared their independence; they were admitted as a member state of the United Nations on 22 May 1992.[45] In a few short weeks Karadzic made good on his promise and conflict engulfed the region, with more than one million Bosnian Muslims and Croats forcibly removed from their homes by Karadzic's Serbian forces. The capital Sarajevo was encircled, effectively blockaded, and was continually bombarded by Serb forces for over a year, while Srebrenica, in the north-east of the country, would bear witness to some of the worst crimes against humanity the world has ever seen.

In April 1993, the United Nations declared the Muslim enclave of Srebrenica, a 'safe area' under UN protection. Such a declaration would prove to be meaningless, for in the summer of 1995 the Bosnian Serb Army, under the command of General Ratko Mladic, the so-called

'Beast of Bosnia', together with a Serbian paramilitary unit called The Scorpions, stormed Srebrenica and pillaged their way across the land. The vastly outgunned and outnumbered Dutch battalion of UN peacekeepers stationed there could do nothing but watch. As a consequence, over 8,372 Muslim men and boys were slaughtered, while some 25,000 to 30,000 Muslim women and girls were raped, abused and forcibly transferred. 'They had big weapons, big armoured personnel carriers, they had helicopters, they had close air support, F16s, Apache (helicopter gunships) but we had nothing,' Derk Zwaan, one of the Dutch peacekeepers told *The Independent* newspaper. It has since transpired that the Dutch commander repeatedly called for aerial backup as the Serb forces besieged the enclave, but his requests fell on deaf ears. Joris Voorhoeve, the Dutch Defence Minister at the time, now admits that a strong application of air force could have bought the UN time to evacuate the Muslim population. Instead Mladic summoned scores of buses and separated the men and boys from the women. 'The buses with the males went in a different direction,' said Voorhoeve, 'and we knew the horrible effects'.[46]

The menfolk were initially evacuated to various holding sites, primarily in areas north of Srebrenica, before being executed. These included a football field in Bratunac, a school in Orahovac, a factory in Karakaj and several meadows and fields near Vlasenica and Nova Kasaba. Once killed, their bodies were thrown into an infinite number of mass graves dotted throughout the landscape; it has been estimated that the Serbs used ninety-one different burial sites. Several months after the Srebrenica massacre the US Secretary of State released a statement confirming that with the use of satellite photography, intelligence officials believed they had found a large number of mass grave sites. It hadn't been easy. To hide their crimes the Bosnian Serb Army had dug up the primary mass graves, using heavy equipment, and reburied the bodies in more remote areas of Bosnia. For example, in the mid-1990s, in the region of Grbavci and Orahovac, two mass graves were found by investigators. Excavation of the first commenced in 1996, by a joint team from the Prosecutor's Office and the Physicians for Human Rights. The grave contained the remains of 243 individuals, all male, and evidence showed that the vast majority had died of gunshot injuries. In addition, 147 blindfolds were located in the grave. The bodies in the second site were exhumed between July and August 2000, by a team from the

International Criminal Tribunal for the former Yugoslavia and included 130 men, twenty-three of whom were later identified as missing from Srebrenica. After a full investigation of the burial sites had concluded, it was revealed that the bodies from both mass graves had, at one point, been removed and reburied in a secondary grave site, sometime between 1995 and 1998. When interviewed, Adam Boys, Chief Operating Officer of the International Commission on Missing Persons related a similar tale: 'We once uncovered the remains of one man in four different gravesites, fifty kilometres apart. We had to carry out thirteen separate DNA tests to identify him.' By 2006, seventy-four mass graves had been found dotted around Srebrenica. Just over ten years later, 6,938 genocide victims had been successfully identified through DNA analysis.[47]

In 1994, NATO initiated air strikes against the Bosnian Serbs to prevent further bloodshed. A year later US-led negotiations in Dayton, Ohio, otherwise known as the Dayton Peace Accords, finally ended the war in Bosnia.[48] In October 2000, Wolfgang Petritsch, the International High Representative for Bosnia and Herzegovina, declared that land in Potočari, Srebrenica, would be transformed into a memorial cemetery for the victims of the genocide. Spread over a twelve-acre site, the initial memorial was held in July 2002 with more than 20,000 people in attendance, the first 600 victims were buried in March 2003. Potočari Cemetery was officially opened in September 2003 by American President Bill Clinton. On the twenty-fifth anniversary of the Screbrenica genocide, on 11 July 2020, the remains of a further eight men and boys were finally laid to rest, buried in a collective funeral at the cemetery site.[49]

In 2004, in a unanimous ruling on the case of Prosecutor v. Krstić, the Appeals Chamber of the International Criminal Tribunal for the former Yugoslavia ruled that the massacre of Srebrenica's male inhabitants constituted genocide, a crime under international law. The ruling was also upheld by the International Court of Justice in 2007. Many of the perpetrators have since been tried and convicted for their crimes, including the Bosnian Serbian leader Radovan Karadzic, who was given a forty-year sentence. General Ratko Mladic, the orchestrator of the Srebrenica genocide, recently lost his appeal case and was finally convicted on charges of crimes against humanity, extermination, murder and war crimes. He was given a life sentence and will spend the rest of his days behind bars.[50]

5

A Watery Grave

One of the largest burial grounds in the world is also the least explored. Water covers more than seventy per cent of the Earth's surface yet the subject of water burials is an area of history very little studied, which is hardly surprising when you consider its fluid-like nature often renders the fate of the corpse unknown. Still, the association between water, death and the afterlife permeates throughout our cultural history. According to Ancient Egyptian beliefs, the soul of the dead would accompany the sun god Ra in his boat as it embarked upon its eternal journey in the Upper Waters (the heavens) as shown in their temples and tombs. Whereas in Greek mythology it was the River Styx that formed the boundary between the Earth and the Underworld. To cross this watery divide the deceased were required to recompense the ferryman, Charon, for his services. If the amount was correct, Charon would ferry you across. If not, your soul would be haunted forever. Even within the Christian faith, followers are reminded that travel through the waters of death will result in a place full of joy. There is also increasing archaeological evidence to suggest that the choice of interment site was frequently influenced by water. At Sutton Hoo it appears that the large primary barrow burials were purposely constructed to be visible to those sailing inland from the coast, or from the North Sea. Likewise, studies of a large burial mound in Taplow, Buckinghamshire, thought to be the last remnants of a significant barrow cemetery, indicate that it was explicitly positioned in relation to two bends of the River Thames, thereby dominating the landscape for those sailing along the Thames Valley. Archaeologists therefore believe that burial grounds such as these are more than just territorial markers; they also act as a protective force, keeping both coastal and river routes secure under the watchful eye of the dead.

Excavation of western mound, Uppsala, Sweden, 1874. (*Henri Osti Swedish National Heritage Board, CCO*)

Excavation of Viking-era Oseberg ship burial, Norway, 1904. (*Museum of Cultural History, Norway, CC A 4.0*)

Palenque pyramid burial ground, Mexico. (*Jan Hardenberg, CC A 4.0*)

Replica of Guanche Mummy cave in Parque del Drago, Icod de Los Vinos, Tenerife, Spain. (*Diego Delso, CC BY 3.0*)

Spirit box house, St Nicholas Cemetery, Eklunta, Alaska. (*Courtesy of Cheri Horkman at www.randomcurrents.com*)

Burial ground of 20,000 saints, Bardsey Island, Llyn Peninsula, North Wales. (*Stray, C CC A 2.0*)

Above: Test-pitting in Kirkmichael shows human remains buried underneath the nave floor. (*Author's own*)

Left: Sedlec Ossuary beneath the Cemetery Church of All Saints, Kutná Hora, Czech Republic. (*Laika, AC CC A 2.0*)

Deviant Vampire burial, Grave number 3a, Zamkowa Street, Poland. (*R. Biskupski, CC BY 4.0*)

Grave of English witch Meg Shelton, St Anne's Churchyard, Woodplumpton, England. (*Alexander P. Knapp, CC A 2.0*)

Overhead view of Crossbones graveyard site, London. (*Professor DEH, CCO*)

Graves of Billy Clanton, Frank and Tom McLaury, cowboys who were killed at the O.K. Corral. Boot Hill Graveyard, Tombstone, Arizona. (*Tony Marine, CC A 3.0*)

Mass grave of Spanish Civil War victims, Estepar, Burgos, 2014. (*Mario Modesto Mata, CC A 4.0*)

Mass graves of clansmen at Culloden Battlefield, Scotland. (*Dave Ahern, CC0*)

Mass grave at Kigali Genocide Memorial Centre, Gizozi, Rwanda. (*Fanny Schertzer, CC A 3.0*)

Srebrenica Massacre - Exhumed graves of victims in Potocari, 2007. (*Courtesy of Adam Jones adamjones.freeservers.com, CC A 3.0*)

Burial at sea for crewmen killed when the USS *Houston* was torpedoed off Formosa on 14 October 1944. (*Courtesy of Natural History and Heritage Command*)

Corpses being burnt and consigned to the River Ganges, Varanasi, Uttar Pradesh. (*CC BY Wellcome Collection*)

Lion guarding the entrance to Neptune Memorial Reef underwater cemetery. (*Todd Murray, CC A 2.0*)

Ship graveyard, Nouadhibou Bay, Mauritania. (*Sebastian Lo Sada, CC BY 2.0*)

Abandoned trains in the Red Star Train Graveyard, Budapest. (*Rodrigo Argenton, CC A 3.0*)

South Park Street Cemetery, Kolkata, India. (*Ankur P., CC A 2.0*)

View of Pere Lachaise Cemetery, Paris, France. (*Reprinted from Courvoisier-Voisin, Library of Arts, France, CCO*)

Entrance to the Egyptian Avenue at Highgate Cemetery, London, England. (*John Armargh, CC0*)

Entrance to Hartsdale Pet Cemetery. The oldest commercial pet cemetery in the United States, it was established in 1896 in the village of Hartsdale, New York. (*Steve Strummer*)

Above: Graves of the 47 Ronin at Sengakuji Temple, Tokyo, Japan. (*Stefan Le Du, CC BY SA 2.5*)

Left: ANZAC grave with a makeshift wooden cross, Gallipoli, Turkey. (*1915 CC BY Wellcome Collection*)

Douaumont Cemetery with ossuary in the background, Verdun, France. (*Jean-Pol Grandmont, CC BY 3.0*)

View from the second floor of the Neptune Society Columbarium, San Francisco, California. (*Frank Schoenberg, CC A 3.0*)

Tree burial used for babies who died before teething, Toraja, Indonesia. (*Michael Gunther, CC A 4.0*)

A Watery Grave

Individuals who spent a lot of their lives at sea, or lived in close proximity to it, might have been given a sea burial in remembrance for their deeds during life. The great Elizabethan sea captain and raconteur, Sir Francis Drake (1540-1596), is believed to have been buried at sea, just off the coast of Panama, placed inside a lead casket to ensure that nobody, especially the Spanish, would find his body. Recent claims by a group of treasure hunters that they have found his corpse are yet to be proven.[1] The remains of the eighteenth-century explorer Captain Cook, rescued from Pacific natives by his crew, were also placed in a coffin and subjected to pomp and ceremony before being discharged overboard. In Hawaii, bodies of deceased fishermen were often wrapped in red cloth and placed into the ocean to be eaten by sharks, as it was believed that the spirit of the departed would inhabit the shark's body.[2] Similarly, in other Pacific cultures it was customary to place the dead in a canoe and cast it adrift into the water. Away from the sea, we have already touched upon the Mayan convention of depositing their dead in cenotes – water-filled caves of the Underworld – whereas in the American Great Salt Lake Desert, in an area appropriately named 'Skull Valley', the local Goshute Indians traditionally used to bury their dead in local springs, which they weighted down with stones or sticks to prevent the corpse from resurfacing.[3]

A well-known form of funerary custom involving water is the Viking ship burial. As we have seen in the opening chapter, boat symbolism played an important part in both Germanic and Viking burial rites, and due in part to the recent success of the History Channel's *Vikings* TV series, the idea of a Viking burial at sea has captured the public imagination more than ever. This was demonstrated in September 2014 when the US Coastguard fulfilled the dying wishes of Norwegian-born Second World War veteran, Andrew Haines, by placing his cremated remains onto a wooden replica Viking boat, towing the boat out into open water, and setting it on fire.[4] One remarkable account of a Viking ship burial has survived, in the writings of Ahmad Ibn Fadlan, an Arab explorer and chronicler who was sent on a mission from Baghdad to observe and make contact with those people who resided in the far north. Dating to the tenth century, he documents the funeral of a Viking Rus chieftain, who had been laid in a temporary grave while preparations for the funeral ship were made. After several days, Fadlan described how the ship was pulled to the shore and the body of the chieftain was laid out on a bed within. He stated:

> I was told that when their chiefs die, they consume them with fire ... . The family of the dead men drew near, and taking a piece of wood, lit the ship. The ship was soon aflame, as was the couch, the man, and everything in it, as it fell into the watery depths.[5]

The deep waters of the world's oceans have also served as a useful disposal site for individuals of a rather heinous nature. On 1 June 1962, following the cremation of Adolf Eichmann, one of Adolf Hitler's Nazi henchmen, the burnt remains were thrown into the Mediterranean Sea, within designated international waters, as Israel did not want Eichmann to be buried upon Israeli soil, where he had been taken to after his capture. They also did not want him to have a land-based grave anywhere else, as they feared such a place could easily become a pilgrimage site for those with far-right leanings.[6] By the same token, in 2011 the US Government stated that the body of the slain al-Qaeda leader Osama bin Laden, killed by a Navy SEAL team in Abbottabad, Pakistan, was given a customary Islamic burial and then buried at sea. The location remains unknown, amid high secrecy. It was also recently announced that the remains of the world's most wanted terrorist, Abu Bakr al-Baghdadi, were quickly disposed of at sea, hours after he blew himself up during a US raid on his compound in north-west Syria, in October 2019. Speaking at the Pentagon, Chairman of the Joint Chiefs of Staff General Mark Millet said: 'His remains were disposed of appropriately in accordance with the law of armed conflict.'

During the so-called Age of Sail, which extended from the sixteenth to the nineteenth century, burials at sea were commonplace. After all, life at sea was a precarious occupation – an accidental stumble overboard during a storm or a fall from the mast often resulted in an untimely death. According to British naval historian Michael A. Lewis, so many risks emerged from normal operations at sea during the Napoleonic Wars that as few as six per cent of the fatalities recorded on British naval vessels were attributed to combat.[7] A burial at sea was generally viewed as less preferable than a burial on land, but without the aid of refrigeration, or

A Watery Grave

any other practical way to preserve a body at this time, there was no real alternative. It was also considered a very bad omen to have a dead body on board. Sailors are extremely superstitious folk by nature, and the corpse was often regarded as a potent storm-raiser. But to their credit, even though it would have been easy to dispose of a body overboard, the majority of sailors considered it their solemn duty to provide a formal burial service to the deceased.[8] Records of individual ceremonies have survived, such as the one documented by Frederick Perry in 1876, an officer aboard the American clipper ship *Continental*:

> His body was reverently carried into the carpenter's shop and was laid out on a bench. The sail-maker and the carpenter prepared it for burial by washing and dressing him up in his best suit of 'go-shore' clothes, then sewing him up in a heavy piece of new canvas for a shroud, and with a couple of old iron cable shackles fastened at his feet, they laid the body on the sliding board, covered with the ship's ensign ... . The Captain performed a brief service proclaiming 'I am the resurrection and the life; we commit this body to the deep.'[9]

A recent dive, excuse the pun, into British Merchant Navy records has provided a wealth of information. In particular, many sea captains came forward to give their own personal accounts of what happens when there is a death on board one of their ships. One captain, of many years' experience sailing both commercial and top of the range cruise liners, gave the following description in November 2008:

> I have done a few burials at sea, mostly for passengers on both Cunard and Canadian Pacific. On those ships the passenger's family had a choice, take them home or bury them at sea. There was a charge for a burial at sea, for the canvas, the men's bonus and the traditional rum ... the watch on deck usually did the sewing up of the body in canvas with old shackles and any other bits of iron at the feet. We had a board with six inch angled sides on and two handles at each end, it was painted white gloss. We placed the body on the board, covered it with a Red Ensign, made fast at

Burying the Dead

the corners so it would not flap about in the wind ... . At six in the morning the ships engine was stopped, and if any relatives were on board they would assemble on the deck, with the Staff Captain or a Minister. They would then read the Burial at Sea Service, where it says we commit his body to the Deep and we tipped up the board and the body would gently slide overboard and out and into the ocean ... . If the relatives want a sea burial the ship's Doctor usually does a Post Mortem and everything is logged, body samples may be taken and preserved as evidence.[10]

Another example, this time from a crew member, read:

In early December 1951, I was an Apprentice on *MV British Baron* when a Chief Steward who had joined us at Ellesmere Port, died on board just before we reached Gibraltar. We received instructions from Head Office that we were to do a burial at sea. The Boson [officer in charge of crew and equipment] was given the task of sewing the body up in canvas and given a bottle of rum to help him! I reminded the Boson of the old naval tradition of putting the last stitch through the nose. He also sewed some heavy metal in the canvas as well to make the corpse sink. After we had passed through the Gibraltar Straits, we held a formal burial service. The ship's crew assembled on the main deck and the body was placed on a wooden chute lashed to the deck railings. The other Apprentice and I were the ones elected to lift up the inboard end of the chute at the appropriate time. We then sounded six loud blasts on the ship's siren, in honour, and proceeded to go on our way.[11]

Visual records of such events are rare, but they do exist. The US Navy photographic archives have some wonderful images depicting the burial-at-sea service of astronaut Neil Armstrong, the first man to walk on the moon, whose remains were committed to the Atlantic Ocean via the USS *Philippine Sea* in 2012. The US Naval History and Heritage Command also have some sobering photographs of sea burials dating to the Second World War. A unique black and white photograph has also emerged recently documenting the tragic aftermath of the sinking of the *Titanic*. For those of you who are unfamiliar with the story, in brief, the RMS *Titanic* was a British passenger liner that sank in the North Atlantic Ocean during its maiden voyage from Southampton to New York City after hitting an iceberg. On the night in question, Sunday, 14 April 1912, at 11.40 pm the stationed lookout sounded the alarm and telephoned the bridge stating 'Iceberg, right ahead!' The warning came too late. The *Titanic* struck the massive chunk of ice, ripping open a series of holes along the side of its hull. Three hours later, in the early hours of 15 April 1912, the ship lay at the bottom of the Atlantic Ocean. There were an estimated 2,224 passengers and crew aboard, and it is believed more than 1,500 died, making it one of the deadliest commercial peacetime maritime disasters in modern history. In the immediate aftermath the ship's owners, White Star Line, contracted a Canadian cable repair ship, *Mackay-Bennet*, to recover what bodies they could. It left Halifax, Nova Scotia on 17 April 1912 and arrived at the wreck site on 21 April. Out of the 306 bodies they successfully recovered from the waters, 166 were buried at sea – many of which had no means of identification as the remains were too damaged to preserve, or they were third-class passengers who could not afford a proper funeral. The aforementioned photograph, originally taken by a *Mackay-Bennet* deckhand, depicts numerous bodies stacked up on the windswept deck, two or three high in places, while two crewmen tip up a makeshift stretcher to drop the corpses over the side. The ship's priest, the Reverend Hind, can be clearly seen holding a prayer book as he conducts a service for each victim, saying, 'The wild Atlantic may rage and toss but far below in the calm untroubled depth they rest in peace.'[12]

Can one choose to have a sea burial today? Well, yes you can. Anyone can choose to be buried at sea, although its popularity in the UK has declined somewhat in recent times. Research published on the Funeral Zone website states that between 2001 and 2013 only 140 people were officially buried at sea in the UK. This number declined further still between 2011 and 2012 to only eight people. Why is this so? A number of contributing factors have been suggested. A recent study by Co-op Funeral Care found that cremation now accounts for almost three-quarters of all funerals in the UK. Not only is it significantly cheaper, compared to other forms of burial, but one in ten families surveyed stated they would prefer to scatter the ashes of their loved ones over water rather than commit the entire body to the deep. [13] There are also new types of burial now on offer, such as green funerals, in picturesque woodland burial sites, an option that has gained much popularity over the past few years. But if one did want a sea burial, how would one proceed? First, you would need to apply for an official license from the Marine Management Organisation (MMO). There are currently only three designated burial sites in British coastal waters, namely Newhaven in East Sussex, the Needles Spoil Ground near the Isle of Wight, and Tynemouth in Tyne and Wear. If you would like to bury a loved one in a different location from these, you can propose a new site when you make your application. However, you are required to submit the exact coordinates and evidence to demonstrate that this site is suitable for a burial at sea, as the proposed site must not interfere with commercial fishing nets. In addition, there must be minimal risk of the body returning to shore by strong currents.[14]

The rules concerning the type of coffin you can use are also specific. The MMO states that the coffin must be both non-toxic and biodegradable and must not contain any contaminants, such as plastic, lead, copper or zinc. It must have around forty to fifty fifty-millimetre holes drilled throughout, corners must be butt-jointed and strengthened with mild steel, right-angle brackets are required to be screwed internally or substantial wooden bracing struts, fifty by thirty-eight millimetres in size, can be used as an alternative. Around 200 kg of iron, steel or concrete must be clamped to the base of the coffin, to act as ballast to ensure the coffin stays weighted down on the seabed. The weight must be distributed evenly to prevent the coffin from turning to the vertical. Finally, two long mild steel bands, running the length of the coffin, and several mild steel bands secured across, at approximately thirty-centimetre intervals along its length, are deemed necessary to prevent any impact damage. John Lister, managing director of the Devon-based Britannia Shipping Company said: 'After eighteen months a body will have completely disappeared, and after three years the coffin will have broken up.'[15]

So, what are the downsides of choosing a sea burial? Well, apart from the stringent criteria regarding coffin manufacture, the deceased must also not be embalmed and should be dressed in light, biodegradable clothing. Applicants need to provide a certificate from a doctor to confirm that the deceased is clear of fever and any infectious disease and, in some instances, the coroner might have to be informed. Attending the chosen burial site can also be fraught with difficulties as it can take over five hours, in cold, choppy waters, to reach one of the designated sea locations. Furthermore, if the weather is extremely inclement then the funeral could be cancelled for days. Because of this, many families choose to have a ceremony on land before saying goodbye to their loved one from the quayside.[16] In rare cases strong currents have been known to dislodge the coffin and/or body from the sea bottom, as occurred in September 2013 when the corpse of a woman, who had been buried at sea, just off the island of Jersey, was found drifting towards the shore. Her remains had to be recovered by the local lifeboat. Commenting on the unfortunate situation the MMO said:

> Despite steps which must be followed prior to a burial at sea taking place, there is still a risk of the body being returned to shore or being caught up in fishing gear. Such rare events naturally cause considerable distress to relatives, friends of the deceased and all concerned, as well as considerable cost to the relevant authorities to identify the body.

Since this particular incident, it has been suggested that a DNA sample should be taken from the deceased before a sea burial is administered, to aid identification if the unfortunate should happen.[17]

Similar rules regarding sea burials are enforced by other countries. Burial within Australian territorial waters is covered by the aptly titled Sea Dumping Act 1981 and is administered by the Department of the Environment. Like the UK, a permit is required for sea burials and they are only usually granted to those who have a strong connection to the sea, for instance individuals who served in the navy. The body must not be embalmed or placed in a casket; it may only be sewn into a weighted shroud and it must be buried in water deeper than 2,000 metres.[18] In the USA, the Environmental Protection Agency is responsible for the burial of human remains at sea, again with specific requirements. Bodies which have not been cremated must be buried at sea no closer than three nautical miles from land, and in water no less than 100 fathoms deep. It must be clearly shown that all necessary measures have been taken to ensure that the remains sink to the bottom rapidly and permanently. Designated burial sites include the waters of St Augustine, Cape Canaveral, Tortugas, and Pensacola in Florida, and the Mississippi River Delta in Louisiana.[19]

For centuries, the old, the sick and dying of India have flocked to the ancient city of Varanasi, in the northern Indian state of Uttar Pradesh. Located on the banks of the sacred River Ganges, it is one of the world's oldest inhabited cities, as well as one of the holiest. Followers of Hinduism believe that if a person's ashes are scattered into the river at this precise spot, then their soul will be purified and thereby reach the divine state of Nirvana (Moksha). As such, over 100,000 cremated bodies are thought to be deposited into the Ganges here each year, making it arguably one of the largest burial grounds to date. But before the remains can be ceremonially offered to the waters, they must be burnt. In accordance with tradition, the body must be disposed of within the first twenty-four hours of death, and only a close male relative, preferably the first-born son, is permitted to perform said rites. Women are not allowed to be present as their tears are regarded as pollutants. Once at the river, the body is immersed in the sacred waters before being laid out to dry for a few hours on a ghat, an embankment of stone steps, sited along the river bank, that have become synonymous with Varanasi. When sufficiently dried the body is anointed with a form of clarified butter (ghee), to aid the burning process, before being carried to a 'burning pit' by members of the family. Once there it is draped in a cloth, lashed to a platform and set alight.[20] Describing the burning ghats at Varanasi in 1933, historian Patrick Balfour wrote:

> Through stagnant water, thick with scum and rotting flowers, we drifted towards the burning ghats, where a coil of smoke rose into the air from a mass of ashes no longer recognizable as a body. One pyre, neatly stacked in a rectangular pile, had just been lit, and the corpse swathed in white, protruded from the middle. An old man surrounded with marigolds, sat cross-legged on the step above. Men were supporting him and rubbing him with oil and sand, he submitted limply to their ministrations, staring, wide-eyed, towards the sun ... . 'Why are they massaging him like that?' I asked the guide ... . 'Because he is dead.' And then I saw them unfold

him from his limp position and carry him towards the stack of wood. They put him face downwards on the pyre, turned his shaved head towards the river, piled wood on top of him and set it alight with brands of straw, pouring on him butter and flour and rice and sandalwood. When I drifted back, some ten minutes later, the head was a charred bone and a cow was placidly munching the marigold wreaths. The body takes about three hours to burn. Sometime less if more wood is added. The richer a family is the more wood they can afford. When the wood is burned to ashes, the breastbone of the deceased is often still intact. It is given to the eldest son who tosses it in the Ganges. After the family of the deceased leaves, children descend on the ashes looking for coins, nose studs or gold teeth.[21]

Although cremated ashes are the only form of human remains traditionally scattered into the Ganges, it is not uncommon to see partially decomposed bodies floating downstream. The majority of Indian families cannot afford the high cost of a funeral pyre and even the cheapest wood is beyond their reach, so when a loved one passes away, their corpse is generally cast away into the river. Moreover, Hindu custom dictates that unwed girls, and small children under the age of 2, are not to be cremated. In the majority of these cases the body is usually weighted down with a heavy object before being casually discarded into the waters.[22] It is not uncommon for bodies to break free of their weights, as was demonstrated in 2015, when over 100 corpses were found floating near the banks of the River Ganges in Uttar Pradesh's Unnao district. Villagers noticed something was amiss when they saw vultures circling the area. It is believed the bodies had surfaced due to receding water levels.[23] To address the issue the Indian Government introduced a rather dramatic, if not ingenious, solution to the ongoing problem – a snapping turtle breeding programme, whereby young hatchlings were fed on a diet of rotting human flesh. When the reptiles had reached a desirable weight, 25,000 of the beasts were released into the Ganges at regular intervals. Although they posed no threat to the living, who often bathe or swim in the river, the government soon reported that the turtles were consuming up to a pound of decaying human flesh a day.[24]

It may come as a surprise to many to learn that the UK has its own version of the River Ganges, namely the River Soar in Leicestershire. Although there are no temples or funeral pyres on its banks, the river has been officially approved by the Environment Agency as an alternative site to the Ganges and is, therefore, licensed to carry out Hindu burials. A spokesman for the agency said:

> We have designated a secluded place on the river, so that ashes are disposed of with due consideration for other river-users. We have forbidden offerings such as photographs and metal and plastic items, which could litter the riverbank. Our officers analyse the water on a monthly basis, but have never found anything amiss.

When asked to comment, Shastriji Prakashbhai Pandya, a Hindu priest who officiates at Hindu ceremonies, said he believes the Soar is an acceptable alternative:

> When I close my eyes, this could be the Ganges. Often it is difficult for people to go to India to scatter the ashes. It is expensive, and older family members may not be able to travel. That is one reason why people are coming here. The second reason is that the River Soar is greener than the Ganges, and the scenery is better. Unlike the Ganges it is quiet here, and the water is clean and clear. Instead of people living along the riverbanks, there are ducks.[25]

There are some burial sites throughout the world that initially began their life on dry land but, due to one reason or another, now find themselves deep underwater. Environmental disasters have been a contributing cause. For instance, in the 1870s, the eruption of Mount Vulcan, in Catarman, Philippines, caused both the cemetery and the surrounding city of Camiguin to sink below sea level. A giant cross, rising out of the water, now marks the spot where people once buried their dead.[26] Human interference has also played its part, such as the Lake Murray Dam in South Carolina, constructed between 1927 and 1930 to create a source of electricity for the nearby city of Columbia, and its ever-growing number of mills. Stretching for approximately 50,000 acres, with more than 800 kilometres of shoreline, in order to construct the dam, the power company bought more than 1,000 parcels of land, predominantly forest, from around 5,000 local residents. As the building works began, most of the cemeteries, comprising old slave cemeteries and family plots, were left in situ as the townspeople did not want the power company to dig them up. As such, more than 2,300 graves now sit at the bottom of Lake Murray.[27]

In 1956, Liverpool City Council attempted to sneak through a parliamentary bill at Westminster allowing for the flooding of the Tryweryn Valley in Wales, in order to create a reservoir that would supply water to Liverpool's residents. The village of Capel Celyn, located in the heart of the valley, was one of the last Welsh-speaking communities in existence and was, understandably, outraged at such a proposal. The residents embarked on a lengthy campaign of resistance to overturn the bill but they failed. Nine years later, a huge torrent of water was released, engulfing the valley below and drowning everything in its path. This included two churches, one graveyard and one Quaker burial ground, which remain underwater today. Despite assurances from Liverpool City Council that all the interred bodies would be exhumed and relocated to another cemetery on dry land, only eight bodies were ever reburied. Moreover, promises that both sites would be covered with a layer of gravel and then encased in concrete to protect the graves from the rising water, did not come to pass. It wasn't until 2005 that Liverpool City Council finally apologised for the distress caused by the drowning of the Tryweryn Valley.[28] A similar event befell the citizens of Kentucky, USA, in 1966, when two huge man-made lakes, Lake Barkley and Lake Kentucky, were created by flooding vast swathes of land. Before the flooding commenced, the local residents were forced out of their homes and their property seized under a US Government directive entitled 'eminent domain'. The Army Corps of Engineers were then given the unpleasant task of digging up the local cemeteries and removing all the remains for reburial elsewhere. Nonetheless, it appears that many cemeteries were not transferred intact and some headstones did not make it to their new location. Those bodies from poorer backgrounds, such as slaves and paupers, who could not afford a headstone and were thus buried in unmarked graves, disappeared from the records entirely.[29]

Regrettably, there is no way of telling just how many graves were left behind once the flooding began.

In August 2019, I was contacted by a funeral company called Memorial Reefs International, who kindly sent me some information regarding their new enterprise. Based in Mexico, according to the literature their aim is to provide families with an eco-friendly alternative to a traditional land burial, while at the same time creating a series of artificial reefs in the waters most affected by the global climate crisis. Using a patented technology, the process involves mixing cremated remains with a concreted sphere, known as a reef ball, and then securing the ball to the ocean floor. The concrete is specially formulated to have the same PH as seawater and the reef ball is fully texturised to ensure coral polyps have an ideal landing pad for propagation. At the time of writing prices start from around $6,000 for a single one-metre diameter ball, rising to around $9,995 for a family-sized ball, which can hold up to four sets of remains. At present, they have one operational burial site, the Slicer Memorial Reef, located a few miles off the Yucatan Peninsula, but they hope to expand into the Cancun region of Mexico.[30]

Artificial memorial reefs are not a new phenomenon. In 2007, just off the coast of Miami, Florida, around five kilometres east of Key Biscayne, one of the largest underwater custom-built burial grounds opened to the public for the first time. Covering more than 600,000 square feet of ocean floor, and reaching to a depth of twelve metres, the Neptune Memorial Reef was conceived by American diver Gary Levine, who wanted to build an underwater columbarium, a form of cemetery inside a living reef. Its design is unconventional, to say the least, and reminds one of a sunken ancient Greek city, or a fabled Atlantean utopia. Comprising a tall columned entrance way, guarded by two large lion statues, the burial ground inside includes a series of stone roads, towering gates and crumbling ruins. The memorial process begins when the cremated remains of the deceased are delivered to the company's office, either in person or by mail. The ashes are then mixed together with concrete and poured into a shell or starfish-shaped mould. Once set, a diver descends into the sea and places the mould into a designated burial space, together with a plaque inscribed with the person's name, date of birth/death and any accompanying condolence message. The mould and plaque are then secured to the reef. The concept was an instant hit with nautical folk;

one of its most famous residents is diver Bert Kilbride, known as the 'last pirate of the Caribbean,' who died in 2008 aged 93 and whose ashes now lie on top of the reef's main entrance gate. With prices starting from $8,000, since it opened the reef has interred the remains of over 1,500 people and recent expansion plans intend to increase the site's capacity to potentially house another 4,000 memorials.[31]

Chuuk Lagoon, in the South Pacific, is a sheltered body of water located within the eastern Caroline Islands, around 1,800 kilometres north east of New Guinea. Consisting of a series of low coral islands, surrounded by a protective reef, it is the true definition of what many would deem to be a tropical paradise, with shimmering white sands, clear turquoise seas and a vast array of marine life, such as sharks, manta rays, and turtles. Yet if you look closer into the watery depths, at times only fifteen metres below the waves, your eyes will zero in on one of the world's largest underwater graveyards. For it was in this spot, during the Second World War, that Japan sited its main base of operations in the South Pacific. Not only did it offer a perfect natural harbour to protect the Imperial fleet against Allied forces, but the surrounding ground provided an excellent location to build a heavily fortified military centre. In no time at all the Japanese were constructing new roads, trenches, bunkers, five airstrips, a seaplane bass and even a torpedo boat station. Naturally such a frenzy of activity caught the attention of Allied forces and, after much discussion, plans were made for an offensive. Codenamed Operation Hailstone, on the morning of 17 February 1944, American forces unleashed a full-scale assault on Chuuk Lagoon, employing five fleet carriers, seven battleships, submarines, destroyers and over 500 aircraft. In the midst of the bombardment, which lasted a full two days, more than sixty Japanese warships ended their days on the floor of the lagoon. Many still lie exactly where they sank all those years ago. Additionally, more than 250 Japanese aircraft were destroyed – some had just arrived from Japanese factories and had not yet been fully assembled. Tragically, the majority of crew members also perished and went down with their respective ships; an estimated 400 Japanese sailors were killed in the sinking of one ship alone when they became trapped in the cargo hold. Over the following decades the events at Chuuk Lagoon were largely forgotten about, until the summer of 1971 when the wreck site became the subject of a major TV documentary, *Lagoon of Lost Ships*, filmed by underwater adventurer Jacques Cousteau. As Cousteau explored the site, to his dismay he discovered that many of the wrecks still contained the corpses of Japanese sailors. When this unhappy fact was made public, the horrified Japanese people pressurised the Japanese Government to take action. A large-scale recovery programme was implemented with the remains returned to Japan for a formal burial. However, it is still believed that thousands of sailors remain entombed at the bottom of the lagoon, and the site, today, is regarded as an official Japanese war grave.[32]

In February 2018, *The Guardian* newspaper reported that the remains of sailors who had died on British and Dutch warships in the Java Sea, during the Second World War, had been dug up and secretly dumped in an anonymous mass grave by scavengers, as they rifled through war wrecks that had been illegally removed from the seabed. The bodies were allegedly left in a grave near the port of Brondong in East Java. The ships were then taken apart, piece by piece, for any remaining valuable metals. Those that were scraped included the Royal Navy destroyer HMS *Electra*, on which 119 men perished, HMS *Exeter*, a 175-metre heavy cruiser on which fifty-four died, and HMS *Encounter*, which was scuttled to avoid capture by the Japanese. A Ministry of Defence spokesperson denounced those who had disturbed the dead and said: 'The British Government condemns the unauthorised disturbance of any wreck containing human remains.' Exhibiting no remorse for his actions, one of the contractors responsible for processing the ships, Haji Ghoni, was quoted as saying: 'Sometimes the remains are there and sometimes not.'[33]

Under international law, sunken warships and associated artefacts enjoy protection through sovereign immunity. International law also provides protection for war graves, but in recent years the seas surrounding Indonesia, Singapore and Malaysia, an immense graveyard containing the wrecks of over 100 ships and submarines, have become the playground of unscrupulous individuals who secretly go searching for submerged wrecks in order to strip them of anything of worth. For instance, the US Navy recently announced that the wreck of the USS *Houston*, which sank in the Java Sea during the Battle of Sunda Strait, had been subjected to 'unauthorised disturbance'. It is the final resting place of almost 650 marines. Similar discoveries have caused outrage in Holland when it was announced that three Dutch ships, also dating from the Second World War, had vanished from the Javanese seabed.

A Watery Grave

Sonar readings still showed the imprints left by each vessel on the ocean floor, but the ships themselves were no longer there. After a thorough investigation the Dutch Ministry of Defence confirmed that the wrecks of two of its warships, the HNLMS *De Ruyter* and the HNLMS *Java*, had completely vanished, while large parts of a third, HNLMS *Kortenaer*, were missing. All three ships sank during the Battle of the Java Sea in 1942, with the loss of over 2,000 individuals, including 900 Dutch nationals and 250 people of Indonesian Dutch origins. Furthermore, in 2019 researchers discovered that the wrecks of two Dutch submarines, which sank off the Malaysian coast in 1941, had also disappeared, along with the remains of the seventy-nine men who perished on board. Just a few pieces of HNLMS *O 16* and a mere outline in the seabed of the hull of HNLMS *K XVII* were all that remained. The ministry stated: 'The desecration of a war grave is a serious offence,' while Theo Vleugels, director of the Dutch War Graves Foundation said: 'The people who died there should be left in peace.' In March 2019, Dutch Foreign Minister Stef Blok travelled to Kuala Lumpur to discuss the issue with his Malaysian counterpart. The outcome was a signed agreement between the two countries committing to a better protection for war graves in Malaysian waters.[34]

6

Boneyards of Steel

When decisions had to be made about what to include in the book or not, as the case may be, I simply could not resist adding a brief chapter exploring those graveyards of a more non-organic nature. After all, a vehicular graveyard, be it car, plane, or train is still in every respect a graveyard and deserves to be recognised as such. Many boast some fairly unusual stories, whereas others are a sad indictment of times now past. Each has their own narrative to tell, as is demonstrated by my current situation. For as I commence writing this chapter, I find myself sitting on the shoreline of Scapa Flow, a 312-square-kilometre body of water, just off the northern tip of Scotland, that forms a natural harbour with the Orkney Mainland on one side and the islands of Graemsay, South Ronaldsay and Hoy on the other. It is a stunningly beautiful place, its peace briefly interrupted by the arrival of the Houton Ferry or the screeching flypast of an irate oystercatcher. But more than 100 years ago, in June 1919, things looked a little different here. Following the German defeat in the First World War, seventy-four warships of the German High Seas Fleet were interred at Scapa Flow, waiting to hear their fate, which was being discussed during peace negotiations at Versailles. But, after nine long months had passed, and believing the negotiations had failed, the commanding officer of the German Fleet, Rear Admiral Ludwig von Reuter, gave the order to scuttle every last vessel, to prevent the fleet from falling into British hands. At 10.30 am, on 21 June 1919, while most of the British Navy was on leave, von Reuter's flagship, SMS *Emden*, sent out the following message 'Paragraph Eleven; confirm.' It was the instruction his men had been waiting for. Leaping into action, the sailors hoisted their respective German flags and opened all the portholes, watertight doors, hatches and torpedo tubes. As the remaining German crews took to the lifeboats, the ships rapidly began to take on water. The few British

Boneyards of Steel

sailors on duty desperately tried to prevent the fleet from sinking, but could only save twenty-two vessels. The remaining fifty-two ships, the vast bulk of the German High Seas Fleet, sank into the murky waters. The only civilian witnesses to the scuttling were thirty primary school children from Stromness, who were on a day trip to view the German fleet. They also witnessed the death of nine German sailors, who were fired upon by British forces as they fled the sinking ships. They were the last casualties of the First World War.[1]

Corpses of warships lurking in the deep are not the only type of ship graveyard in existence. There are a number of sites throughout the world, especially in the poorer nations of the Indian subcontinent, where ships which have outlived their usefulness go to die. With cheap labour on tap, and environmental protection laws rarely abided by, huge ocean-going vessels, predominantly from Europe, are towed into ports, or beaches, along the Bay of Bengal and stripped of every last bit of value they have. Gadani Beach in Pakistan is probably the best example with its shoreline of skeletal hulks resembling one large metallic necropolis. In Bangladesh, along the Dhaka-Chittagong Highway, there are well over seventy ship-breaking graveyards that bring in a staggering 800 million pounds a year to the nation's economy.[2] Other examples include ships that run aground, are abandoned or are broken up in storms. Evidence of this could once be seen strewn along the shores of Nouadhibou in Mauritania, on the west coast of Africa. Once the coastline was littered with 300 rusting vessels, ranging from fishing trawlers to naval cruisers, and it is still regarded as one of the largest ship graveyards ever to have existed. The first metallic corpse, so to speak, was a French Navy cruiser, *Chasseloup-Laubat*, which sank offshore in June 1926. It later became a floating stage, but since then ships have been brought in from all over the world to be abandoned in Nouadhibou's shallow waters, particularly during the 1980s when financial hardships led the authorities to turn a blind eye to ship owners who offered bribes to dump their used vessels in the harbour. A few enterprising Mauritanians even began to offer salvaging services, but their efforts effectively amounted to nothing. In recent years the Mauritanian Government, with assistance from China, has attempted to clean up the shoreline and announced their intention to transform the graveyard into an artificial reef, to act as a haven for fish and other wildlife. Their efforts have become an ecological success story, with many of the submerged hulls now acting as breeding grounds for fish, revitalising an otherwise decimated local fishing industry, together with an increase in birdlife which are utilising the offshore vessels as safe nesting sites.[3]

In today's throw-away society, breakers yards and scrap metal merchants are doing a roaring trade. Motivated by environmental factors, economic pressures or merely a desire to follow the latest fashion, it is apparent that mechanical vessels, in all their forms, are being thrown onto the trash heap at an alarming rate. Cars, in particular, are susceptible to consumer folly, with little discrimination between the rich or poor. During the recent world economic crisis, the appropriately named 'Supercar Graveyard' became an overnight phenomenon, particularly in the oil-rich countries of the Middle East, where numerous luxury cars were abandoned in their droves. In Dubai, for example, individuals who had once profiteered from the global trading market simply dumped their vehicles at the airport carpark, many with the keys still in the ignition, before fleeing the country with what assets they had left. More than 3,000 cars, including Ferraris, Porsches, Jaguars, Audis and BMWs, were abandoned in this manner, the majority were later sold by the Dubai Government for rock-bottom prices. Unbelievably one of the rarest cars in the world, a limited-edition Ferrari Enzo, worth millions of pounds, was discarded in one of these makeshift graveyards.[4] Similarly, in the summer of 2014, the Qatari newspaper *Doha News* reported that it had found a gigantic vehicle cemetery located in the desert, around a kilometre outside the city of Al Wukair. The site composed of two enormous yards containing the skeletal remains of trucks, buses and high-end sports cars. It is estimated that around 20,000 vehicles found their way to Al Wukair's sandy graveyard, many being sold on to various salvage companies at very low prices.[5]

The abandonment of automobiles is not necessarily a new trend. Châtillon, one of the oldest villages in Belgium, was once the site of the largest vintage car graveyard in the world. Numbering at least 500 cars at its height, many of them dating back to the Second World War, there are two competing theories as to how the graveyard came into being. One says the cars were left behind by American GIs, who were stationed in southern Belgium during the war. Once hostilities had ceased, they were unable to ship their cars back home to America, so they drove them into Châtillon Forest and left them there. The other theory, uncovered by American auto journalist Ronan Glon, argues that the graveyard's existence was due to the actions of a local mechanic who specialised in selling and fixing up American cars used by Canadian troops based in the area. When the Canadian forces moved to a new base, in Lahr, Germany, they asked the mechanic to accompany them, as good mechanics were extremely hard to come by. He declined their offer and chose to stay in Châtillon. The problem was he was unable to dispose of the cars, which had amassed into the hundreds. Before long Châtillon's graveyard had spilled out from its forest home, onto land surrounding his repair shop, along the backstreets, and eventually terminating on a garage forecourt located at the other end of town. Although the local residents appeared nonplussed, in 2010 the Belgian courts deemed the site to be an environmental hazard and ordered the graveyard to be cleared. Within a few years the Châtillon necropolis was no more and every car had been removed for scrap.[6]

There are some sites that defy explanation. 'Mystery Car Graveyard Discovered Inside a Welsh Cave' screamed the newspaper headlines in February 2016, and mysterious it most certainly was, for sixty-one metres down an abandoned mineshaft, deep in the heart of the Ceredigion valley, lay the remains of approximately 100 cars, all dating from the 1970s. How they ended up at the bottom of the mineshaft, or by whose hands, is unknown, but the graveyard has certainly caught the imagination of the potholing/cave diving community. One such explorer who had entered the cave, was quoted as saying, 'There was something so surreal about this exploration, it was totally dark, wet, slippery and very dangerous. And then you see the most unexpected thing, a mountain of old cars.'[7] Another oddity can be found 320 kilometres north of Charlotte in North Carolina, a stock-car cemetery devoted to relics from the National Association for Stock Car Auto Racing (NASCAR). Owned by racing driver Dale Earnhardt Junior, this unusual cemetery, often called Dirty Mo Acres, sits deep inside the woods upon Earnhardt's property and consists of approximately eighty car wrecks strategically placed inside bushes, down ditches, buried in the high grass or even, in the case of Will Powers' race-winning IndyCar, hanging from a tree. Many of the remains once took centre stage in some of NASCAR's most famous racing moments, such as Dave Gilliland's No. 38 car and Justin

Allgaier's No. 51 car from their Kansas wreck in 2014. NASCAR racer Brad Keselowski has sent several of his cars to the graveyard, while there is also a vintage No. 24 DuPont Chevy gifted by a local restaurant. In 2014, when asked about his bizarre car cemetery by *The Sporting News*, Earnhardt Jr replied: 'There are all kinds of quirky stuff back there. I don't know why I want them or even why I go get them.'[8]

The advancement in automobile technology, combined with the advent of cheap, affordable air travel, has had a detrimental effect on one particular mode of transport, the train. I am a big advocate of train travel and use it often when embarking on a grand new adventure. When it works, there is no finer way of being transported from A to B, in my humble opinion. There is also something romantic about the ideal. Commuter travel aside, names such as the Orient Express or the Trans-Siberian Railway evoke images of exotic enterprises from a bygone era, at times in opulent surroundings. In addition, we must not forget that trains were once at the forefront of transporting much-needed goods and materials around the world. Sadly, it seems these days are now over and large numbers of working trains that once proliferated the landscape lie abandoned and forgotten, rotting away in some deserted backwater.

On the outskirts of a desert trading village, high in the Bolivian Andes, there sits the Salar de Uyuni, the world's largest salt plain. At approximately 11,000 square kilometres, the area was once a prehistoric lake, but has since become dry, leaving behind a desert-like landscape of bright-white salt, rock formations and cacti-studded islands. Deemed one of the world's foremost natural wonders, what you don't expect to find here are rows of rusty old steam engines and railway carriages baking under the desert sun. How did this happen? Well, in the late nineteenth century, when the mining industry in Bolivia was at its height, the region of Uyuni became one of the most important transportation hubs in South America. So much so, that a team of British engineers was invited to Bolivia to construct a new and improved railway network that stretched from the heart of Uyuni province all the way down to the Pacific coast. Despite repeated protestations and acts of vandalism by the local Aymara tribe, who viewed the railway as a threat to their indigenous way of life, the line was finally completed in 1892. It was not in service for long, for fifty years later the Bolivian mining industry collapsed, the railway line subsequently fell into disuse, and the trains and other associated equipment were no longer required. Vast numbers were abandoned at Uyuni, where they have been left to decay. Plans to turn the train graveyard into a museum are currently ongoing.[9] A similar fate befell Suriname, the smallest independent nation in South America, located north of Brazil. First explored by the Spaniards in the sixteenth century, Suriname also became a victim of the boom and bust years of the mining industry, in particular gold mining, when large quantities of minerals and ore were once transported via a thriving railway network. The small town of Onverwacht, in the eastern Para District, is very proud of this past train heritage. Not only can you explore a quaint mini-locomotive graveyard, but throughout the town the rusted and charred remains of many old steam engines are strategically displayed. Onverwacht has even adopted a 2-4-2 steam loco as its official town emblem, which can be seen displayed on formal government signs, as well as on the sides of public vehicles, bus shelters and council buildings.[10]

The collapse of the Iron Curtain during the late 1980s was, among many things, a good time for steam train enthusiasts. Most of the Eastern bloc communist countries had continued to use old engine stock until as late as 1989, and as the Berlin Wall fell, one keen train enthusiast from rural Brandenberg bought dozens of old communist trains. Unfortunately, he had nowhere to put them. So, after an exhaustive search throughout the Brandenberg region, in the mid-2000s he eventually found an old abandoned train repair shop and moved his collection there. The graveyard site is vast, crammed with rusting locomotives as far as the eye can see. Most of the time the trains are hidden behind highly guarded fences, but for two days of the year the owner opens the train graveyard to the public, allowing them inside to marvel at his obsession.[11] Another site that benefited from the collapse of the Eastern Bloc is the Red Star Train Graveyard, located in Istvántelek, Budapest, Hungary. Once the site of a colossal train repair shop, the corpses of trains now inhabit an area stretching over twenty-two hectares, with a wide-ranging selection of dilapidated old steam engines parked top-to-tail. Once the most important repair yard in Hungary, keeping an entire communist state running like clockwork, today, bar a few determined urban explorers, the graveyard is largely forgotten.[12] One particular train graveyard, with an exceptional backstory, lies in the Russian city of Chernobyl, located around ninety-six kilometres north of Kiev, at the site of one of the world's worst nuclear disasters. On 26 April 1986, when a reactor at the Chernobyl Nuclear Power Plant exploded, the entire local railway network, including the station and trains, was showered in lethal levels of radiation with the passengers and train operators forced to exit the trains. The trains themselves, including carriages and engines, were abandoned in situ on the tracks. The railway station was largely made safe during the clear-up operation, but the trains still reside within the designated exclusion zone, too contaminated to ever be of use again.

Although the aviation industry has put paid to the necessity of train travel, it too has not escaped the ravages of time. The existence of plane graveyards is not a new phenomenon, with many of them dating back to the Second World War, but witnessing the once-proud hulks of mighty fighter planes, bombers, helicopters and commercial airliners turning to rust is a sobering sight. A few years ago, the US Army released a series of remarkable aerial images depicting several aviation graveyards strewn across America. Predominantly located in the deserts of Arizona, California and New Mexico, the images showed hundreds of retired planes, neatly lined up in formation, sprawled over vast areas of sandy wasteland. The largest of these graveyards is located around five miles south of Tucson, Arizona and is officially known as the Davis-Monthan Air Force Base. Unofficially it is referred to as 'The Boneyard' and it houses the remains of more than 4,500 planes, including F-14 fighters, made famous in the film *Top Gun*, and the iconic B-52 bomber, which was scrapped in 1991 and put into storage in an arms reduction agreement with Russia. The base is currently home to the 309th Aerospace Maintenance and Regeneration Group, whose task is to care for the twenty-two billion pounds worth of aircraft stored within its boundary. The Boneyard stretches for around 2,600 acres, with each aircraft categorised and deposited onto a specific site: category 1000 refers to those planes preserved and able to fly again if required; category 2000 is used for spare parts; category 3000 contains planes in good condition which are likely to be redeployed; category 4000 is outdated aircraft likely to be scrapped for parts or in some cases museum pieces. One can visit the site in person and weekly bus tours are available. The US Army has also provided a high definition interactive online graveyard map providing remarkable close-up details of each aircraft on display.[13]

Boneyards of Steel

Similar sites to The Boneyard include the aviation cemetery attached to Mojave Air and Space Port just outside the city of Mojave, around ninety-five miles north of Los Angeles, California. First opened in 1935, as a small, rural airfield serving the local gold and silver mining industry, today it is used by some of the largest commercial airliners in the world – such as Boeing and Airbus – as a repository. Another graveyard can be found eleven miles south of Roswell in Chave County, New Mexico. Famed for its association with UFOs, the site is also the last resting place for American Airlines' planes which have outlived their usefulness. Its tarmac once housed a 1962 Lockheed JetStar owned by Elvis Presley, it spent over thirty years languishing at Roswell before being sold at auction in 2017 for a paltry $430,000.[14] Africa also has a number of airplane graveyards worthy of mention, such as the one in Benin Airport, Nigeria, where in a forgotten corner of the airfield the grounded planes of the now obsolete Okada Air have been left to rot, their vast decaying hulks clearly visible on Google Earth.[15] The runways of Goma International Airport in the Democratic Republic of Congo, a country devastated by decades of conflict, have also become an unwitting cemetery for abandoned commercial airliners, their carcasses baking in the African sun. The largest commercial airplane graveyard in Southern Africa is Lanseria Airport just north of Johannesburg, which houses the metallic remains of over forty abandoned commercial planes, including a Boeing 727, dumped in a field by a derelict runway.[16]

The sight of aircraft left to decay on runways is a common feature of old Cold War airfields. The collapse of the Soviet Union was a hasty affair, with little or no time to arrange the removal of manpower let alone military hardware. As such, forsaken aircraft can be found strewn throughout old Eastern Bloc countries. Some graveyard sites are even located on the doorsteps of major cities, in plain view, such as Dolgoye Ledovo, on the eastern side of Moscow, whereas others can be found in some of the most remote areas imaginable, such as Ugolny Airport on the outskirts of eastern Siberia. The heart of the Soviet Union's bomber fleet, all manner of airborne firepower was kept at Ugolny, from Tupolev-Tu-95 Bears to supersonic Tu-22M Backfires, all patiently waiting for the order to attack the West. But the order never came, the military base was subsequently deserted, and the aircraft were left behind. Many fighter planes would become victims to the harsh Siberian climate, while those abandoned in aircraft hangers slowly withered away in their concrete mausoleums.[17] Perhaps the most fascinating aircraft cemetery of them all can be found in Albania, at the Kuçovë airfield, around sixty-five kilometres south of Tirane. Originally constructed in 1952, with a little Soviet assistance, the cemetery was recently brought to the public attention via the popular BBC motoring programme *Top Gear*, when it showed its presenters, Jeremy Clarkson and James May, salivating over an endless column of deserted fighter jets. The site currently houses the remains of over seventy of the most iconic fighter planes of the Soviet era, including the famous MiG-15, 17 and 19 jets, all now crumbling away on the tarmac. Surprisingly, in 2018, it was announced that the graveyard was soon to become a NATO airbase.[18]

While many aircraft cemeteries remain above ground, there are those that follow a more traditional path, with their incumbents given the usual subterranean ending. One such graveyard was stumbled upon by accident during the Second Gulf War. In 2003, coalition forces entering the Al-Asad Airbase in western Iraq, to secure the surrounding territory, found to their surprise that the retreating Iraq Airforce had buried more than fifty Soviet-era fighter jets, including the high-performance MiG-25 Foxbat, deep under the sand. Likewise, an identical MiG-25 Foxbat jet was found buried at the vast Al-Taqaddum Airbase, located some seventy-two kilometres west of Baghdad.[19] During the 1980s, the Australian Government purchased forty-three F-111 fighter planes from the US, to bolster their air power, but after decades of use the decision was taken to dispense with the fleet. Twelve of the planes were decommissioned and preserved for posterity, with a number of these donated to relevant museums. Eight had already crashed in action, while the remaining twenty-three were scheduled to be scrapped. But rather than allow the planes to rust away beneath the baking Australian sun, the government decided to bury them deep underground. Consequently, in November 2011, the last of the F-111 fighters was sent to an undisclosed burial site, with only a series of GPS coordinates, which remain classified to date, acting as a grave marker.[20]

Visiting any military cemetery can be an emotional experience. The names of the young frequently inscribed on stone grave markers, cut down in the prime of their lives, continually reiterate the futility of war. There does exist, however, a number of memorial grounds that do not honour the human casualties of war, but rather the carcasses of mechanical ones. These metallic beasts, whether it be tanks, armoured vehicles or aquatic submarines, were all once formidable weapons of battle, striking terror into enemy forces. Now, many lie forlorn, deteriorating in some forgotten hinterland, discarded where they were last switched off. Just a few have been lucky enough to be given a new lease of life, residing in some museum as a poignant reminder of past endeavours. Since the First World War, tanks have played a front-line role in almost every major conflict in the twentieth century. As such, their burnt-out shells can often be found prostrate in surprising places. For instance, outside the Eritrean capital city of Asmara, on the north-east coast of the Red Sea, a rare African tank graveyard acts as a lasting reminder to its once-ongoing conflict with neighbouring Ethiopia, in which more than 200,000 people lost their lives. Since hostilities commenced in 1974, hundreds of the metallic beasts have been stacked here, one on top of another, in a series of rows. Predominantly Soviet in origin, many have now been reclaimed by the sand, but they are far from forgotten. 'We keep this place as a reminder,' said a spokesman from the Department of Tourism, 'since these rusting ruins are not an expression of needless deaths but are a reminder of the numerous loyal citizens who gave their lives to free Eritrea.' The war officially came to an end in 1991, but continual skirmishes along the Eritrean/Ethiopian border between 1998 and 2000, killed a staggering 70,000 people. Although peace terms were agreed in 2019, disputes still remain over the highly militarised frontier.[21]

Did you know that Fort Knox in Kentucky, widely known as the home of America's main gold reserve, is also a tank graveyard? I'm ashamed to say I didn't. Named after Henry Knox, the country's first secretary of war, for sixty years Fort Knox was home to both the US Army Armor Centre and the US Army Armor School, which used the area extensively as target practice for the M1 Abrams battle tank. Fort Knox is thus littered with tank parts, with many of the leftover pieces painstakingly put together to form new tank shells, earning them the nickname 'Frankentanks'. Although Fort Knox is predominantly off-limits to the public, on the last Monday of May, commonly known as Memorial Day, it opens its doors to visitors, allowing them to explore this bizarre tank necropolis.[22] Thousands of the aforementioned M1 Abrams battle tanks have also been abandoned in a cemetery environment on the

Burying the Dead

Sierra Army Depot Army Base in the small town of Herlong, California. The base was originally established during the Second World War to act as a storage facility for general supplies and confidential Treasury Department material, as it was deemed to be far enough inland to avoid potential Japanese attacks. Following the end of the war, the depot's remit was expanded to include munitions, both live and otherwise, used during the Korean War. This was expanded further to include various militarised vehicles, such as tanks and trucks, left over from more recent conflicts in Iraq and Afghanistan. Unwittingly the depot has now become one of the largest armoured vehicle cemeteries in the world.[23]

Another large tank graveyard can be found in the Ukrainian city of Kharkov, around forty-eight kilometres from the Russian border, where some 400 Russian tanks have been laid to rest. Throughout the Cold War the site was a thriving tank repair workshop, servicing around sixty tanks a month, and specialised in the overhaul of the T-64 tank, the predominant Soviet-era battle tank of the 1960s, the T-72 tank, which was to become one of the most popular and widely produced tanks of the 1970s, and the T-80 tank, which was the first gas-propelled tank to be utilised in military operations. Yet again, with the collapse of the Soviet Union, output came to an immediate cessation and the site, together with its tanks, were simply abandoned.[24] A similar situation occurred during the Russian occupation of Afghanistan, a country that has been a battleground for as long as I can remember. In recent years a bloody conflict between coalition forces and Taliban insurgents has decimated the country, but throughout the 1980s it was the Soviet Union who was the main protagonist. With superior fighting power in both numbers and military equipment and after waging a futile war for almost ten years, against an unrelenting guerrilla insurgency, in 1989 the Soviets took the decision to pull out of Afghanistan for good, leaving behind a great deal of military equipment. One of their dumping grounds was located approximately fourteen kilometres to the east of the country's capital, Kabul, and it was left strewn with old decaying Soviet tanks. Although many date from the 1960s, Soviet hardware is extremely robust, built to withstand the inhospitable conditions of the Afghanistan terrain and it has provided a valuable resource to the Afghan military. Those tanks that cannot be salvaged, or provide valuable parts and spares to keep other more modern tanks running, are left in peace in the desert graveyard.

Boneyards of Steel

There is something rather evocative about a submarine graveyard. Visions of a James Bond-type villain hiding away in some secret underground base, mulling over their plans for world domination, comes to mind. In many instances, this isn't too far away from the truth. Take the Soviet Union's Simushir Island submarine base, concealed inside an old volcanic caldera, around 204 kilometres off the coast of Japan. Secretly constructed by the Soviet military during the late 1970s, the base was tasked with extensive reconnaissance, monitoring antagonist activity and, rumour has it, clandestine placement of underwater explosive charges running across the entire northern end of Japan, just in case there was an immediate deterioration in relations with its Cold War enemies. Believed to house around 3,000 people at its height, once the base was detected its primary objective became somewhat lessened and it was quietly demobilised. All that remains is a few rusty signs and a couple of long-ago damaged submarines interred forevermore inside the volcanic cemetery.[25]

Staying with the Russian theme, high in the Arctic Circle, encircled by the Barents Sea to the north and the White Sea to the south and east, sits the Kola Peninsula. The area hit the headlines in 1993 when the US Navy's nuclear attack submarine USS *Grayling* and the Russian Navy's nuclear ballistic missile submarine K-407 *Novomoskovsk* accidentally collided some 150 kilometres north of the Russian naval base Severomorsk. A cause of huge embarrassment to both parties, *Novomoskovsk* suffered only a large scratch on her starboard bow, while the American submarine limped away with minor damage. The event is rarely spoken about.[26] It was during the Soviet era that this particular region witnessed intense militarisation; the Kola Peninsula became the major naval base for a large portion of the Soviet naval and strategic air forces. However, by the time the Cold War ended, vast expanses of the peninsula had become totally inhabitable, contaminated by the dumping of thousands of tonnes of military waste products. One such area, which still remains highly restricted today, is Nezametnaya Cove, close to the town of Gadzhiyevo, whose secret was recently revealed by the release of certain Google Earth images. Despite the Russian's best efforts to keep the site's true purpose hidden, the photographs in question showed the remnants of a large submarine graveyard, housing the remains of various K-ships, which were once the backbone of the feared Soviet Northern

Fleet, semi-submerged in the icy waters. As a result, the Russians attempted to dispose of the submarine corpses, dragging at least one of the submarines out of the water, whereas the others have reportedly been scrapped.[27]

Not all submarine graveyards are sited in remote areas, away from prying eyes. Some can be found right under your nose. One such place can be found in the UK, in Devonport, Plymouth. Devonport is currently the largest naval base in Western Europe, stretching over 650 acres, and has been home to the Royal Navy since 1691. Within the vast site there are fifteen dry docks, four miles of waterfront, twenty-five tidal berths and five basins. There is also a cemetery of submarines, nine with their nuclear cargo intact, just a stone's throw away from a large residential area. Once the frontline of Britain's Cold War defence, at present thirteen submarines are housed in this impromptu graveyard, the majority of which were removed from active service some thirty years ago. They include HMS *Tireless* and HMS *Conqueror* – the latter being responsible for the sinking of the Argentinian ship *General Belgrano* during the Falklands War. Even though officials from the Ministry of Defence claim the submarines are perfectly safe where there are, understandably the local inhabitants are somewhat concerned about the possibility of radiation leaks. In the nearby housing estate, mother-of-one, Christelle Gilbert, confesses she is more than a little worried about her next-door neighbours: 'They need to get rid of the submarines, it's disgusting that it is taking so long,' she said. 'It's just too long for the submarines to be sitting there as a potential threat to the city. It's a lack of responsibility on the government's part not to get them moved. I have a son and I don't want his future jeopardised by it.' It is estimated that safe disposal of the decaying submarines will cost at least ten billion pounds over the next twenty-five years, and will continue well into the 2040s. Until then, the submarine necropolis will remain very much part of the Plymouth landscape.[28]

7

The Return of the Cemetery

Around 160 kilometres south of Baghdad, to the west of the mighty Euphrates River, lies the holy city of Najaf. Reputedly founded in AD 791, it is home to the largest cemetery in the world, namely the Wadi al-Salam, meaning 'valley of peace'. Stretching over 1,500 acres, the cemetery comprises thirteen per cent of the city's total mass and extends from the heart of the city centre to the north-west boundary. Encompassing a jumbled mass of tombs and graves, it has a special place in the hearts of Shi'ite Muslims as it surrounds the mausoleum of their first Imam, Ali ibn Abi Talib, a cousin and son-in-law of the Prophet Mohammad. Other notable burials include the kings of Al-Hira and leaders from the Al-Sassani era, AD 637-226, as well as princes from the state of Hamdania, Fatimia, Al-Buwayhyia, Saffawayia, Qajar, and Jalairiyah. For over 1,400 years people have been burying their dead here, including Shi'ite pilgrims who travel vast distances to inter their loved ones within its sacred ground. Just how many bodies lie within the cemetery confines is difficult to ascertain, estimates range from five to ten million depending on what reports you read.[1] This number has increased expeditiously in recent times as the 'valley of peace' became anything but. Amid the battle against the hardline Sunni Islamic State, the lack of available burial plots in Wadi al-Salam became a real issue with many existing grave sites illegally resold or stolen. 'The pace of daily burials rose to 150-200 after Islamic State overran the country in 2014,' says cemetery historian Jihad Abu Saybi. 'Before that the rate was around eighty a day.' In fact, so great was the number killed that some of the largest Shi'a militias opened burial offices in Najaf to effectively manage the interment of their fighters, which included the cost of transporting the corpse from the field of operation, as well as paying for the funeral and headstone inscription. Once a diorama of sandy brown, the cemetery is now interspersed with brightly coloured posters memorialising those killed in the fighting.[2]

A vast, desert-bound necropolis such as Wadi al-Salam is arguably the antithesis of most people's portrait of a cemetery. A wide, open green space encompassing rows of decorated gravestones, together with foliage aplenty, is more the norm. Before the nineteenth century, laying a loved one to rest normally took place in a local churchyard or burial ground. But with the onset of the Industrial Revolution, as vast numbers of people left the countryside and headed towards the cities, urban areas began to face extreme pressure on their burial provision. Space in traditional churchyards filled rapidly, resulting in extremely cramped and unhygienic conditions. The solution to this predicament was the development of the more familiar garden cemetery we see today, first by private joint-stock companies and later by public authorities. Often sited on the fringe of urban settlements, cemeteries were unlike traditional burial grounds as they did not cater for regular religious worship and their sole purpose was for interment. Moreover, unlike traditional churchyards, they also accommodated both consecrated and unconsecrated patrons alike. That is not to say that cemeteries did not have a chapel within, most of them had at least two, but these were solely for funerary services. In effect, cemeteries were originally conceived as public landscapes, characterised by a combination of pleasing fauna together with some of the finest monumental sculpture on view. Many of them were professionally designed and laid out by the same people who created public parks.[3]

Early examples of this new breed of cemetery first appeared in India during the eighteenth century. South Park Street Cemetery in Calcutta, which opened in 1767, once served as a cemetery for European expatriates who settled in the country during the colonial period. Named after a private deer park, it stretches for approximately eight acres and has a total of 1624 registered graves, including that of the founder of The Asiatic Society, Sir William Jones, who first came to India in 1783; Lady Anne Monson, a great granddaughter of King Charles II, who died in 1776; Colonel Robert Kyd, a botanist who founded the Botanical Garden of Calcutta and George Bogle, a diplomat who led the first British expedition to Tibet. The eastern wall also contains a number of grave tablets from the now defunct North Park Street Cemetery. Many of the graves commemorate more than one person, and there is a fine display of pyramids, obelisks, mausoleums, cairns, urns and sarcophagi. It also houses the famous 'bleeding tomb', a small, pyramid-shaped structure belonging to the Dennison family that is rumoured to ooze a blood-like substance during monsoons. Due to a lack of burial space, the cemetery finally closed its gates in the 1830s and is now a national heritage site, managed and maintained by the Archaeological Survey of India.[4] Another stunning example in India is the Roman Catholic Cemetery in Agra, which contains several members of the French Bourbon royal family as well as the remains of the first Englishman to be buried in India, John Mildenhall, an ambassador to Queen Elizabeth I, who arrived in Agra in 1603 to negotiate access to Mughal ports. Unlike other colonial cemeteries, the majority of the monuments here are designed in the traditional Mughal style, with the addition of a Christian cross on top. The earliest tomb, Marty's Chapel, dates to 1611 and consists of an octagonal-domed monument complete with arched entrance. A place of Christian pilgrimage, inside lie the bodies of at least five Armenian priests together with twenty-six Jesuits. The cemetery also has a magnificent red sandstone copy of the Taj Mahal, aptly named the Red Taj. Costing 100,000 rupees to construct, approximately £1,170 in today's money, it belongs to Dutch mercenary and former Commandant of Agra Fort, John William Hessing, who journeyed to India in 1763 to join the service of the Nizam of Hyderabad, where he remained until his death in 1803.[5]

Similar cemeteries also began to appear in the southern states of America around this time, notably in New Orleans, which by 1725 already had a small cemetery just outside the city limits. This was replaced in 1789 by St Louis Cemetery No. 1, famously located a few blocks away from the mighty Mississippi River and a short walk from the popular French Quarter. The city itself is unusual in that it is built on top of a swamp, so with a higher than normal water table, the dead have to be buried above ground. Thus, the design of St Louis Cemetery No. 1 has a rather urban street feel about it, with a procession of decorative crypts resembling a townscape environment. Henceforth, the cemetery landscape of New Orleans would commonly be referred to as the 'cities of the dead'. Owned by the Roman Catholic Church, the cemetery is thought to contain the remains of thousands of individuals, including

Étienne de Boré, wealthy pioneer of the sugar industry and the first mayor of New Orleans; members of artist Edgar Degas' family and the renowned Voodoo priestess Marie Laveau, believed to be interred in the Glapion family crypt.[6] A relatively recent addition to this list is the Hollywood actor Nicolas Cage, who though not presently dead, recently purchased a nine-foot pyramid shaped tomb to house his remains upon his passing. Today, due to ever-increasing vandalism, the cemetery is closed to the public and is only accessible via a certified guided tour.

In 1832, when the city council believed an outbreak of yellow fever and cholera was caused by bad air emanating from St Louis Cemetery No. 1, a new cemetery was hurriedly consecrated. It was titled St Louis Cemetery No. 2. Famed for its Greek-revival tombs and ornate ironwork, notable burials include jazz and blues legends Danny Barker and Ernie K-Doe and Andre Cailloux, an African-American Union Army hero who was killed in combat during the American Civil War. St Louis Cemetery No. 3 followed in 1854, full of high-quality marble vaults and mausoleums together with a designated Greek Orthodox section. In 2005, cemeteries 2 and 3 were badly affected by Hurricane Katrina; the latter experienced particularly heavy flooding, but remarkably the tombs remained intact.[7] Perhaps the most famous cemetery in New Orleans is Lafayette Cemetery, sited among the lush greenery and opulent homes of the Garden District. Opened in 1833, it is the oldest city-run cemetery and prides itself on being the only non-denominational, non-segregated burial space within the city's environs. It has also become the final resting place for many of the city's outcasts, including those from the Independent Order of Odd Fellows, the German Presbyterian Community, the Home for Destitute Orphan Boys, and the New Orleans Home for the Incurables.[8] Lafayette gained notoriety in the 1990s when it was used as a backdrop by best-selling author Anne Rice for her fictional Mayfair Witches tales and vampires stories, in particular that of a vampire named Lestat, whose character was vividly brought to life by Tom Cruise in the 1995 Hollywood blockbuster *Interview with a Vampire*. Last but not least there is Greenwood Cemetery, founded in 1855, which is one of New Orleans' largest cemeteries, containing over 20,500 burials. Tombs in this cemetery are arranged to create maximum capacity and include the Firemen's Monument, a neo-gothic design inspired by Sir Walter Scott's Monument in Edinburgh, and the Elk's tomb, erected in 1912 as a symbol of fraternity.[9]

The Return of the Cemetery

The inspiration for Britain's quintessential Victorian garden cemetery did not come from these early examples in the New World, but from a cemetery far closer to home – Cimetière du Père-Lachaise in Paris. Established by Napoleon in 1804, and named after Father François d'Aix de La Chaise, official confessor to King of France Louis XIV, the site is located to the east of the city, making full use of a disused quarry, and contains the remains of over one million people. Spanning approximately 110 acres, the cemetery is strictly non-denominational. Fashioned by architect Alexandre-Théodore Brongniartit, to resemble the appearance of an English country park, a fine array of funerary sculpture is interspersed with herbaceous flower beds and shrub-lined paths. Yet, the cemetery did not have an auspicious beginning. Many Parisians believed it was too far away from the city to be a viable option.[10] It also had little appeal to those from a religious background, especially followers of the Roman Catholic Church as the land had not been blessed by the proper religious authorities and remained unconsecrated. What followed next was a stroke of marketing genius. To entice a wider audience, and effectively more custom, the cemetery gained permission from the relevant authorities to dig up the famed seventeenth-century fabulist and poet, Jean de La Fontaine, together with Molière, the renowned actor and playwright, from their original grave sites, and rebury them in Père-Lachaise. The stunt worked. Records show that in 1804 only thirteen burials took place within the cemetery. After the illustrious reburials had taken place, this number increased to forty-four, rising to 833 by 1812. The exercise was repeated in 1817 when the purported remains of medieval French philosopher and theologian Pierre Abélard, together with his lover Héloïse d'Argenteuil, were also transferred to the cemetery. Soon Parisians were clamouring to be buried in Père-Lachaise, lying among the rich and famous. In 1830, documents show that the cemetery housed more than 33,000 graves.[11]

In 1804, the Parisian authorities passed a law that allowed the sharing of cemeteries between various religions, and so a new Jewish enclosure in Père Lachaise opened on 18 February 1810. Initially enclosed by a wall, this part of the cemetery included a purification room and a pavilion for the caretaker. It was soon followed in 1856 by a Muslim enclosure, the first of its kind in France, complete with mosque, a waiting room, a lavatorium, intended for the purification of Muslims, and a counter for religious effects.[12] There is also an ossuary, located behind the 'To the

Dead' monument that houses the bones removed from cemeteries all over the city. Père-Lachaise is still a working cemetery, although finding a grave plot is nigh on impossible. Recently the cemetery adopted a new practice of issuing thirty-year leases on grave sites and if the lease is not renewed the remains are removed and space is made for a new grave. The abandoned remains are boxed, tagged and moved to the ossuary.[13] Moreover, burial in Père-Lachaise is only afforded to those who either live in Paris or who have died within the city's boundary. Burials of note include writer Oscar Wilde; Jean-François Champollion, the decipherer of Egyptian hieroglyphs; French singer Edith Piaf; the father of Spiritism, Allan Kardec; eighteenth-century stage performer Étienne-Gaspard Robert, whose monument is decorated with skulls, skeletons and ghouls, and the 1960s rock legend Jim Morrison, lead singer of The Doors.[14]

The idea of utilising a disused quarry for burial provision, as Père-Lachaise had, was enthusiastically adopted by architects in England, with one of the first garden cemeteries, St James's in Liverpool, taking full advantage of such little valued land. Opened in 1829, at a cost of £21,000, St James was solely a commercial venture, aimed at Anglicans, and was built within a strategic twelve-acre abandoned hillside quarry. Its architect, John Foster, felt it was important to create a pleasant environment to attract paying customers, so his design encompassed a neo-classical oasis, complete with catacombs dug into beautifully landscaped terraced ramps, mixed with ornamental accoutrements and eye-catching flora and fauna. It was a success, making an eight per cent profit in its first year. Similar examples soon followed, including Key Hill Cemetery in Birmingham (1836) and Church Cemetery in Nottingham (1856).[15] Another cemetery that took inspiration from Paris was the Glasgow Necropolis, which opened in 1832. Described by many as one of the most significant cemeteries in Europe, its proprietors, who were eminent members of Glasgow's influential Merchants' House, wanted to create an inclusive necropolis for all denominations, which reflected the wealth, brilliance and diversity of Glasgow at that time. Located in the old rocky Wester Craigs area of the city, adjacent to Glasgow Cathedral, the cemetery spans thirty-seven acres and comprises some 50,000 burials. Due to its natural surroundings, a high percentage of the tombs have stone walls and brick partitions, while others, sited on top of the necropolis, initially had to be blasted out of the rock face.[16]

The Return of the Cemetery

Many of the new cemeteries took their lead from horticultural journalist John Claudius Loudon, regarded by many as the godfather of cemetery design. Born in Lanarkshire, Scotland, in 1843 he published the highly influential writings, *On the Laying Out, Planting and Managing of Cemeteries*, which gave detailed and effective advice on the construction and management of cemeteries. Sadly, he died that same year so never got to experience its impact. The ideas he extolled are still in use today, such as the use of a rectangular grid system for burial plots and the utilisation of broad sweeps if the cemetery is sited on an incline. He recommended that 1,361 graves per acre was sufficient, interspersed with a variety of roads and paths wide enough so a funeral could be performed without treading on any other grave. Chapels were to be placed in a central position and every cemetery should be enclosed with a surrounding boundary wall, together with a main gate and lodge house. One of Loudon's primary recommendations was in the use of vegetation. He stipulated 'no flowers at all', rather trees and shrubs should only be used, in particular dark green, weeping and fastigiate varieties, such as yews, junipers, firs and pines, which offered a symbolically mournful effect.[17]

Between 1800 and 1850 the population of London more than doubled, placing enormous strain on the city's infrastructure, especially its churchyards, which were too small and overcrowded to cope with the influx. In a short space of time it became impossible to bury bodies at an adequate depth, many were left above ground to rot, while relatively fresh graves were often broken into and the resident corpse dismembered in order to make room for another one. It was not uncommon to see bones sticking out of the ground or numerous coffins piled six metres high in burial shafts. Some coffins were even broken apart, by unscrupulous individuals, to sell as firewood to the poor, the contents simply discarded onto the ground. The outcome of this ensuing chaos was that decaying human matter began to enter London's water supply, which at that time was either located in close proximity to churchyards or, more often than not, actually inside them. For instance, water from St Clement's Well and St Giles's Well came through their respective burial grounds, while communal water pumps once existed within the now defunct Stepney Churchyard, St Mary-le-Bow Churchyard and St George's in the East. With regards to the latter, it is reported that the Reverend of St George's once hung a placard around the churchyard water pump which read 'Dead

Man's Broth', in a vain attempt to prevent the locals from drinking from it.[18] In 1831 his fears were realised when London experienced its first great cholera epidemic; the general consensus at the time was the disease had been caused by 'foul emanations from overflowing churchyards'. Prompt action was called for and in response Parliament passed the 1832 Bill entitled 'Establishing a General Cemetery for the Interment of the Dead in the Neighbourhood of the Metropolis'. What followed was the formation of seven private cemeteries, based upon the commercial model of Père-Lachaise. The first, Kensal Green, opened in 1833 and the last, Tower Hamlets, opened in 1841. Today they are more commonly known as the Magnificent Seven.

Kensal Green Cemetery – 1833

Kensal Green had a somewhat troubled beginning. Its owner, the General Cemetery Company, initially purchased land for the cemetery in 1831 and immediately endorsed a nationwide competition for its design, with the brief including two chapels with catacombs, an entrance gateway with lodges and a landscaped layout for monuments. There were forty-eight entrants and the winner was architect Henry Edward Kendall, who specialised in the Gothic style of design. Unfortunately for him, the chairman of the General Cemetery Company preferred a more neo-classical approach, and persuaded the company surveyor, John Griffith, to secretly draw up new designs in the Greek Revival style. It would be his designs, not Kendall's, that would prevail. The cemetery would eventually open its gates in 1833. Comprising seventy-two acres of grounds, designed by Richard Forrest, the former head gardener at Syon Park, it was divided into a consecrated Anglican section and an unconsecrated one for Dissenters. Provision was also made for infants. Along the northern boundary wall is a series of catacombs, defined by a colonnade of Greek architecture, which holds around 2,000 coffins, and in 1939, to the west, the West London Crematorium and Gardens of Remembrance were developed. Over 250,000 people have been buried in Kensal Green, including 500 titled nobility, such as the 5th Duke of Portland; Prince Augustus Frederick, Duke of Sussex; the 9th Duke of Queensbury; three marquesses of Sligo; Lord Palmerston and numerous servants of Queen Victoria. Other notable burials include Isambard Kingdom Brunel; the poet Thomas Hood; 'the father of computing' Charles Babbage, and novelists Anthony Trollope and William Makepeace Thackeray. In 1989, the Friends of Kensal Green Cemetery was established to aid the conservation of the cemetery and they were fundamental in the restoration of the Dissenters' Chapel, which has now become their headquarters.[19]

West Norwood Cemetery – 1836

Designed by architect Sir William Tite, West Norwood Cemetery was the first cemetery in the UK to be constructed in the new Gothic style, and included two Gothic chapels, a consecrated one facing west and a Dissenters' chapel facing north. It is believed to hold the finest collection of sepulchral monuments in London, including a dedicated Greek Orthodox necropolis with nineteen listed mausoleums and monuments. Built on the site of the Great North Wood, hence the name Norwood, the cemetery opened in 1836, receiving its first burial soon after, and spans forty acres. Blending a mixture of monumental sculpture, manicured lawns and leafy fauna, Tite's original design included a number of mature tree specimens taken from the ancient woodland; a recent tree survey identified one particular oak that dated from 1540. By the year 2000 there had been 164,000 burials in 42,000 plots, 34,000 cremations and several thousand interments within its catacombs. There are 136 Commonwealth burials dating to the First World War and fifty-two dating to the Second World War, plus eighteen cremations. In 1969, the remains of 11,500 bodies were removed from the closed burial ground of St George's, in Hanover Square, cremated and reinterred in West Norwood. More than 200 individuals buried in the cemetery are recorded in the *Dictionary of National Biography*. Notables include pottery magnate Sir Henry Doulton; Dr William Marsden, founder of the Royal Free and Royal Marsden hospitals; artist David Roberts; architect William Burges; Isabella Mary Mayson Beeton, aka Mrs Beeton, the Victorian cookery writer; Sir Hiram Maxim, inventor of the automatic machine gun and Paul Julius Baron von Reuter, founder of Reuters news agency. West Norwood is currently closed for burials but the cemetery's crematorium still operates and cremation plots are available.[20]

Highgate Cemetery – 1839

Built by the London Cemetery Company, Highgate, in its original form, was located on a south-facing hillside, just below Highgate village. It was first consecrated in 1839 by the Bishop of London. In 1854, the area to the east of the site, across Swains Lane, was purchased to form the eastern part of the cemetery. Designed by architect Stephen Geary, who is buried within, Highgate caters to followers of the Church of England and Dissenters alike. The cemetery's tombs and buildings are constructed in an imposing Victorian Gothic style, set among trees, shrubbery and wildflowers. At the heart of the West Cemetery lies the world-renowned Egyptian Avenue, entered via a decorative arch, which consists of sixteen vaults arranged on either side of a broad passageway. Each vault is fitted with a number of shelves that can hold at least twelve coffins. From the avenue, the passageway leads neatly into the Circle of Lebanon, built in the same Egyptian style, which comprises twenty vaults on the inner circle with a further sixteen that were added in the 1870s. Above this, a separate Gothic style catacomb, the Terrace Catacombs, was added. It was completed in 1842. There are over 170,000 people buried in Highgate Cemetery in 53,000 graves, including forty-eight Fellows of the Royal Society, six Lord Mayors of London, and over 850 burials of note. This includes the novelist George Eliot; archaeologist and anthropologist Peter Ucko; Scottish folk musician Bert Jansch; Elizabeth Lilley, midwife to Queen Victoria, and Highgate's most famous resident, German political philosopher Karl Marx. Highgate Cemetery is still open for burial, although there are a limited number of plots available. To buy a plot in advance you must be over 80 or be suffering from a terminal illness.[21]

Abney Park Cemetery – 1840

Named after Sir Thomas Abney, Lord Mayor of London, Abney Park Cemetery, in Stoke Newington, opened in 1840 as a non-denominational garden cemetery and arboretum, the first of its kind in Europe. Its designers, architect John Hoskins and horticulturalist George Loddiges, wanted to create a space that combined burials with public land, which would display trees from all over the world. As such, there are now over

2,500 trees and shrubs carefully arranged around the cemetery's thirty-one-acre boundary, the oldest being a 170-year-old holly bush. Abney Park also boasts the earliest complete design for a permanent Egyptian Revival entranceway anywhere in the world. Its Gothic chapel was designed by architect William Hosking and remains unconsecrated; the thirty-six-metre steeple is the tallest structure in the vicinity. There are over 200,000 people buried in Abney Park, including William Booth, the founder of the Salvation Army, and his wife Catherine; Welsh nurse Betsi Cadwaladr, a contemporary of Florence Nightingale; Frank Bostock, a Victorian lion trainer and educator on African and Asian wildlife and many from the entertainment industry, including comedian and actor Herbert Campbell, and Nelly Power, male impersonator and panto star.[22]

Nunhead Cemetery – 1840

Spanning fifty-two acres, Nunhead Cemetery was originally owned by the United Cemetery Company and is the second largest of the Magnificent Seven. It was consecrated in 1840 and the first burial was Charles Abbott, a 101-year-old grocer from Ipswich. It contains a fine Anglican church, designed by Thomas Little and also houses the remains removed from the now demolished St Christopher le Stocks Church in the City of London. Landscaped with avenues of trees and country-like paths, there are many fine examples of monumental sculpture here, including a large obelisk dedicated to the Scottish Political Martyrs – the leaders Thomas Muir, Maurice Margarot, and Thomas Fyshe Palmer were transported to Australia in 1794 – together with simpler gravestones of poorer folk. Initially slow to attract custom, Nunhead quickly became a repository for communal graves, where up to forty coffins could be placed in a single grave. At one point the demand for burial plots became so acute they had to bury the dead along the pathways. By the middle of the twentieth century the cemetery had reached its capacity, and thus its profitability, so was duly abandoned by the United Cemetery Company. With no-one to maintain the premises, the cemetery quickly fell into disuse, becoming littered with detritus and overgrown with vegetation. It wasn't until the early 1980s, when the Friends of Nunhead Cemetery was formed, that the cemetery received much needed due care and attention.

Today, it is a successful local nature reserve and a Site of Metropolitan Importance for Wildlife.[23]

Brompton Cemetery – 1840

Brompton Cemetery was opened in 1840 by the West London and Westminster Cemetery Company, whose intent was to provide a garden for public recreation, in addition to burial space. It is currently owned by the Crown, managed by The Royal Parks, has several listed buildings and is a Site of Nature Conservation Importance. Spread over forty acres, the cemetery was designed in a neo-classical style by architect Benjamin Baud, who had previously worked at Windsor Castle, and constitutes an immense open-air cathedral complex with a central avenue that runs for 609 metres, through a ninety-one-metre circle, to meet a spectacular domed chapel. The entire design is said to have been inspired by the piazza of St Peter's in Rome. The central avenue was once lined by a double row of lime trees, surrounded by pines, but the pine trees have long since disappeared. Two prominent colonnades flank the central avenue and great circle, underneath which are to be found a series of catacombs. Another series of catacombs originally ran the entire length of the cemetery's west wall, with a raised earthen terrace traversing the east wall. Unfortunately, they were not a financial success and only 500 were sold. Brompton also has a small columbarium and a secluded garden of remembrance at the northern end for cremated remains. The cemetery was originally designed to accommodate 60,000 burial plots; those on the east side were private graves and typically contained brick-lined vaults placed beneath large monuments or mausolea. On the west side, large sections of cheaper common graves housed several unrelated coffins, in some places the graves were dug around seven metres deep and could hold up to ten adult burials at any one time. A stipulation for the provision of common graves was that no memorial headstone could ever be erected. By 1900 there were some 155,000 burials, rising to today's figure of 250,000. It is still a working cemetery and those buried in Brompton come from all walks of life. A few noteworthy burials include suffragette Emmeline Pankhurst; sculptor, artist and Egyptologist Joseph Bonomi the Younger; missionary and academic Agnes de Selincourt;

The Return of the Cemetery

middleweight bare-knuckle fighter Nat Langham and Robert Fortune, the botanist who introduced the tea plant to India.[24]

Tower Hamlets Cemetery – 1841

Tower Hamlets Cemetery was formally consecrated on the morning of Saturday, 4 September 1841 and the first burial took place that same afternoon. Spanning twenty-seven acres, the cemetery is divided into consecrated and unconsecrated sections, but unlike the other Magnificent Seven cemeteries, Tower Hamlets was predominantly for the working-class people who hailed from the East End of London, many of whom could not afford a proper burial, let alone a headstone. Accordingly, you will find numerous common burial plots containing many unrelated individuals, including unmarked graves of orphans from Barnardo's homes. Some graves are even said to be twelve metres deep in places, housing up to thirty bodies at a time. In the first two years after opening, sixty per cent of burials were in common graves and by 1851 this number had increased to eighty. In total around 350,000 people are thought to be buried in Tower Hamlets Cemetery, including 279 service personnel who died during both world wars. In 1966, the cemetery ceased trading and was purchased by the Greater London Council, whose aim was to clear the cemetery of all the graves and turn the land into a leisure park. This idea was met with staunch opposition from the local community, who forced the Greater London Council to shelve their plans. Mind you, not before a small number of graves had already been removed. Although Tower Hamlets may not have the gravitas of other Magnificent Seven cemeteries, it does have its fair share of noteworthy burials, including Dr Rees Ralph Llewellyn, who performed the autopsy on Mary Ann Nichols, the first victim of Jack the Ripper; Will Crooks, trade unionist and first Labour Mayor of Poplar; Major John Buckley, one of the first recipients of the Victoria Cross and Clara Grant, educator and social reformer. Today the cemetery is a local nature reserve, managed and conserved by The Friends of Tower Hamlets Cemetery Park.[25]

One of the last commercial enterprises to open its doors was Brookwood Cemetery in Woking, Surrey. Founded in 1852, by the London

Necropolis and National Mausoleum Company, and opened to the public in 1854, it is the largest cemetery in the UK, and one of the largest in Europe, with approximately 250,000 people buried within its grounds. Comprising around 2,000 acres of prime heathland, with more than 400 acres given over for burial provision, it is divided into two large Anglican and Nonconformist sections, together with a number of separate plots put aside for specific communities, denominations and institutions, such as the unique Parsi burial ground, the Oddfellows, the Ancient Order of Foresters and the London and South Railway.[26] It also houses Brookwood Military Cemetery, the American Cemetery and Memorial and Britain's oldest Muslim cemetery, not to mention the remains removed from at least twenty-one London churchyards that were demolished during the massive civil engineering projects of the mid-nineteenth century. It even had its own railway line, the London Necropolis Railway, which linked directly to a receiving station at Waterloo. Included were two separate stations, serving each cemetery section, platforms, waiting rooms and refreshment options. Special hearse vans were constructed inside the train, allowing for the transportation of both corpse and grieving relatives, with compartments divided and ticketed depending on one's social status. The remains of a pauper would cost 2 shillings 6d, while those from the upper echelons of society would be charged 5 shillings. Mourners would pay £1. For over eighty years a daily service ran from Waterloo to Brookwood, carrying over 2,000 bodies annually. It came to an end in 1941 when the Waterloo receiving station was mostly destroyed by a bomb that fell during the Second World War. 'It was pioneering; it was revolutionary,' says railroad historian John Clarke. 'As far as I know, it was the first use of the railway for a dedicated service from one private station, directly into a cemetery at the other end.'[27]

Although private companies continued to run their cemeteries without any interference from the government, a second devastating cholera outbreak in 1848 forced Parliament to pass a number of Acts known collectively as the Burial Acts, aimed at improving burial conditions in urban settings, see Appendix 1. With a few exceptions, such as the aforementioned Brookwood Cemetery and Undercliffe Cemetery in Bradford, from 1850 all new cemeteries would be managed by public bodies called Burial Boards. Appointed by the local parish, their responsibilities would include the sale of grave plots, burial of the dead, as well as the upkeep and management of the cemetery and its associated buildings. Some even offered those with limited financial means the option of being buried in a shared marked grave called a 'guinea grave', complete with headstone and inscription, which unlike paupers' graves would display the name and age of the deceased plus their date of death. The finest surviving example can be seen in Beckett Street Cemetery in Leeds. Opened in 1845, and one of the earliest publicly funded cemeteries in England, along the cemetery path are several lines of guinea graves complete with identical headstones. Burial Boards would continue to function until the late 1890s when cemeteries became the responsibility of local authorities.[28]

Unlike the confined churchyards that came before, cemeteries provided ample space for those with financial means to construct lavish monuments. A new industrial means of cutting stone allowed firms of monumental masons to flourish and a host of styles became available for the discerning customer. Gone were the days of mortality symbols and trade emblems, by 1840 white marble was being imported from Italy and the Victorian client had a taste for the exotic.[29] Harking back to civilisations of old, neoclassical designs were the way to go, with many influenced by one culture in particular, namely ancient Egypt. I should confess that I may be somewhat biased here, as being a qualified Egyptologist I do have an unhealthy fixation of seeing ancient Egyptian influences wherever I turn. I am not the only one. The eminent Egyptologist, I. E. S. Edwards, was in no doubt that the Egyptians would exert an enormous influence on later architectural developments, while Amelia Edwards, pioneering founder of the Egypt Exploration Society, notes that: 'It would be difficult to find a more interesting subject of inquiry than the extent of that debt which is owed to the teaching and example of the Ancient Egyptians.'[30] In truth the public was, and still is, enthralled by the mysteries of ancient Egypt, especially the Egyptian way of death. Ultimately, it is a matter of judgment and personal opinion, but mausoleum-type structures, torus mouldings, stand-alone columns, pylons, shrine plinths – which appear as grave monuments and statue bases in numerous cemeteries – serpents, winged discs and alike, all have their roots in the deserts of Egypt.

Expanding on this theme in only a few paragraphs will be somewhat challenging. After all, the appropriation of Egyptian-style monumental architecture for funerary desires can easily be traced back to classical times. For example, the city of Rome once had two known pyramids, both grave monuments. The first was Meta Romuli, located close to St Peter's, which was removed during the enlargement of the church during the sixteenth century, while the other, which still stands today, can be found close to the English Cemetery, and belonged to the Roman official Gaius Cestius. Descriptions of Egyptian tombs and temples were first brought back to Britain in the mid-seventeenth century by John Greaves, professor of Mathematics at Oxford University, who was the first to record and draw on site, the external and internal measurements of the Giza pyramids.[31] Shortly after, in Scottish graveyards, a winged disk symbol began to appear on stone markers, reminiscent of an Egyptian form known as py-wer, 'the great flyer'. Positioned as the uppermost decoration on headstones, the Scottish version is characterised with unique facial features on a central disk; an early example, dating to 1697, can be found in the rural burial ground of Westerkirk in Dumfriesshire.[32] During the seventeenth and eighteenth centuries, further influences would be brought home by those who had completed the Grand Tour, a period of foreign travel commonly undertaken by gentlemen in order to complete their education. Many would experience their first taste of ancient Egypt while residing in Rome. Napoleon's Egyptian Campaign (1798–1801), in particular its extensive scientific study of Egyptian remains and culture, would flame a full-scale Egyptian Revival, augmented a few years later, in 1822, by Jean-François Champollion who succeeded in deciphering Egyptian hieroglyphs. Undoubtedly the work of Scottish artist, David Roberts (1796-1864) was most effective in spreading awareness of Egyptian forms, while in 1922, Howard Carter's discovery of King Tutankhamun's tomb set off a final wave of ancient Egyptian fever, commonly known as Egyptomania. By the time the recording and conservation of Tut's tomb, and its contents, had been completed, the craze was all but over.

Since then ancient Egypt's unique architectural forms, in particular its powerful symbols of commemoration, have had a profound effect on contemporary monumental sculpture, especially within a burial setting. The pyramid style is probably the best known. It is believed the early stepped versions were seen by the Egyptians as staircases to heaven, whereby the pharaoh's soul could ascend the surrounding night sky regarded as the gateway to the realm of the gods. They are not prolific in a cemetery/graveyard context, but they do exist, an early example being the 1684 pyramid-capped mausoleum in Penicuik, St Andrews, Scotland. Other examples from my private research list include a four-and-a-half metre pyramid built for physician Dr Francis Douce in St Andrew's Churchyard, Nether Wallop, Hampshire; the pinnacle of the pyramid is capped off with a flaming torch, and one side of the pyramid bears a tablet which holds a coat of arms and an inscription. There is also the nine-metre pyramid tomb, dating to 1851, constructed for civil engineer William Mackenzie in St Andrew's Presbyterian Churchyard, Liverpool and the Star Pyramid in Valley Cemetery, Stirling, a striking stone pyramidal structure, dating to 1863, that commemorates the martyrs of the Scottish Reformation and Covenanting era. In Ireland a nineteenth-century nine-metre replica of the Great Pyramid of Giza can be seen in Kinnitty Graveyard, Birr. It currently houses the remains of six members of the Bernard family, once the wealthy landowners and owners of nearby Kinnitty Castle. There is also the large Howard Mausoleum pyramid in Old Kilbride Cemetery, Arklow, where eighteen members of the Howard family were laid to rest. Elsewhere in the world, the Serbian playwright, satirist and novelist, Branislav Nusic, was entombed in a pyramid in Belgrade in 1938 and at the entrance to Laglio's Cemetery, Lake Como, a pyramid tomb houses the remains of eminent Italian doctor Joseph Frank, who was interred in 1852. Numerous American tycoons have purposely incorporated the Egyptian pyramid-style into their own mausoleum designs, such as the Schoenhofen Pyramid Mausoleum in Graceland Cemetery, Chicago, built in 1893 as a family mausoleum for the brewery magnate Peter Schoenhofen; the Van Ness/Parsons tomb, Green-Wood Cemetery, Brooklyn, New York; and the pyramid of George W. P. Hunt, an American politician and businessman, in Papago Park, Phoenix, Arizona.[33]

If circumstances had been different, the most audacious pyramid of them all, outside of Egypt, could now be sitting atop Primrose Hill in north London. In 1829, before Parliament agreed on the construction of new cemeteries, architect Thomas Wilson proposed that a giant necropolis, in the shape of a pyramid, could be the answer to London's funerary problems. Called the Metropolitan Sepulchre, it would be significantly larger than the Great Pyramid at Giza, with its base covering eighteen acres and rising to a height of ninety-four storeys, effectively four times the height of St Paul's Cathedral. Wilson estimated that there would be enough room for the bodies of five million Londoners. Constructed from brick, but faced with granite, in order to obtain funding for the project Wilson founded the Pyramid General Cemetery Company, a private undertaking that would sell shares to investors. At a rate of £50 per vault for families or parishes, and based upon 40,000 burials per annum, he believed it would make a tidy return for his investors of somewhere between ten to eleven million pounds per annum. Sadly, the pyramid was not to be. A pity, as I am sure you would agree the Metropolitan Sepulchre would have made a fascinating addition to the London skyline.[34]

Like the pyramid, hybrid versions of the sphinx, the recognisable Egyptian leonine figure, were extremely popular in cemeteries throughout the USA. Examples include the 1872 Martin Milmore sphinx monument in Mount Auburn Cemetery, Cambridge, Massachusetts, which is dedicated to the fallen who died fighting against slavery, and the blue sphinx tomb containing the remains of Matthew Lawler in Spring Grove Cemetery, Cincinnati. There is also a wonderful example in Rakowicki Cemetery in Krakow, Poland, on the tomb of Leszek Zinkow, which depicts an Egyptian-style sphinx, complete with a pharaonic headdress, crushing a skull underfoot. But perhaps the most stunning representation of them all, and one that I would highly recommend going to view, presently guards the mausoleum of Alfred Illingworth, in Undercliffe Cemetery, Bradford. A former member of parliament and founder of Whetley Mills, Illingworth was buried in a grey granite mausoleum resembling a mastaba, a style of ancient Egyptian tomb typical of the Old Kingdom period, c. 2686-2181 BC, where the burial chamber is located underground. A bronze door once sat at the tomb entrance, complete with Egyptian decoration, with the name Illingworth carved across the lintel, which is still in situ, adorned with an Egyptian winged solar disc flanked by an uraeus, a representation of a sacred serpent. The base of the mausoleum is extended at the front and is guarded by a pair of stone sphinxes, whose design mirrors those from Egypt's Middle Kingdom Period, c. 2050-1652 BC, such as the ones belonging to Pharaoh Amenemhat III. Interestingly, an almost identical design, the Tate Mausoleum, can be seen in Bellefontaine Cemetery in St Louis, Missouri.[35]

The obelisk, the tapered monolithic pillar erected in pairs at the entrances of ancient Egyptian temples, is one of the most prominent mourning symbols of the eighteenth and nineteenth centuries, yet many people are unaware of its origins. They come in all shapes and sizes, fat ones, thin ones, small ones that often denote the untimely death of a child, tall ones with urns, why I have even seen one in a Scottish cemetery wearing a crown. To the Egyptians the obelisk, or tekhenu, was intimately connected to the cult of the sun and was, therefore, considered a sacred symbol of the sun god Ra. The tip of the obelisk was often decorated in a shining metal, either gold or electrum, in order to catch the first rays of the sun, just before dawn, thus amplifying the illuminating and life-giving power of the creator. Moreover, the obelisk also represented the benben, the primordial mound upon which the god Atum stood at the creation of the world. As a consequence, obelisks were repeatedly associated with the bennu bird, the Egyptian precursor to the Greek phoenix, who, according to some Egyptian myths, was the very first living creature whose cry awoke creation and set life in motion. The bird was also intimately linked to the end of the world; as its cry had initiated the creative cycle, so it would sound again to signal its completion. Identifying with life, death and rebirth, the obelisk was a gateway to the next world. Whether the discerning Victorian, or later Georgian, customer was aware of such potent symbolism is nigh on impossible to say. But with an overriding obsession for mourning, a desire to be reborn and concerns over the safeguarding of the soul, it is no wonder ancient Egypt struck a chord in their psyche.[36]

No discussion about cemeteries would be complete without briefly mentioning our four-legged friends. After all, pets are valued members of the family too and should be remembered in death. The earliest example of a pet cemetery can be found in Hyde Park, London. Hidden behind Victoria Lodge, and rarely open to the public, it was founded in 1881 by lodge keeper, Mr Winbridge, who was asked by friends if they could bury their much-loved Maltese terrier, Cherry, in his back garden. He agreed and Cherry was laid to rest with a memorial tombstone that read 'Poor Cherry Died April 28 1881'. Over the next two decades more garden space was set aside to accommodate pet interments, approximately 300 burials in total, including 'Poor Prince', a Yorkshire terrier who belonged to the actress Sarah 'Louisa' Fairbrother, wife of HRH Prince George, Duke of Cambridge, and Topper, another terrier who belonged to Hyde Park Police Station.[37] Like London, Paris also has a pet cemetery, located in the small suburb of Asnières-sur-Seine. Opened in 1899, it is called the Cimetière des Chiens et Autres Animaux Domestiques and over 40,000 animals are buried within its grounds, including Rin Tin Tin, the canine Hollywood star, and Barry the Saint Bernard who, according to his memorial inscription, was responsible for saving the lives of forty people in the Swiss Alps. The cemetery is still in use today and for a small entrance fee people are allowed to walk among the tombs.[38] America's first pet cemetery sits in the sleepy hamlet of Hartsdale, Greenburgh, in Westchester County, New York. Nicknamed 'The Peaceable Kingdom', it was established in 1896 by local veterinarian Dr Samuel Johnson, and houses over 100,000 animals on its five-acre site.[39] Tokyo in Japan, has seven pet cemeteries spread around the city's environs, the largest is Jindaiji Temple Pet Cemetery in the suburb of Chofu City. The cemetery consists of a series of vaulted corridors where, for a small monthly fee, ashes can be kept in a ceramic urn inside a cubbyhole-style altar. More expensive stone graves are available outside in the temple grounds. Over 20,000 pets' ashes have been interred in Jindaiji, many now lie beneath a thirty-metre tall tower, aptly called the Tower of Souls.[40]

8

Lest We Forget

In the heart of Tokyo, Japan, in the vicinity of Shinagawa Station, sits a small unobtrusive Buddhist temple called Sengakuji – or Spring-Hill – Temple. Opened in 1612, from the outside it resembles any other temple dotted throughout the city, but behind its walls, shrouded from the public gaze, you will find the graves of the 47 Ronin, famous samurai warriors of old whose deeds still resonate throughout Japanese society today. Their story, recently made into a Hollywood film starring Keanu Reeves, is based upon a historical event dating to the beginning of the eighteenth century, when the samurai's feudal lord, Asano Naganori, was unfairly sentenced to death for illegally drawing his sword against another court official, Lord Kira Hozukenosuke. Because of his high status, Naganori was given the rare honour of *seppuku*, where one is permitted to commit ritual suicide, but once dead his estates were immediately confiscated, his family was disinherited and his retinue of 300 serving Samurai were ordered to disband, thus rendering them 'Ronin' or masterless warriors. Nonetheless, forty-seven of their number vowed to avenge their master's disgrace and restore his honour. Headed by General Oishi Kuranosuke, they met secretly to plan their revenge. To avoid suspicion many of them gave up their swords, as ordered, and become farmers or merchants. Kuranosuke even moved to Kyoto, where he disguised himself as a gambler and a drunk. The ruse worked, and two years later, having reconvened at a designated time and place, the 47 Ronin put their plan into action. Storming the palace of Lord Hozukenosuke, whom they blamed for the demise of their master, and killing his guards, they found him cowering in a corner. As had been afforded their master, they gave him the option of an honourable death. When he refused he was beheaded on the spot. Making their way to Sengakuji Temple, where their master was buried, the 47 Ronin offered the head of Houzukensuke, in a bucket, to Naganori's spirit, thus declaring that his honour had been restored. With their task now complete, one by one, they gave themselves up to the authorities. Although sympathetic to their plight, Japan's overall leader, the Shogun, had no option but to pass a sentence of death. Nevertheless, as their act of loyalty and bravery was deemed the ultimate form of the samurai spirit, instead of being executed as common criminals he passed the judgment of *seppuku* and permitted their bodies to be buried alongside their master. Today, their final resting place has become an important historical shrine and each year, on 14 December, hundreds of Japanese flock to Sengakuji to burn incense around the graveyard site, honouring the warriors of old.[1]

Memorialisation of the heroic dead is as old as time itself. Honouring those who have given their lives to benefit others or who have fought against tyranny or persecution, is a defining human characteristic. Memorials can take on many forms, from large stone monumental structures, such as the Helles Memorial at Gallipoli, Turkey, to simpler ones, such as the humble umlahlankosi bush, the Zulu 'tree of the kings', found throughout southern Africa. War cemeteries, in all their many guises, also act as memorials, as well as centres of commemorative reflection. What defines a war cemetery though is not absolute. Some argue that it represents a burial ground solely for service personnel who died during battle, as opposed to a garrison cemetery which might also contain the remains of the families of servicemen or those who died of disease.[2] I would further subdivide this category into those who died during active duty and those who died while being held as a prisoner of war (PoW).

Unbeknownst to many, during the Napoleonic Wars of 1809-1816 and the Anglo-American War of 1812-1815, 1,200 French and 271 American PoWs died while in custody at Dartmoor Prison in Devon. A surviving journal, entitled *The Prisoners' Memoirs*, records how many were held in appalling conditions, with one prisoner declaring: 'Death itself, with the hope of a hereafter, seemed less terrible than this gloomy prison. The place is deprived of everything that is pleasant or agreeable, and is productive of nothing but woes and misery. Even riches, pleasant friends and liberty could not make it agreeable.' Once a foreign inmate passed away, he was buried in a simple unmarked grave, in an unassuming field, located to the west of the prison confines. Yet after receiving numerous complaints from local farmers regarding body parts dug up during ploughing, Governor of Dartmoor Prison, Captain Stopford, decided to formalise the PoW interment and thus created two separate burial grounds, one for French prisoners and one for the Americans. Unfortunately, as there was no way of telling which bones belonged to which nationality, they were all dug up and divided into two assemblages, which were then reburied in one of two new cemeteries. The American Prisoner of War Cemetery is located to the north of Dartmoor Prison, outside the prison confines, and is enclosed by a granite stone wall, around one metre in height. A large commemorative obelisk stands proudly in the middle and the inscription reads: 'In memory of the American Prisoners of War who died between the years 1809 to 1814 and are buried here – *Dulce et decorum est pro patria mori*' (It is sweet and honourable to die for one's country). In 1928, the National Society United States Daughters of 1812 added a granite memorial gate to the American Cemetery, based upon the entrance gate to Dartmoor Prison. A pair of cast iron gates was later added in 2002 and in 2012 two marble memorials, inscribed with the names of the 271 American captives, were erected behind the obelisk. Immediately to its west lies the French Prisoner of War Cemetery, laid out in a similar design, comprising a large lawn with earthen banks, an enclosure wall and a commemorative obelisk.[3]

Understandably the lot of a PoW was not a happy one and their treatment was largely dependent on the benevolence of their captors. In times gone by, those unluckily enough to be captured were usually executed or forced into slavery, thus their burial sites largely remain unknown. In medieval conflicts the exchange of prisoners for financial gain was not unheard of, the ransoming of noblemen being particularly profitable, whereas during the American Civil War a system of parolees was in operation, whereby captives agreed not to fight until they were officially exchanged. Until then they remained in PoW camps. This arrangement appeared to work well, until 1863 when the Confederacy suddenly refused to exchange black prisoners. The resulting tensions meant that those already held in camps remained where they were with the numbers increasing rapidly as the conflict intensified. One such example is a sixteen-acre facility on Johnson's Island in Sandusky Bay, Lake Erie, Ohio. Opened in April 1862, the prison was originally designed to hold no more than 1,000 captured soldiers, but with the system of parolees no longer viable, the inmate population rose dramatically, reaching a peak of 3,256 in January 1865. With starvation commonplace and disease rife, more than 200 Confederate officers died in captivity and were buried in a one-acre cemetery plot, situated at the northern end of the island, called the Confederate Stockade Cemetery. Today the cemetery is all that remains of the island's Civil War past, with each fallen soldier marked by a simple marble gravestone. The cemetery also has four separate memorials, including a bronze statue of a Confederate soldier looking out over the graves of his fellow compatriots.[4]

There also exists a significant number of burial grounds around the world that incorporate the remains of PoWs who were forcibly removed from their homeland, only to die some hundreds, if not thousands, of kilometres away in captivity. Three examples come to mind. The first is the Apache Prisoner of War Cemetery on the Fort Sill Army Base in Oklahoma. Here lie the graves of over 300 Apaches of the Chiricahua, Warm Springs, and Nedni nations, who were captured after the Geronimo campaign of 1886, taken from their tribal homelands of Arizona, New Mexico and northern Mexico and sent as PoWs first to Florida, then on to Alabama, finally reaching Oklahoma in 1894. The cemetery houses the remains of some of the most prominent Apache leaders in history, including Geronimo, Chief of the Apaches; Chief Loco of the Warm Springs who stood for peace; Chief Nana, the original desert fox; Chief Chihuahua of the Chiricahuas and the sons and grandsons of Manus Colorados, Victorio, Cochise and Naiche.[5] In the same manner, during the Second Boer War (1899-1902), in South Africa, with more than 20,000 Boer captives languishing in PoW camps in or around the Cape Colony, a notable Boer stronghold, the British Army persuaded the British Government to ship out the most difficult prisoners to its other colonies around the world, such as Bermuda, India, and present-day Sri Lanka. As a consequence, there now exists the strange sight of Boer cemeteries in places you would least expect to find them, such as the British overseas territory of St Helena, an island located 1,950 kilometres off the southwestern coast of Africa. More than 6,000 prisoners were detained on St Helena Island between 1900 and 1902, with the first group arriving on board SS *Milwaukee* on 14 April 1900. Few ever saw Africa again, with many now buried in a small district cemetery called Knollcombes.[6] The final example is Labuan War Cemetery, which dates to the Second

World War, located on the small island of Labuan, just off the north-west coast of Borneo. In February 1945, believing that an Allied invasion of Borneo was imminent, the Japanese decided to move all its PoWs further inland. This forcible relocation is often referred to as the 'Death March to Ranau', where more than 2,000 PoWs were marched more than 250 kilometres from camps in Sandakan to Ranau. These included British and Australian soldiers who were captured after the fall of Singapore. Having sustained a barrage of brutality while confined in the prison camps, where beatings, torture and starvation were commonplace, few were fit enough to make such an arduous journey, and only 260 survived the ordeal, the majority of whom died soon after. Initially buried in Sandakan, the remains were later transferred to a new cemetery at Labuan, built by the Commonwealth War Graves Commission. The total number of graves in Labuan War Cemetery is 3,905, of which 2,700 are believed to have been those who perished on the march. Sadly, nearly half of this number still remain unidentified.[7]

The aforementioned Commonwealth War Graves Commission (CWGC), is a truly remarkable organisation. Initially called the Imperial War Graves Commission, its existence is due to the sheer determination of one extraordinary man, Sir Fabian Ware. A former editor of *The Morning Post*, in 1914, as the first shots of the First World War were being fired, Ware signed up as a volunteer with the British Red Cross. At 45, he was too old to fight, and was deployed to France where he was given the command of a mobile unit. Shocked and saddened by the huge loss of life, his unit began to systematically record and care for any grave they came across, ensuring no soldier would be forgotten. By 1915, their invaluable efforts were given official recognition by the War Office and incorporated into the British Army as the Graves Registration Commission. This would become the Imperial War Graves Commission, after receiving its official Royal Charter on 21 May 1917. The Prince of Wales was to be its first president, Ware was made vice-chairman and the board included the high commissioners from Canada, Australia, New Zealand and South Africa, as well as representatives from countries such as India and Malaysia. Three eminent architects, Sir Edwin Lutyens, Sir Herbert Baker and Sir Reginald Blomfield, were chosen to design and construct a series of new cemeteries and accompanying memorials to house those who had died on the battlefield, while writer Rudyard

Kipling, who had lost his only son in action at the Battle of Loos, was appointed official literary advisor with regards to inscriptions.[8]

One of Ware's first priorities was to obtain suitable land for the burial of Allied soldiers in the name of the French state. The French Government would then purchase the land from its owner and give it as a gift, in perpetuity, to the British. Before any site excavation could commence, agreements had to be reached in respect of design. The French insisted that graves were to be placed nine to twelve inches apart and a path not exceeding one metre wide was to be laid between each row. Once the land had been guaranteed, the enormous task of recording the dead could begin. By 1918, some 587,000 graves had been identified and a further 559,000 casualties were registered as having no known grave. Sir Frederic Kenyon, director of the British Museum, was also chosen by Ware to appraise the differing approaches of the principal architects. His report, which can be viewed on the CWGC website, outlines the principles by which the commission still abides to today. They are as follows: each of the dead should be commemorated by name on the headstone or memorial; headstones and memorials should be permanent; headstones should be uniform and there should be no distinction made on account of military rank, race or creed.[9] 'It is easy to forget now how revolutionary the cemetery idea was,' says Peter Francis, head of external communications at the Commonwealth War Graves Commission. 'It came, I think, from a realisation that this war was different, in scale and character, to anything before. This was not a war fought by a largely unloved and little known professional army. It was fought after its first year mostly by volunteers, in effect it was fought by fathers, sons and brothers.'[10]

It should be noted that not everyone was in favour of the CWGC's plans. There were many petitions and heated debates in Parliament regarding the 'no repatriation' rule and the 'unchristian' cemetery design. Others viewed the memorials' listing those missing at Ypres and the Somme as a vain attempt to sweeten the memory of unimaginable horror. Nevertheless, since its establishment in 1917, the CWGC has constructed 2,500 war cemeteries and plots, erected headstones over graves where the remains are missing and inscribed the names of the dead on hundreds of permanent memorials. No identified soldier is ever overlooked – the British Cemetery in Kathmandu, Nepal has only one war grave.[11] They also painstakingly maintain each and every cemetery, sometimes under extremely difficult circumstances. For instance, the recent troubles in the Middle East have had a profound effect on working practices. In 2006 and 2009 respectively, the Gaza War Cemetery, also known as the British War Cemetery, was badly damaged by Israeli forces, who not only callously bulldozed a large section of the site but also caused the destruction of hundreds of graves by their offensive bombing of neighbouring Gaza. Adverse publicity forced the Jewish state to pay £90,000 in compensation.[12] Likewise due to the political instability in Iraq, many of the CWGC cemeteries have been no-go areas for years. Despite such constraints, more than a million burials are now commemorated at 23,000 military and civil sites in more than 150 countries and territories. Clearly it is impossible to explore each and every one, so here are just a few of note.

The largest CWGC cemetery in the UK is Brookwood Military Cemetery in Surrey. Stretching for approximately thirty-seven acres, it contains the graves of over 1,600 servicemen of the British Empire who fought in the First World War and over 3,470 from the Second World War. Located on the south-eastern side is a large Royal Air Force section, which also contains the graves of Czechoslovakian and American airmen. The opposing western area of the cemetery contains approximately 2,400 Canadian soldiers who were killed in action during the Second World War, including forty-three men who died of wounds following the Dieppe Raid in August 1942. At the southern end of this Canadian area are two memorials, one for each world war, which commemorate those Commonwealth service personnel who have no known grave. The intriguing Brookwood 1939-1945 Memorial, designed by Ralph Hobday, pays tribute to 3,500 Commonwealth men and women who could not officially be commemorated on any of the campaign memorials, such as special agents who lost their lives while in the hands of the enemy or those working with Allied underground movements. Brookwood also houses a number of war graves of other nationalities and is home to the American Military Cemetery and Memorial, currently in the care of the American Battle Monuments Commission.[13]

The largest CWGC cemetery in the world is Tyne Cot Cemetery, located on the old Ypres Salient battlefield area in Belgium. Named after a barn that once stood near the road from the killing fields of Passchendaele to Broodseinde, it was designed by Sir Herbert Baker, assisted by John Reginald Truelove, and is currently the final resting place of around 11,962 soldiers from the First World War – 8,374 of whom are unidentified – plus special memorials to more than eighty casualties known or believed to be buried among them. There are also four German soldiers buried within its boundary, three of whom are unidentified. After the Armistice, the remains of those who died at Passchendaele and Langemarck were brought to Tyne Cot for interment as well as those buried in a few smaller surrounding burial grounds, such as the Iberian South Cemetery, the Iberian Trench Cemetery, Oostnieuwkerke German Cemetery and Waterloo Farm Cemetery. To the rear of the cemetery is the Tyne Cot Memorial, also designed by Baker, which commemorates the 35,000 servicemen from the UK and New Zealand, with no known grave, who died in the Ypres Salient after 16 August 1917.[14]

Another notable cemetery in Belgium, also dating from the First World War, is St Symphorien Military Cemetery, which contains an almost equal number of German and Commonwealth casualties who died at the Battle of Mons in August 1914. The cemetery was originally established by the German Army, who had earlier exhumed the remains of soldiers buried in the local church and nearby cemeteries and reburied them in this single location. St Symphorien is acclaimed for housing the burials of Private John Parr and Private George Lawrence Price, traditionally believed to be the first and last Commonwealth soldiers killed in action during the First World War.[15] The CWGC took over maintenance of the cemetery from the German authorities after the war ended. Another interesting burial site is Cabaret-Rouge British Cemetery, which lies south of Souchez in France. It is unique in that for most of the twentieth century it acted as an 'open cemetery', whereby the remains from any newly discovered servicemen in the area would be buried. Designed by Frank Higgins, an officer from the Canadian Army, the cemetery contains more than 7,650 graves of servicemen who fell during the First World War, mostly from British, Irish, Australian, New Zealand, Indian and South African units. Seventy officers from the Royal Flying Corps and Royal Air Force are also interred here. The area was first used as a burial site in March 1916, by various Commonwealth troops, but it wasn't until after the war that the site was formalised with the bodies of around 7,000 soldiers transported to Cabaret-Rouge for reburial from over 100 cemeteries in the surrounding area. The Canadian Infantry has a particular close affinity with Cabaret-Rouge, as hundreds of Canadian soldiers who fell during the Battle of Vimy Ridge in 1917 were later buried within its grounds.[16]

Significant European Second World War cemeteries in the commission's care include the Reichswald Forest War Cemetery in Kleve, Germany, which is the largest Allied war cemetery in the country. Created after the end of the war, it houses the remains of land forces killed throughout western Germany, together with airmen who died while supporting the advance into enemy territory. There are 7,594 Commonwealth servicemen buried here, 179 burials are unidentified, while seventy-eight graves belong to other nationalities, predominantly from Poland.[17] Moro River Canadian War Cemetery, in the Italian province of Chieti, was chosen as a burial site by the Canadian Corps in January 1944 to house the remains of their fellow compatriots who died during ferocious fighting along the Moro River and in the town of Ortona. In just one month alone, in December 1943, the 1st Canadian Division suffered over 500 fatalities. Burials other than Canadian forces, totalling 1,615, have been given their own designated plots.[18] In Greece, the Phaleron War Cemetery, which lies a few kilometres south east of Athens, began life as a burial ground for casualties of the Greek Civil War, until the Greek Government, together with the Army Graves Service, decided it would make a suitable site for a Second World War cemetery. As such, there are now 2,029 Commonwealth servicemen buried or commemorated within its grounds, including seventy-four soldiers from India, cremated due to their religious beliefs.[19]

Moving eastwards, we come to the beaches of Gallipoli, Turkey, the scene of some of the most ferocious fighting of the First World War. Tens of thousands of Allied troops died on these beaches, the majority of whom came from Australia and New Zealand. In fact, so many men perished in the first few months of the campaign that in May 1915 an Armistice was agreed between the Allies and the opposing Turkish forces to allow the dead to be buried. The majority were hurriedly interred in mass graves or in abandoned trenches, whereas those who died on Allied hospital ships were often buried at sea. Soldiers from other Commonwealth regiments, such as the Sikhs and Gurkhas, were usually cremated. The latter were eventually commemorated on memorials at various cemetery sites, such as Hill 60, Chunuk Bair, Lone Pine, and

Cape Helles. Although efforts had previously been made to survey and record all the burial sites, in particular by Chaplain Walter Dexter, it wasn't until four years after the war had ended that a team from the Graves Registration Unit (GRU) arrived at Gallipoli to locate, identify and bury any uninterred Allied soldiers they came across. They faced a number of immediate problems, including the total disappearance of many of the cemeteries; the simple wooden crosses that had been used to denote grave sites had been torn up by the Turks and used for firewood. Furthermore, in 1916, when Pope Benedict XV sent an envoy to Gallipoli to monitor the Allied cemeteries, the Turkish War Office quickly had to rebuild Shrapnel Valley Cemetery – one of the largest cemeteries in the region – from scratch, thereby creating a series of fictitious burial mounds. It soon became apparent that these mounds did not tally with any of the original graves underneath, and even with Dexter's meticulous plans at hand, the GRU only had a general position and direction of any Allied graves. Utilising an old archaeological trick, the team began to plunge a series of metal rods into the ground, the premise being if the rod progresses easily into the soil, the area may have previously been dug and could contain bodies. Although time-consuming, it was a success and the GRU team found thousands of graves in this manner. When their task was complete, responsibility for the future upkeep of all the graves fell to the Imperial War Graves Commission, who would plan, build and maintain a series of permanent cemeteries at Gallipoli.

The architect chosen for the job was Sir John Burnet, who had also personally designed the Helles Memorial, an imposing thirty-metre pylon, standing on high ground above the Dardanelles. It was agreed that most of the permanent cemeteries would remain in their original positions, with graves in isolated areas moved to safer confines. By the end of 1924 most of the work on the permanent cemeteries had been completed and each identified soldier had been allocated a pedestal stone grave marker. Graves that contained multiple burials were left to grass. Men who were known to be buried within one of the cemeteries but their gravesite unknown were commemorated on a series of special grave markers which read, 'Believed to be buried in this cemetery'. Today there are thirty-one CWGC cemeteries at Gallipoli together with associated memorials.[20]

Africa would become the backdrop to many military operations throughout the twentieth century. During the First World War, the East African Campaigns were particularly brutal and by the time the German forces finally surrendered, on 25 November 1918, the Allied dead numbered a staggering 60,000, of which 50,000 were soldiers and porters from East Africa. Voi, a Kenyan town approximately 160 kilometres from Mombasa, has a small CWGC cemetery dedicated to those who fell during this conflict. In total, 137 Allied soldiers are buried here, including thirty-seven bodies transferred from Bura Military Cemetery, seventeen from Maktau Military Cemetery and six from Tsavo Military Cemetery. Further south, in Tanzania, once the heartland of German East Africa, a CWGC cemetery has been built in Moshi, a city located in the southern foothills of Mount Kilimanjaro. It houses ninety Commonwealth burials from the First World War and a further eighty-four from the Second World War, including two German war graves.[21] Arguably the most famous war cemetery in Africa can be found in Egypt, at El Alamein, approximately 130 kilometres west of the city of Alexandria. Designed by Sir John Hubert Worthington, it houses those who perished during the 1940-42 Western Desert campaign, and includes 7,240 Second World War burials, 815 of which are unidentified, as well as 102 graves of other nationalities. The entrance to the cemetery is marked by the famous Alamein Memorial, which commemorates almost 12,000 servicemen from both the land and air forces, while the Alamein Cremation Memorial, sited in the south-eastern part of the cemetery, pays tribute to more than 600 men who were, once more, cremated according to their beliefs.[22]

Soldiers from the Indian subcontinent made a significant contribution to both world wars, fighting throughout the Western Front during the First World War, notably at the battles of Neuve Chapelle, Ypres Salient and Gallipoli, as well as seeing active service in Burma, Singapore and the deserts of Egypt during the Second World War. Although many never returned home, the CWGC does maintain a number of cemeteries throughout India, such as the Delhi War Cemetery, approximately eleven kilometres from the centre of New Delhi. Designed by architect H. J. Brown, who worked on several CWGC cemeteries and memorials throughout India and Pakistan, it was built in 1951 primarily to receive war dead from burial sites in northern India, such as Dehra Dun, Allahabad, Lucknow and Cawnpore. Today, the remains of 1,022 Commonwealth casualties from the Second World War are buried within, together with a number of war graves of other nationalities, predominantly Dutch. The Delhi War Memorial forms the entrance to the cemetery, with an identical memorial sited on the approach to the Karachi War Cemetery in Pakistan. Neither is inscribed with the names of the dead. Instead a Roll of Honour is housed at each cemetery, one in Hindi, the other in Urdu, which lists the names of those commemorated.[23] In Pakistan the aforementioned Karachi War Cemetery was created by the CWGC to house those burials scattered throughout the northern part of the country whose care could not be guaranteed. The cemetery has 642 Commonwealth graves dating to the Second World War, in addition to two war memorials; the 1914-18 memorial commemorates 568 men who served in various garrisons, while the 1939-45 memorial honours more than 25,000 servicemen of an undivided India who died in so-called non-operational zones.[24]

Neighbouring British colonies in the Far East also suffered greatly during the Second World War, primarily at the hands of Japanese forces. For example, on Christmas Day 1941, after a brief but intense period of fighting, Britain's prized territory of Hong Kong fell to the invading Japanese. Casualties were heavy among the defending forces, with most of those killed in the fighting buried in Sai Wan War Cemetery, located to the north east of the island, on the western slope of Pottinger Peak. Designed by Colin St Clair Oakes and built in 1946, there are 1,528 Commonwealth casualties from the Second World War buried within, of which 444 are unidentified. There are also memorials to a further sixteen casualties that were initially buried in Kowloon No. 3 Muslim Cemetery, but whose graves were subsequently lost. There are seventy-seven war graves of other nationalities, the majority Dutch, together with the remains of prisoners who died in Taiwan, mainland China and the Philippines. The entrance is marked by the Sai Wan Memorial, also designed by Oakes, which bears the names of more than 2,000 Commonwealth servicemen who died in the Battle of Hong Kong. Additional panels form the Sai Wan Cremation Memorial, inscribed with the names of those who were cremated in accordance with their faith.[25]

Not all those residing in CWGC cemeteries played a combative role, but rather fulfilled a vital civilian function. An excellent example of this currently lies in a farmer's field in the small village of Nolette, France.

Dating to the First World War, the Noyelles-sur-Mer Chinese Cemetery contains more than 800 graves of the Chinese Labour Corps, labourers who were employed by the British Government to provide logistical support along the Western Front. The men were predominantly recruited from northern China, with the first contingent arriving in France in April 1917. Noyelles-Sur-Mer had been their base depot throughout the war, so the CWGC decided it would be the ideal place for a remembrance cemetery. Designed by Sir Edwin Lutyens, and assisted by John Reginald Truelove, all the headstones are engraved in Chinese characters, while the cemetery gateway, in the form of a pailou (Chinese architectural archway), bears a Chinese inscription to honour the dead together with monograms bearing symbols of eternity. The accompanying inscription, chosen by Shi Zhaoji, Chinese ambassador to Great Britain during the Great War, reads, 'This site commemorates the sacrifice paid by 1,900 Chinese workers who lost their lives during the 1914-1918 war, these are my friends and colleagues whose merits are incomparable.'[26]

Although the CWGC is the largest organisation of its kind, other countries have similar operations, such as the German War Graves Commission, or Volksbund Deutsche Kriegsgräberfürsorge, which was founded as a private charity in December 1919 and is responsible for the maintenance and upkeep of German war graves in Europe and North Africa. Within its remit it has 833 military cemeteries in forty-six different countries, but it consciously works with foreign partner countries in bilateral war grave agreements, such as the one signed by the British Government and the Government of the Federal Republic of Germany, on 16 October 1959, for the establishment of a new cemetery for German nationals who died in internment camps in Britain during both world wars. Designed by architect Diez Brandi, the site selected for the new cemetery was a steep wooded valley in Cannock Chase Forest in Staffordshire. More than 5,000 Germans are buried here, including the crew members of four zeppelins shot down over England during the First World War – the members of each crew are buried in a single grave – as well as a small number of Ukrainians. Opened to the public on 10 June 1967, notable burials include Karl Ritscherle, German flying ace and Luftwaffe major, killed during the Battle of Britain, and German Field Marshal Ernst Busch. As with their British counterparts, the German War Graves Commission offers an accessible online database listing almost five million individuals who were killed during both world wars.[27]

Similarly, the American Battle Monuments Commission, an agency of the US Government, maintains twenty-six American cemeteries and twenty-nine memorials, monuments and markers in sixteen different countries, on behalf of Americans who died overseas during the Second World War. Aside from their cemetery at Brookwood, Surrey, there is also the Cambridge American Cemetery, located approximately one kilometre west of the University of Cambridge. Spanning over thirty acres, the land was originally donated by the university, but was later given to the United States by the British Government in perpetuity. The cemetery contains the remains of 3,811 war dead, with a further 5,127 names recorded on the 'Walls of the Missing' located on the south side of the cemetery. The majority of those commemorated died in the Battle of the Atlantic, or in the strategic air bombardment of north-west Europe. An accompanying cemetery chapel has also been built, complete with stained glass windows depicting various state seals and military decorations, together with a mosaic ceiling honouring the dead of the air forces.[28]

The French War Graves Agency, or Ministère des Pensions, is responsible for the care of French military cemeteries from the First World War to the present day. Created on 27 January 1920, it has 265 military cemeteries in its charge that house the remains of over 730,000 bodies, of which 240,000 are uniquely buried in communal ossuaries. One such remarkable structure is the Douaumont Ossuary, which lies at the heart of the battlefield of Verdun in northern France. War commentators generally agree that the Battle of Verdun was one of the most savagely fought battles of the First World War. Commencing on 21 February 1916, after 300 days of heavy fighting an estimated 800,000 soldiers were either dead, missing or wounded. Established in 1932, the Douaumont Ossuary was designed by Léon Azéma, Max Edrei and Jacques Hardy, in the guise of a church cloister, and it currently houses the skeletal remains of 130,000 French and German troops who died on the surrounding battlefield. Many of the bones, in particular the skulls and femurs, are on public display, deposited in a series of tombs along the interior north wall. There are forty-six tombs in total, corresponding to the forty-six main sectors of the Battle of Verdun, and above each tomb is a vault containing the bones of an unknown soldier. At the apex of the ossuary is an imposing tower, forty-six metres high, upon which is a rotating red and white 'lantern of the dead' that shines across the battlefield at night. Directly in front of the ossuary lies the single largest French military cemetery from the First World War, containing 16,142 graves, laid out in neat rows typical of French military cemeteries. This figure includes 592 Muslim soldiers of the French Colonial Forces who were laid to rest facing Mecca. Tragically the bodies of 160,000 men have never been found, their remains still lie on the battlefield where they fell.[29]

Much thought was given as to whether to include the following two examples or not. Highly contentious and politicised in nature, both reflect the current turmoil and tensions that exist in the Middle East, but from opposing ends of the spectrum. One side acts furtively, often under the cover of darkness, so as not to draw attention to its activities, while the other is openly proud of its militant martyrs, displaying their sacrifice in a somewhat ostentatious manner. In essence, both types of cemetery exist due to the ravages of war and thus deserve to be included. As the conflict between the two antagonists remains ongoing, each example also uniquely conveys a powerful message to their perceived enemy.

In the land of modern-day Israel there exists a number of secret cemeteries referred to as the 'cemeteries of numbers', so-called because each body is buried in an unnamed grave, with just a small numbered metal plate marking it location. Away from the public eye, they are all cited on closed military zones and exist solely to house the remains of Palestinians or Arabs believed to have carried out attacks on Israel, together with those who have died in captivity but may still act as a catalyst for terrorist atrocities committed in their name. According to Palestinian reports the Israel authorities do this for two reasons: firstly, to deter other Palestinians from carrying out attacks on Israel and secondly, so the bodies can be used as bargaining chips in any future prisoner exchanges with various armed Palestinian militia.[30] In 2003, the Israeli military reluctantly confirmed the existence of two such cemeteries, Amiad Cemetery, close to Safed, and Jisr Adam Cemetery in the Jordan Valley. A few years later it became apparent that there were at least a further five, including one previously unknown example in Beersheba, as well as Jisr Banat Yaqub Cemetery, close to the occupied Syrian Golan Heights. The latter hit the headlines in 1999 when the Israeli

Supreme Court demanded that the bodies of two Palestinian fighters, Issa Zawahra and Bassem Sobh, be released to their respective families. Bar a few highly placed government officials, no-one outside the Israeli military was even aware that the cemeteries existed. Now exposed, it quickly became apparent that many of the bodies had been dumped in unmarked graves, with no identifiable documentation and with no numbered plate to identify who they were. Worse still, the bodies in Jisr Banat Yaqub Cemetery were buried directly into the ground, without a layer of protective concrete, so rainwater had seeped into the graves destroying many of the skeletons. The cemetery was forced to close in 2001 and the remaining corpses are thought to have been exhumed and transferred to Amiad Cemetery.[31]

In 2014, Salem Khelleh, coordinator of a national campaign to recover the bodies of missing Palestinians, stated that around 262 bodies were still unaccounted for, including those of Jordanians, Moroccans and Iraqis. He told the website Al-Araby Al-Jadeed that the Jerusalem Legal Aid and Human Rights Center had petitioned the Israeli Supreme Court earlier that year, demanding that the Israeli military disclose the number of secret cemeteries, where they are, the condition they are in, and the names and the total number of bodies held within them. Even though some bodies were recovered, including militants dating from as far back as the 1970s, together with the remains of Palestinian suicide bombers from the Second Intifada, which began in late 2000, the sheer scale of these clandestine cemeteries in today's ever-increasing climate of violence is simply unknown.[32]

In contrast to Israel's covert cemetery policy, in neighbouring Lebanon there exists a burial ground where soldiers of the main Shia party, Hezbollah, are currently interred. Created in the early 1980s, Hezbollah, meaning the 'party of God', has become Israel's most powerful enemy over the intervening years. It forced the Israeli Army out of Lebanon in the year 2000, ending decades of occupation, and during the thirty-four-day war in 2006, withstood over a month of Israeli attacks, allowing its then leader Hassan Nasrallah to declare overall victory. Today, in the West, Hezbollah is regarded as a terrorist organisation. The cemetery in question lies in the Horsh district of downtown Beirut, just to the south of the existing British and French war cemeteries, and is called 'روضة الشهيدين' in the Arabic tongue, which means the 'place of two martyrs'. It is more commonly referred to as the 'Martyrs' Cemetery'. Located in one of the city's few remaining green spaces, it consists of a large outdoor cemetery, together with a roofed cemetery hall, the latter housing the remains of those who died in the conflict with Israel in 2006, and those who were killed in more recent battles across the border in Syria. The hall contains a series of white polished marble grave slabs, placed in rows, each adorned with a photograph of the martyred deceased, usually shown wearing military uniform. Additional decoration can include flowers, lamps or copies of the Quran. Shia Muslims take great pride in caring for martyred family members, especially when they died during political conflict, and often visit the graves to pay their respects. It is not uncommon to see a grieving mother sitting in quiet contemplation by the side of her martyred son, reciting quietly from the Quran. Along with the average soldier, the hall also contains the bodies of many prominent members of the Hezbollah hierarchy, including the military commander Imad Mughniyeh and notable spokesman Hadi Nasrallah, the slain son of the organisation's secretary general. A recent burial of note was Mohammed Abdel Malik al-Shami, a senior Yemeni Houthi official, who was critically injured in a suicide bomb attack, carried out by Islamic State, at the Al Hashahush mosque in Sanaa, Yemen. Airlifted to Iran for medical treatment, he succumbed to his injuries in hospital and died. Deemed a hero to both Hezbollah and Iran, on 13 April 2015 he was laid to rest in the Martyrs' Cemetery alongside his Shi'ite comrades.[33]

9

Thinking Outside the Box

According to the Population Reference Bureau there are approximately 101 billion dead people on the planet, with another seven billion set to join these ranks within the next century.[1] As pressure for burial land intensifies, and with suitable urban spaces becoming scarce, countries around the world are facing a united problem – what to do with their dead. To illustrate, researchers have found that in some parts of the US, land the size of Las Vegas will be needed to bury those who die between the years 2020 and 2042.[2] In Sydney, Australia, the situation is particularly dire with the *Metropolitan Sydney Cemetery Capacity Report* stating that all cemeteries are projected to be full by 2051 with some inner-city cemeteries, such as Waverley, exhausted by 2020.[3] China, in particular, is facing a huge dilemma as unlike the US, which currently has approximately 50,000 cemeteries, unbelievably China has only around 3,000, with many experts predicting that the country will run out of allocated areas for interment within only six years. With a lack of options on offer, what burial plots do exist are now changing hands for exorbitant prices. One prime spot in Shanghai recently sold for a staggering $3.5 billion.[4] Similarly, in those countries where cremation is the preferred option, finding a space for an urn can be exceptionally taxing. Thousands of families currently living in Hong Kong have no option but to store the ashes of their loved ones in sacks at funeral homes, patiently waiting for a space to become available in either a private or public cemetery.[5] Whereas in Japan, which has one of the world's largest ageing populations, one astute businessman recently opened a 'hotel for the dead' to combat the city's overworked crematoriums. Here bereaved families can temporarily store the remains of their loved ones while they wait for a slot at the crematorium to become available.[6] Still, the number of unclaimed urns has reached staggering proportions, with the southern

Thinking Outside the Box

city of Fukuoka recently reporting that it had accumulated nearly 6,000 urns in its care, while the city of Yokosuka was so overwhelmed it began to combine the ashes of various cremations into much smaller urns and then store them in a nearby cave.[7]

The UK is facing a similar crisis with a recent report predicting that, in England, half the land for cemetery use will run out in the next twenty years.[8] London is particularly feeling the pressure. 'On my doorstep there are already a number of boroughs that do not have any burial space left,' states Gary Burks, manager of the City of London Cemetery and Crematorium. In fact, certain London boroughs, such as Tower Hamlets and Hackney, are no longer able to provide burial provision to their residents at all, with families having to use the facilities of neighbouring boroughs, which can cost an extra fifty per cent on top of the standard burial fees. Likewise, in Islington, most of its burials now take place in Barnet.[9] Further pressures are brought about by London's multicultural fabric. 'There is a shift in the ethnic landscape of London,' says Londonist writer Harry Rosehill. 'Jews, Muslims and Buddhists are ninety per cent more likely to opt for burial rather than cremation, and tend to prefer one plot per person.'[10] As in the past, the government has been looking at possible alternatives. In the Mayor of London's 2017 *Draft New London Plan Policy S7 Burial Space*, which can be downloaded via the Mayor of London/London Assembly website, some of the following points were made:

> 5.7.1 In assessing the requirements for burial space, account should be taken of the fact that different faith groups have different needs for burial provision. In London, the demand for burial space for particular faith groups is not always well matched with the availability of burial space. Some boroughs have little or no burial space available. For inner and central London boroughs, this requires them to seek provision in outer London or beyond. This can cause problems of access and cost which has a disproportionate effect on London's poorest communities. It also risks undermining community cohesion and social integration. The Mayor favours the principle of proximity as a general rule, but there may be cases where meeting the needs of residents in one borough may require burial provision to be located in another

borough. This may require a sub-regional approach to the provision of burial space.

5.7.4 When making new provision, boroughs are encouraged to take into account the Mayor's broader aims for green infrastructure and the natural environment, including, but not limited to, the creation of new parks and open spaces, the enhancement of existing open spaces and natural environments, and the provision of enhanced links to London's green infrastructure. Woodland or parkland burial grounds can offer broad burial provision as well as wider public access. Amenity provision and environmental enhancements should be encouraged.

5.7.5 Boroughs should continue to make traditional burial provision but innovative approaches to the provision of community burial space, particularly in inner and central London, may also need to be taken. These could include creating public gardens for the burial of ashes on underused pockets of open land, parkland and brownfield land. Such gardens could also offer broader community utility, improved amenity provision and environmental enhancement.[11]

As has already been discussed in Chapter 7, the lack of suitable burial space in highly populated areas is nothing new. In Paris, before the advent of the garden cemetery, the situation had become so grave, excuse the pun, that in 1763, King Louis XV issued an edict banning all future burials within the capital. It was largely ignored by the Church, until the summer of 1780 when, during a period of extremely heavy rainfall, the walls surrounding Paris's largest cemetery, Les Innocents, collapsed resulting in hundreds of rotting corpses spilling out into neighbouring properties. Although temporary repairs were made, overcrowding was still an issue. Thereupon, in 1785, Les Innocents was finally closed and the Council of State ordered its contents to be removed. But where to? With time of the essence, and with no available space above ground, the eyes of those in authority fell upon the disused quarry system that snaked its way beneath the Parisian streets. With miles of unused storage space, it seemed the perfect solution. Accordingly, on 7 April 1786 the Tombe-Issoire quarries were officially consecrated by the Church and the first bodies from Les Innocents began to arrive. Today, the Tombe-Issoire is more commonly known as the Paris Catacombs.[12]

It would take a mind-blowing two years to empty Les Innocents, with the remains of approximately two million individuals transferred to the underground quarry. Out of respect for the living, the corpses were always moved at night, on wooden carts, with a solemn procession of priests walking behind, offering prayers to the deceased. Over the following decades the remains from other cemeteries, such as Errancis Cemetery, Madeleine Cemetery, Saint-Étienne-des-Grès and Notre-Dame-des-Blancs-Manteaux, would also be reinterred here. At first there was no structure to the reburial process let alone any official documentation. The bones were simply dumped into two quarry wells before being stacked haphazardly into numerous side galleries. Despite the chaos, visitation was permitted, but it was strictly by appointment only. It wasn't until 1810 that Louis-Étienne Héricart de Thury, director of the Paris Mine Inspection Service, began to formalise the reburial process, and renovate the underground caverns. In addition to overseeing the assemblage of skulls and femurs that are on display today, he was also responsible for procuring any surviving tomb decoration that could be salvaged from the mass cemetery closures, to complement the array of designs on the quarry walls. He also built a specialist room to house unusual remains that depicted a wide-ranging series of deformities. Today access to the catacombs is still permitted, but is limited to only a fraction of the network.[13]

In Cairo, Egypt, one of the most populated cities in the world, there exists a rather unique situation where the dead and the living find themselves sharing the same space. Below the Mokattam Hills, in the south east of the city, is the Qarafa el-Arafa, an Islamic necropolis otherwise known as 'City of the Dead'. Stretching over six kilometres, the cemetery is divided into two distinct regions; the Northern Cemetery to the north of Cairo's Citadel and the older Southern Cemetery to the south of the citadel. Its foundation dates back to the Muslim conquest of Egypt in AD 642, when Arab commander Amr ibn al-As sited his family's graveyard here.[14] At first it was only the tomb custodians who inhabited the cemetery, but before long others followed suit. It has now grown into a dense maze of tombs and mausolea, with more than half-a-million people believed to be living among the graves. Many of these were forced from their previous residencies in central Cairo by the government's urban renewal programmes. Others had no choice but to move into family tombs when they lost their homes following the 1992 Cairo earthquake. There are those, however, who believe that living beside the shrines of the dead is a blessing that will reap divine rewards in the afterlife. Provision has been made for the living, with many of the tombs having full running water and electricity. It is probably the only cemetery in the world that also has apartment blocks, a medical centre, a post office and two schools! Even so, the City of the Dead is regarded as a slum by many, with very few opportunities for employment, drug use is rife and crime is continually on the rise.[15] In September 2020, the Egyptian government started bulldozing areas of the cemetery.

Grave reuse could be a solution to the current burial crisis. Cemeteries in Germany constantly reuse their grave space every couple of years, while other European countries have been utilising this practice for centuries. In the Old Jewish Cemetery in Prague, when burial space ran dry, a fresh layer of soil was laid out on top of an existing grave to make room for a new body. When the last burial took place, in 1787, the authorities discovered twelve layers of graves stacked one on top of the other.[16] Here in the UK, since 2007, burial authorities have had the ability to reclaim any grave that has been in existence for more than seventy-five years, but few have chosen to go down this route. One exception has been the City of London Cemetery and Crematorium in Newham, which in 2009 began to implement a grave reuse policy. 'Originally a lot of the older plots were designed for six people,' says manager Gary Burks. 'Some were dug two to three metres deep but only housed two burials.' Since the policy's implementation more than 1,500 graves have been recycled, with over sixty per cent of new burials at the cemetery using reused graves. 'We are in a position now where we can provide families with grave space, forever,' says Burks. 'We are the UK's first sustainable cemetery.'[17] Nonetheless, grave reuse is not without its critics.

In 2017, *The Daily Telegraph* reported on a controversial plan by Camberwell Old Cemetery, in south London, who were about to commence burying people on top of war graves, after the Church of England judicature gave them permission to do so. The plan involved clearing scrub land on top of 48,000 existing burials, including forty-eight war graves, to make room for 700 new burials. Understandably local residents were unhappy when they heard the news and began a campaign to stop the proposal; the local authority Southwark Council received more than 660 objections in one week alone. Despite assurances by the council and the Commonwealth War Graves Commission, who advised on the plans, local campaigners were not so sure. After all, until the plans were leaked no-one really knew the war graves even existed, and as the war dead remain unmarked, local campaigners say they are concerned that mistakes will inevitably be made. A spokesman for the War Graves Commission said:

> We have agreed with Southwark LBC [London Borough Council] that the war graves will not be disturbed during the clearance process and that no burials will take place above the war graves. We only have responsibility for the war graves and these have all been identified and will not be affected by the works.[18]

This is not the first time Southwark Council has come in for criticism regarding its burial provision. In order to obtain as much land as possible for new burials their methods have, so far, included the destruction of ancient woodland, removing its own tree preservation orders in the process, and the desecration of countless headstones and tomb memorials. In one example, local resident, David Nicholls, who went to lay flowers at his grandfather's grave, found to his horror that it had completely disappeared. 'We were just flabbergasted,' said the father of three. 'The whole section where the grave was had been completely decimated. They had just put everyone's personal effects – fencing, teddy bears and flowers – into a big pile and everyone's gravestones were missing and we didn't know what was going on.'[19]

Another shocking example of grave reuse malpractice was exposed in May 2018 at Tottenham Park Cemetery, a private burial ground in north London, when a variety of human remains, including a broken skull, shoulder blade and various leg bones, were discovered lying in open ground. Tottenham Park is one of the largest Turkish-Cypriot cemeteries in the UK and families are charged anything from £4,100 for a single burial plot. A few weeks after the initial find, further skeletal remains were observed by the Tottenham Park Cemetery Action Group, who feared that graves were being dug up and reused without consent. Under current legislation it is an offence to remove buried human remains without a licence from the government, or permission from the Church of England if they are buried in consecrated ground. However, one disgruntled customer, David Johnson, who has five members of his family buried in three neighbouring plots, claims that in 2005 he discovered two elaborate marble structures had been erected over his family plots, obviously to commemorate two completely unrelated people who appear to have been buried there. Having contacted the owners of the cemetery to ask what had happened to the remains of his loved ones he was unable to get any answers. 'What have they done with them? We think they have been dumped in a skip,' he said. 'I feel very angry to have this done to my family.' A police investigation has been underway since May 2018 when the first bones were found and Scotland Yard has said a man has been interviewed under caution. It said it was alerted to the discovery of more bones on 29 August 2018 and 'a dismantled human-looking partial skeleton' on 14 September.[20] At the time of writing the company responsible for Tottenham Park Cemetery has gone into liquidation.

For followers of the Jewish faith living in Israel, grave reuse is simply not an option. Neither is cremation. Consequently, the city of Jerusalem is fast running out of burial space, with many funeral directors arguing that thousands of new plots will be needed to meet the current demand from residents and non-residents alike. Unlike other countries, the bulk of financial support for cemeteries within Jerusalem comes from Jews who live abroad; their dying wish is to be buried within its sacred soil. Combine this with Jerusalem's growing population, which currently stands at approximately three-quarters-of-a-million people, it is perhaps not surprising the city's cemeteries can no longer cope with the demand. A recent report revealed that the Sheikh Badr Cemetery, adjacent to the Supreme Court, as well as one beside the Shaare Zedek Medical Center, are now closed to new burials. Burial plots in the private Sanhedria Cemetery are extremely limited and out of reach financially for the vast majority; plots here can cost from $20,000 upwards. The national cemetery of Israel, Mount Herzl, is not open to the general public and only accepts interments from Jewish leaders of note, war heroes and alike, while

Jerusalem's oldest and most famous cemetery, the Mount of Olives, is located in the troubled East Jerusalem quarter, a disputed area between the Israeli and the Palestinian governments. This only leaves Jerusalem's largest cemetery, Har Hamenuchot, open for burials. Opened in 1951, it now spans an entire hilltop on the western edge of the city.[21] In response to this burial crisis, the Jerusalem Jewish Community Burial Society and a local construction firm, Rolzur Tunnelling, have joined forces to create a unique underground necropolis. Unlike the ready-made catacombs of Paris, the fifty-million-dollar project, which commenced in 2015, drills deep under Har Hamenuchot to create a vast underground burial chamber, complete with an elevator system, soft lighting and beautifully carved stonework. It will initially have room for 22,000 burial crypts, arranged from floor to ceiling in three tiers, in a network of intersecting tunnels. The majority of the project's costs will come from private funds derived by the sale of plots to Jews who reside overseas, while most of the plots are free to Jewish Israelis, paid for by their national insurance contributions. Project Manager Yair Maayan says: 'This all about how to make better use, smarter use of the land.' He predicts that all 22,000 burial vaults will be full by 2022 when, he says, 'we will dig deeper and deeper, all over the mountain.'[22]

Purpose-built necropolises do provide intriguing possibilities. In 2014, in a throwback to how our ancestors once took care of their dead, property developer Tim Daw opened a 'Neolithic' long barrow, the first to be built for over 5,000 years. Based in All Cannings, Devizes, Wiltshire, the barrow was constructed using traditional methods, for a hefty cost of £200,000. As in ancient times, the structure has been aligned to receive the sun's first rays on the winter solstice. Inside the barrow mound are five separate chambers, arranged off the entrance passageway, each with a series of niches built into the chamber wall. Each niche is able to hold single or multiple cremation urns. 'I am absolutely thrilled with the way the structure had turned out,' says Daw. 'It's been a lot of hard work. Every stone has been shaped and placed by hand.' In just a few years every available niche has been sold and Mr Daw is considering building another burial mound to meet the demand.[23] The concept has also caught the imagination of others, with Bedfordshire-based company Sacred Stones opening a similar barrow facility near St Neots in Cambridgeshire.[24]

A more modern approach to urn storage has emerged in recent years. In Singapore there exists a private fully automated storage unit, currently holding around 50,000 cremation urns, whereby families can retrieve the ashes of their loved ones by using an electronic swipe card.[25] Identical facilities can also be found in Japan, such as at the famous Ruriden, a small, futuristic charnel house located in Koukoko-ji temple in downtown Tokyo. Here, inside one of the mourning rooms, relatives can view photographs of the departed on computer screens before a frosted glass screen descends to reveal the cremation urn.[26] In a similar fashion, Essex-based funeral directors, Secure Haven, offer a bespoke urn storage facility, housed in a local barn, called Secure Niches. Opened in 2014, cremation urns are kept for a fee of £1 per day (at the time of writing), in an oak-lined cabinet, for as long as required. Each niche has the capacity to house two standardised urns, along with a few personal keepsakes. The facility is not open to the public and bar paying customers, it can only be accessed by Secure Haven staff members.[27] Perhaps the strangest amenity, for want of a better description, is the postmodernist structure that sits in San Cataldo Cemetery, near Modena in Italy. Designed by Italian architect and writer, Aldo Rossi, a plain orange terracotta cube, teetering on top of concrete stilts, stands among the ancient tombstones. With no roof or doors, just an internal courtyard, inside the cube is a framework of empty burial niches still awaiting the deposit of ashes. Unfortunately, in 1976 Rossi was involved in a serious car accident, which prevented him from completing the project and he died in 1997. As such, the building has lain empty to this day, with no sign of any burial on the horizon.[28]

But the most elaborate example of them all, and possibly my favourite, is the San Francisco Columbarium, just north of the Golden Gate Park in a residential district of Richmond, San Francisco. It is one of the last traditional repositories for cremated remains left in the US. Built in 1898 by British architect Bernard J. Cahill, in what was then Odd Fellows Cemetery, it is a building of extreme opulence, comprising baroque and neo-classical features, and consists of a large rotunda, around fourteen metres high, with a width of around nine metres, a mosaic-tiled floor, ornate stained-glass windows and a domed skylight. There are eight rooms on the ground floor which bear the names of the mythological winds, while the first-floor rooms are named after the constellations. The Columbarium has three main halls – the Hall of Olympians, the Hall of Titans and Hall of Heroes – which house 8,500 niches, each one containing a variety of urns and caskets. The building is currently owned by the Neptune Society of California, a nationwide cremation service, which in the 1980s saved the building from dereliction and restored it to its former glory.[29]

High-rise cemeteries, or grave apartments, could be the key to the world's burial crisis, especially if you consider the amount of vacant real estate in existence. In the Marape district of Santos, Brazil, a vertical cemetery has been trading since the mid-1980s. Called the Memorial Necrópole Ecumênica, it inhabits a large apartment building some fourteen storeys high and contains approximately 25,000 tombs, crypts and mausoleums. Each floor has 150 tombs, with each tomb holding up to six bodies. Costs can vary with a three-year plot rental ranging from 10,000 to 35,000 Brazilian reals. A separate family plot, complete with a memorial room is more expensive, costing around 174,000 reals. In addition, the choice of view in the afterlife, be it of the sea, the rainforest or, more importantly in football-crazy Brazil, a view of the Vila Belmiro football stadium, is breathtaking. 'Death is hard enough. We try to do everything to make the difficult hours for the family easier,' said architect Antonio Augusto.[30] Even taller grave apartments are in the pipeline for the citizens of Norway, since the government's planned solution to combat the lack of burial space failed spectacularly. Graves had intended to be recycled every two years, but it became apparent that the specialist material used for wrapping the corpse was failing to decompose the body fast enough.[31] In Tel Aviv, in the over-subscribed Yarkon Cemetery, a high-rise tiered apartment block is under construction, with the potential to hold over 250,000 burials. Plans include a piping system filled with soil from the Holy Land, so that each burial is still connected to the ground, which is a precept of the Jewish faith. Because of this addition, opposition to the project from ultra-conservative Jews was negated and the new construction was deemed 'kosher' by local rabbi leaders.[32]

Grave apartments are also becoming a popular feature in the Far East. Previous vertical options, such as the impressive terraced stepped hillside Pok Fu Lam Road Cemetery in Hong Kong, which was built in 1882, have proved inadequate. Therefore, many have now turned to more artificial choices. Taiwan has a high-rise cemetery provision called the Lung Yen Life Service where a burial niche in the wall costs a family from around $1,000.[33] In Japan, where a burial plot in one of Tokyo's crowded city cemeteries can cost, on average, around $23,000, grave apartments, or *ohaka no manshon* have become an attractive option. In operation since 1987, Shokakuji Buddhist Temple, in Tokyo's Fukagawa district, was the first to open a six-storey building comprising small locker-size stacked tombs. Within a few months over half the available space had either been occupied or reserved. Since then the Tokyo Government has given permission for the construction of 2,480 *kabe bodhi*, meaning 'tombs built into stacked walls', in Kodaira, Tama and Yabashira city cemeteries. 'Looking like storage lockers in bus terminals,' said Shigefumi Matsuzawa, a government official, 'the tiny tombs will be stacked on top of one another on unused green belt land within each cemetery.'[34] In Mumbai, India, a huge apartment block, called the Moksha Tower, is currently under construction and aims to become the world's tallest cemetery, complete with botanical gardens. Catering for all India's major religions, there will be garden burials for followers of the Islamic faith, cremation receivers for India's Hindu population and even a 'tower of silence' for followers of the Parsi Zoroastrian religion, where the deceased's corpse will be exposed to the elements for winged scavengers.[35]

If height is your thing, but the thought of spending the afterlife in an apartment block is not very appealing, then how about being buried in space? The concept is not a new one, as it was first introduced in 1931, in a literary sense, when science fiction author Neil R. Jones wrote about the notion in his book *The Jameson Satellite*.[36] This was later appropriated on the big screen in the 1965 movie *The Loved One*. Since its inception, many have toyed with the idea and today it is very much a viable option to those with the available funds. Although it should be made clear that we are not talking about firing bodily remains, or ashes, directly into orbit. Space is polluted enough, with all kinds of satellite detritus. No, a space burial, as it stands, is where the cremated remains are locked inside a sealed container and placed onto a spacecraft. From here the customer has a number of choices. The simplest one is where the spacecraft is fired into space and returns back to Earth once zero gravity has been achieved. After spaceflight the capsule, still containing the remains, is returned to the bereaved relatives. For the slightly more adventurous there is the Earth Orbit Mission, where the spacecraft orbits the Earth for a designated period, maybe a few years in some cases, eventually burning up upon re-entry into the Earth's atmosphere. Then there is the Moon Mission, whereby the human remains are launched onto the surface of the moon and, finally, the Deep Space Mission, where the remains are carried aboard a spacecraft as it voyages into the outer depths of the Solar System and beyond.[37] There are a number of private companies that offer a space burial, including Celestis, Ascending Memories and Elysium Space, with costs ranging from $9,950. Writing on their website, Elysium Space states that:

> Elysium Space is a unique team of space and funeral experts, combining experience from major NASA space missions and deep-rooted funeral profession knowledge. Our wide background goes from space systems to anthropology and funeral directing. We are dedicated to offer awe-inspiring celestial services to the world and celebrate the significance of lives that have been lived with dignity and honour.[38]

Elysium is also able to provide a specially designed app, free to download on iOS and Android devices, which has a unique digital tracking system that allows friends and family of the deceased to follow and locate their loved one in real time as they hurtle through space. They are also invited to attend the launch event, as it happens and the launch is webcasted live to those close to the deceased who are unable to travel. Families also receive a certificate confirming the success of the launch, including the official spacecraft tracking ID assigned by the North American Aerospace Defense Command.[39]

The first space burial took place aboard the NASA space shuttle *Columbia*, in 1992, when a portion of ashes belonging to Gene Roddenberry, the creator of *Star Trek*, was carried aboard the vessel. He orbited Earth a number of times before returning aboard a private vessel, the Celestis *Founders Flight*. Accompanying him on the return journey were the ashes of Gerard K. O'Neill, a physicist whose particular interest was developing off-world territories, and rocket scientist Krafft Ehricke, who designed some of NASA's earliest rockets. Said flight remained in orbit for five years, before burning up over the coast of Papua New Guinea. Another Celestis flight was launched in 2007, this time carrying the ashes of Gordon Cooper, Mercury Seven astronaut, and James Doohan, the actor who played Scotty in *Star Trek*. This time, the craft failed to reach its objective and it wasn't until 2012 that a SpaceX Falcon 9 rocket could finally transport the remains to their chosen destination. At the time of writing Elysium has two planned launch missions. The Star II Mission, whereby remains will be carried aboard the upcoming Spaceflight's SSO-A Space Falcon 9, will be launched from Vandenberg Air Force Base in California, and the Lunar I Mission is due to be launched in 2021. Each is permitted to carry burials.[40]

When researching the funeral industry as a whole, I was shocked to discover the extent of environmental damage traditional burials can cause. A study in 2016, documented by the website A Course in Dying, found that in the US, in one year alone, 827,069 gallons of toxic embalming fluid were released into the ground; 180,544 pounds of steel were used in the production of caskets as were 5,400,000 pounds of casket copper and bronze and 30,000,000 feet of hardwood coffin boards, plus 3,272,000,000 pounds of reinforced concrete were used for vaults. Furthermore, the process of embalming was found to be extremely hazardous for those working in the industry, especially the use of toxic materials, such as carcinogenic formaldehyde. Research carried out by the American National Cancer Institute found that funeral directors had a much higher incidence of myeloid leukaemia than the national average.[41] Those that do understand the complexities involved are attempting to offset any damage caused by choosing to have a 'green' or 'natural' burial. In essence, this is the interment of the body into the soil using non-toxic materials, such as a biodegradable coffin or wrapping. Wool, wicker and cardboard are all commonly used. A natural burial site is preferable and forests and woodlands are the most popular choice, such as Hillig Meer in the Netherlands, which not only offers a natural forest environment but also has the added bonus of continual burial rights, so there is no fear of loved ones being dug up in the future.[42] In the US, national parks are a popular option – for example one can choose to have a green burial ritual within the Joshua Tree Memorial Park – although the legalities differ in each state.[43]

In the UK there are hundreds of natural/green burial sites, and many are members of the Association of Natural Burial Grounds, an organisation established by The Natural Death Centre to assist people in the process of establishing natural and woodland sites for burial use. Not only do they allow families to organise a funeral without the need of a funeral director, they also guarantee long-term security of the graves, pledging to manage the site ecologically and sustainably. Memorial sculpture is wholly discouraged in natural burial grounds, as is the leaving of sentimental items upon the grave. Most graves are marked by the use of an indigenous tree, or shrub.[44] Not everyone, mind you, has fully grasped the concept of a green burial. The Good Funeral website recently reported on a number of incidents at a natural burial ground in Bridport, Dorset, where customers had complained that the site had become an 'overgrown mess' and resembled a 'sea of grass and weeds'. One woman complained to the local authority that she could no longer see her brother's grave, whereas another, Mrs Henry-Coulson, discovered that due to invading vegetation she had been tending someone else's grave by mistake for well over a year. Having planted a number of flowering bulbs on the wrong grave, she said, 'someone is going to have a surprise in the spring'.[45]

In Japan the concept of a tree burial, or *jumokusou,* has become increasingly popular in recent years. Said funerary rite was once prevalent among indigenous folk worldwide, including those from various Native American tribes, as well as the Toraja of Indonesia, who used to bury the remains of babies inside the trunks of sacred trees. First conceived in 1999, within the confines of a Buddhist temple in Ichinoseki, a city located to the north of the country, the aim of *jumokusou* was to provide sustainable burial provision for the increasing population, while simultaneously rehabilitating Japan's wooded landscapes. Each grave consists of one tree only, chosen from a register of twenty-two varieties, provided by the local tree burial office, together with a simple wooden tablet inscribed with the name of the deceased. Each plot is contracted for thirty-three years, at a cost of 50,000 yen, after which it may be recycled and sold to a new client if no relative or friend of the deceased agrees to take over the contract. To date the temple has buried the remains of over 600 people, has purchased two neighbouring sites, and has inspired over fifty similar temple cemeteries across the country. Yokohama, one of Japan's largest cities, has subsequently made provision for tree burials in their public cemeteries, while in 2005 the Tokyo Ending Centre introduced *sakurasou*, meaning 'burial under a cherry tree' into many of the city's traditional graveyards. Research carried out by historian Sebastian Boret has discovered that many Japanese families are now abandoning the traditional Japanese funeral and adopting the new tree burial concept, with some households removing the remains of their ancestors from the original family gravesite to rebury them in a tree burial space.[46]

Another addition to the green burial movement began life in a small workshop on the edge of Rome's Campo Verano Cemetery, when two Italian furniture designers, Anna Citelli and Raoul Bretzel, put their respective talents together to create a biodegradable egg-shaped coffin pod. Entitled Capsula Mundi, the idea is relatively simple, with the deceased placed in a foetal position inside the pod before the pod is buried in the ground. There are two types of design on offer, the first is a cremation urn-shaped pod, costing £337-£374, where the ashes are placed inside the pod via a hole in the top; the second is a larger pod designed for inhumations but this is not currently available due to legal difficulties surrounding the deposition of human remains. Bretzel explains: 'Culturally people accept the idea and are interested in having them. But rules and regulations around burials have not caught up with cultural attitudes.'[47] If one is not enticed by the thought of being buried in an egg-shaped pod, how about a mushroom death suit? Also known as the 'infinity death suit' this rather bizarre method of burial recently hit the headlines when it was revealed that Hollywood actor Luke Perry, who tragically passed away in 2019, was interred in just such a suit. Centred around the idea of 'reconnecting the body with the earth', the concept was originally designed by Massachusetts Institute of Technology Research Fellow and artist, Jae Rhim Lee. Her premise being that instead of using a traditional coffin or casket, upon death the body is placed in a suit embedded with mushroom spores, which feed upon the body after burial, thereby speeding up decomposition. The suit is accompanied by an 'alternative embalming fluid and decompiculture makeup,' in essence a slurry mixture of liquid spores aimed at preventing toxins in the body from being released into the ground. Understandably there has been some reticence towards the idea. 'I realized that a certain amount of cultural shift was needed to precede the commercialisation of the suit,' Lee said in a recent interview with CNN. 'No matter how we marketed the suit, the culture was not ready for it.' According to the official website, each suit costs $1,500 to purchase, yet none are currently in stock.[48]

Like inhumation, cremation has also come in for criticism, with many arguing that furnace emissions of carbon dioxide, combined with trace elements of mercury from the likes of dental fillings and metal prosthetics, are contributing to today's soaring air pollution levels. As a result, two alternatives have entered the market. The first is called promession, and was conceived in the early 2000s by Swedish marine biologist, Susanne Wiigh-Masak. Unlike traditional cremation, which uses fire, in promession the corpse is immersed in a liquid nitrogen solution, before vibrations shake the body apart, turning the corpse into a fine powder. A separator then filters out any metal dental fillings or surgical implants. The entire process takes place in a closed, fully automated piece of equipment called the promator and, according to its founder, it is 'justifiable in terms of ethical, moral, environmental and technical considerations, and does not subject the body to violent or destructive handling.' Once the corpse has turned to dust, the remains can be interred in a more conventional manner of one's choosing. As yet there is no evidence to suggest the promator has been used in a commercial setting, but in January 2018 it was announced that Spain would be one of the first countries to offer the service to the general public.[49]

Resomation, also known as alkaline hydrolysis, is another liquid cremation process that uses water instead of fire and its founder, Scots biochemist Sandy Sullivan, believes it could become the third significant choice for people when they are choosing a burial method. 'Water cremation,' says Sandy 'is a dignified and respectful option, and an environmentally-friendly choice.' So how does it work? First the corpse is placed in a biodegradable coffin, before being lifted into a resomator chamber filled with a specialist hot water solution. Pressure is then applied to chemically reduce the body to a pure white ash. Bodily fluids, which would normally seep into the soil, are sterilised through the resomator and then drained away to be recycled later. 'Nothing,' explains Sullivan 'goes up the stack'. In America, two big funeral homes and a major university medical facility have already begun using the resomation process and in 2010, three years after launching his concept, Sullivan was granted the John Logie Baird

Award for Early Stage Impact through Innovation together with the *Observer* Ethical Awards' Big Idea trophy for pioneering green funeral work. When asked for her opinion, Rosie Inman-Cook, manager of the Natural Death Centre, replied that resomation would further enhance Britain's status as one of the most liberal – if not the most liberal – country in the world with regards to choice. 'If people love the idea of resomation,' she said, 'wouldn't it be wonderful if it was available for them. If that's what people want, then absolutely, why not?'[50] Resomation is, however, not without its critics. Although water cremation is legal in the UK, the Ministry of Justice currently holds the view that hydrolysis does not constitute 'the burning of human remains' and therefore falls outside the current regulatory framework for traditional flame cremation. This did not prevent the Rowley Regis Crematorium in Sandwell, West Midlands, from hitting the headlines recently when a planning application for the building of a resomation unit in Leeds revealed that they intended to pour any remaining liquids from the process down the drains and into the main sewer system. Understandably Severn Trent Water, the company responsible for the mains sewerage, was troubled when they heard this and has so far refused to grant permission. *The Sunday Times* quoted one source at Water UK, who represent water companies and wastewater service providers, as saying: 'It is the liquefied remains of the dead going into the water system. We don't think the public will like the idea.'[51]

Efforts to provide new and innovative funerary methods that are kinder to the environment are commendable. However, none of the 'green' examples on offer really aid the current burial crisis. Each one, bar resomation, still requires a certain degree of space to bury and/ or commemorate the dead. So, what other alternatives are on offer? Well, if you like a bit of bling you can always turn your remains into a diamond. Available in a wide array of designs and colours, the process involves several ounces of cremated ashes, temperatures exceeding 5,000 degrees fahrenheit, the transformation of carbon remnants to graphite, and a diamond press of 800,000 lbs per square inch. Hair, or fur, can be combined with the ashes for a more intimate feel.[52] If you are not a big fan of jewellery how about a piece of memorial art? For roughly £100, cremated ashes of a loved one can be tastefully incorporated into a one-of-a-kind piece of artwork, whether it is a pencil drawing or photographic design. Digitally manufactured, the ashes are carefully added to a canvas-transfer print, held in place by a specially formulated glaze.[53] But maybe you're an avid music lover? If so, a UK-based company, AndVinyly, founded by music producer Jason Leach, offers people the chance to immortalise loved ones by having their ashes pressed into playable vinyl records. For around £3,000 you can have thirty discs, each with twenty-four minutes of your chosen specialised audio, be it spoken word or otherwise.[54] Or why not go out with a bang? Heavens Above is just one of several specialist companies that can help create stunning displays using memorial fireworks made from your cremation ashes.[55] Tattoo artists are offering memorial tattoos, where cremated ashes are combined with the ink, while for football fans there is the option of having your ashes scattered on your chosen team's football pitch. I am proud to say my home team, Queens Park Rangers, are one of the best for honouring their fans in this manner, where the ashes can either be laid at the goalposts and/or scattered into the soil when the grass is reseeded at the end of the season.[56] Last but not least, there is cryonics, the option for those with more money than sense, where upon death the body is immediately frozen in the hope that years down the line medical science will make it possible for you to be revived. The concept was first propagated in 1962, by Robert Ettinger, in the book *The Prospect of Immortality*. He later went on to found the Cryonics Institute, now based in Clinton Township, Michigan. Here a fully fledged cryonics facility currently houses around 150 people, and pets, in 'cryostasis,' a permanent frozen state. Costs are not cheap – the basic full-body immersion will set you back around $28,000 – but as the company's president Dennis Kowalski states: 'Cryonics is much more than just the science of "freezing," because our objective is life after revival, with renewed youth and extended lifespans. We want to make this a reality.'[57]

    Fiscal matters, lack of available space and an increasing secular society are continually refashioning the funerary landscape. Barrow mounds, cremation caves and underground necropolises are not only viable alternatives, for many they are now the preferred choice. As an archaeologist and death historian I am often asked what form of burial arrangement I have chosen for my own eternal rest. In truth, I haven't given it much thought, which might sound somewhat surprising, until you realise I spend the majority of my waking hours in the land of the dead, metaphorically speaking. One option under consideration, which I have not touched upon, is body donation to a scientific teaching facility. With today's funeral costs excessively high, and rising, plus working in an industry that is renowned for low wages, I would not wish to inflict the financial burden of a traditional funeral on my one remaining family member. I am probably not alone in this matter. Moreover, these old bones could possibly be of use to some budding medical practitioner. In conclusion, the study of burial provision, both past and present, is a developing field of inquiry and it is my fervent hope that the examples given here may encourage readers to embark on their own avenues of research.

Appendix 1: The Burial Acts

The following list is based on my ongoing research and documents all the major Public and General Acts of Parliament relating to burials in England only, complete with web link.

1816   An Act for enabling Ecclesiastical Corporate Bodies under certain Circumstances to alienate Lands for enlarging Cemeteries or Churchyards

http://www.legislation.gov.uk/ukpga/1816/141/pdfs/ukpga_18160141_en.pdf

1847   An Act for consolidating in One Act certain Provisions usually contained in Acts authorizing the making of Cemeteries (Cemetery Clauses Act)

http://www.legislation.gov.uk/ukpga/1847/65/pdfs/ukpga_18470065_en.pdf

1850   An Act to make better provision for the Interment of the Dead in and near the Metropolis

https://archive.org/details/metropolitanint00glengoog

1852   An Act to amend the Laws concerning the Burial of the Dead in the Metropolis

http://www.legislation.gov.uk/ukpga/1852/85/pdfs/ukpga_18520085_en.pdf

1853   An Act to amend the Laws concerning the Burial of the Dead in England beyond the Limits of the Metropolis, and to amend the Act concerning the Burial of the Dead in the Metropolis

http://www.legislation.gov.uk/ukpga/1853/134/pdfs/ukpga_18530134_en.pdf

1855	An Act further to amend the Laws concerning the Burial of the Dead in England
	http://www.legislation.gov.uk/ukpga/1855/128/pdfs/ukpga_18550128_en.pdf
1857	An Act to amend the Burial Acts
	http://www.legislation.gov.uk/ukpga/1857/81/pdfs/ukpga_18570081_en.pdf
1859	An Act more effectively to prevent Danger to the Public Health from Places of Burial
	http://www.legislation.gov.uk/ukpga/Vict/22/1
1864	An Act to make further Provisions for the Registration of Burials in England
	http://www.legislation.gov.uk/ukpga/1864/97/pdfs/ukpga_18640097_en.pdf
1867	An Act relating to the Consecration of Churchyards
	http://www.legislation.gov.uk/ukpga/Vict/30-31/133
1868	An Act to amend The Consecration of Churchyards Act 1867
	http://www.legislation.gov.uk/ukpga/Vict/31-32/47
1880	An Act to amend the Burial Laws
	http://www.legislation.gov.uk/ukpga/1880/41/pdfs/ukpga_18800041_en.pdf
1884	An Act for preventing the erection of Buildings on Disused Burial Grounds
	http://www.legislation.gov.uk/ukpga/1884/72/pdfs/ukpga_18840072_en.pdf
1902	An Act for the regulation of the burning of Human Remains, and to enable Burial Authorities to establish Crematoria
	http://www.legislation.gov.uk/ukpga/1902/8/pdfs/ukpga_19020008_en.pdf
1952	An Act to amend the law relating to cremation; and for purposes connected therewith
	http://www.legislation.gov.uk/ukpga/1952/31/pdfs/ukpga_19520031_en.pdf

Appendix 1: The Burial Acts

1970   An Act to amend the law relating to the provision by parish councils of signs and the administration of burial grounds by burial authorities, and for matters connected therewith

http://www.legislation.gov.uk/ukpga/1970/29/pdfs/ukpga_19700029_en.pdf

1981   An Act to amend the Disused Burial Grounds Act 1884 to enable building to take place on certain disused burial grounds with appropriate safeguards; and for purposes connected therewith

http://www.legislation.gov.uk/ukpga/1981/18/pdfs/ukpga_19810018_en.pdf

Appendix 2: Graveyard Symbolism

If you take a stroll through any cemetery or churchyard today you are, effectively, entering a secret world of hidden meanings and fervent symbolism. The Victorians made great use of symbolism on their monuments and gravestones, as did the preceding generations. In the seventeenth and eighteenth centuries immortality/mortality images, such as the skull and crossbones, were a particular favourite, as were trade symbols, especially in Scotland. Some work-related examples to be found inscribed on grave markers include maltmen: large grain shovel, tongs for handling peat, fire hook; farmers: sheaves of corn, plough instruments; wrights: dividers, square, hammer, ace, saw; weavers: loom frame, reeds and rollers and blacksmiths: anvil, chisel and rasp, pincer tool, horseshoes and bellows. Although there can be many interpretations of even the most popular mortuary symbols, below is the standard guide of definitions, which will hopefully be of use to anyone embarking on their first taphophile exploration.

Acanthus Leaf	Common motif seen on the edges of headstones. Thought to symbolise the immortality of the soul.
Agnus Dei	Latin for 'Lamb of God' = Christ.
Anchor	Often signifies deceased was a sailor. Anchor with a broken chain represents end of life. Symbol was also used in early Christianity as a disguised cross.
Angels	Various symbolism. Angels blowing trumpets signifies Day of Judgment. Angels pointing towards heaven represents guardians of the dead as they escort soul

Appendix 2: Graveyard Symbolism

	to heaven. Weeping angel signifies grief, an untimely death. Flying angels represent rebirth. Two angels identified by the objects they carry: Gabriel, who is depicted with a horn and Michael, who has a sword.
Book	Represents Book of Life. Often depicted as a double-page spread.
Buttercup	Victorian symbol meaning childhood memories.
Candle with flame	Represents life.
Chi Rho	Cross-like shape made from two Greek letters, chi (X) and rho (P) = symbol for Jesus Christ.
Column	Symbolises a person's life. A broken column is seen as a life cut short. A wreath placed over a column equates victory over death.
Crown	Salvation.
Daffodil	Victorian symbol meaning unrequited love.
Daisy	Victorian symbol meaning innocence.
Dart/Arrow	A symbol of death, often carried by skeletons.
Death's Head	Death symbol. On seventeenth-century monuments, the death's head was a skull, portrayed either in partial profile or facing front and gnawing on a femur.
Deid Bell	Small handbell symbolising the bell rung at funerals. Popular motif in Scotland.
Dove	Common bird symbol. Flying down = Holy Spirit. Flying up = soul's journey to Heaven. A dove depicted in profile, sometimes carrying an olive branch = peace.
Father Time	Bearded, robed figure often carrying a scythe and hourglass. Represents mortality.
Grapes	Symbol linked to the blood of Christ.
Hands	Various definitions. Hands pointing up = gone to Heaven. Hands pointing down represents mortality or sudden death. Clasped hands = being guided to Heaven or a final goodbye parting between loved ones.
Hawthorn	Victorian symbol meaning hope.

Burying the Dead

Heart	Represents love.
Hourglass	Time's inevitable passing. Winged hourglass = time flies.
Ivy	Symbolises immortality, memory or friendship.
Laurel	Victorian symbol representing triumph and glory.
Lillies	Flower associated with death.
Moss	Victorian symbol meaning maternal love.
Moon	Death and rebirth.
Myrtle	Victorian symbol representing love.
Olive	Peace and healing.
Ouroboros	Image of a snake swallowing its tail is an ancient symbol for eternity and the cycle of life and death.
Pomegranate	Immortality and resurrection.
Rope	Represents eternity and binding.
Scroll	Symbol of life and time. Often held by a hand, symbolising life being recorded by angels.
Scythe	Symbol of death. Also a symbol for a farmer.
Sexton's Tools	Consists of a spade, pick, turf cutter and mattock. Symbolism represents mortality.
Shell	Symbolic of fertility, resurrection and pilgrimage.
Ship	Usually represents the grave of a sailor.
Skeletons	Symbol of death.
Skulls	Common symbol for death. A winged skull can represent the flight of the soul from mortal man.
Skull and Crossbones	Most recognised symbol of mortality. On gravestones it is often referred to as *Memento Mori*, the Latin for 'Remember You Will Die', and can be found in conjunction with other death symbols, such as hourglasses, cadavers and Sexton's tools.
Snowdrop	Victorian symbol meaning hope.
Stars	Various meanings. One star = Jesus. Six stars = Star of David. Twelve stars often symbolises the Apostles.
Steps	Generally means ascension or levels.

Appendix 2: Graveyard Symbolism

Torch	Represents life when upward and flaming and death when inverted and extinguished.
Tree	A generic tree often represents the Tree of Life.
Tree Trunk Broken	Means a life cut short.
Trumpets	Victory and Resurrection.
Tulip	Victorian symbol for declaration of love.
Urn	Greek symbol of mourning, often draped with a cloth.
Vine	Represents Christ and his followers.
Weeping Willow	Mourning and grief.
Winged Wheel	The Holy Spirit.
Wreath	Victory over death.
Yew Tree	Evergreen tree symbolising immortality. Also Victorian symbol for sorrow.

Notes and References

The Pagan Way

1. Gibbon, Edward, *The History of the Decline and Fall of the Roman Empire*, Chapter XXXVI, p. 84.
2. Meany, Audrey, *Gazetteer of Early Anglo-Saxon Burial Sites*, Oxford. 1964, pp. 104-105.
3. Browne, *Thomas, Hydriotaphia, Urne-Buriall, or, a discourse on the Supulchrall Urnes lately found in Norfolk*, Brome, 1658, p. 202 (5).
4. Lucy, Sam, *The Anglo-Saxon Way of Death*, Stroud, 2000, p. 6.
5. Douglas, James, *Nenia Britannica*, London: Nichols, 1793.
6. Williams Howard, 'Mortuary practices in early Anglo-Saxon England', in Hamerow Helena; Hinton David A.; Crawford Sally, (eds.), T*he Oxford Handbook of Anglo-Saxon Archaeology*, Oxford University Press, 2011, pp. 238-59.
7. Hirst, Sue; Clark Dido, 'The Mucking Anglo-Saxon Cemeteries', York Archaeology Data Service, 2010.
8. Higham, Nicholas J.; Ryan, Martin J., *The Anglo-Saxon World,* New Haven: Yale University Press, 2013, pp. 112-119.
9. Sayer, Duncan, 'Laws, Funerals and Cemetery Organisation: The Seventh-Century Kentish Family', in Sayer Duncan; Williams Howard, (eds.), *Mortuary Practice and Social Identities in the Middle Ages*, The Exeter University Press, 2009, pp. 141-166.
10. Spurrell, F. C. J., 'Dartford antiquities. Notes on British Roman and Saxon remains there found', *Archaeologia Cantiana*, Vol 18, 1889, pp. 304-318.
11. Hirst, Susan, *An Anglo-Saxon Inhumation Cemetery at Sewerby, East Yorkshire*, York University Archaeological Publications 4, 1985, p. 38.
12. Williams, 2011, pp. 238-59.
13. Carr, Christopher, 'Mortuary practices: Their social, philosophical-religious, circumstantial and physical determinants', *Journal of Archaeological Method and Theory*, Vol 2, Issue 2, 1995, p. 161.

Notes and References

14. Boddington, Andy, 'Models of burial, settlement and worship: the final phase reviewed', in *Anglo-Saxon Cemeteries: A Reappraisal*, Southworth, Edmund, (ed.), Sutton, 1990, pp. 177-99.
15. Bradley, Richard, 'Time regained: the creation of continuity', *Journal of the British Archaeological Association*, Vol 140, 1987, p. 199.
16. Carver, Martin; Oswald Hugh, 'Mound-building and State-Building: A poetic discourse', in *The Earliest States of Eastern Europe. Old Rus' and Medieval Europe. The Origin of States*. Russian Academy of Science, 2016, pp. 131-157.
17. Williams, Howard, 'Monuments and the past in early Anglo-Saxon England', *World Archaeology,* Vol 30, Issue 1, 1998, pp. 90-108.
18. Harden, Donald, B.; Leeds, Edward T.; *The Anglo-Saxon Cemetery at Abingdon, Berkshire*, University of Oxford Ashmolean Museum, 1936, p. 9.
19. Welch, Martin, G., *Early Anglo-Saxon Sussex*, Vol 1-2, Part 2, British Archaeological Reports British Series, 1983.
20. Williams, 1998, pp. 90-108.
21. Buckley, David, G.; Hedges, John, D., 'The Bronze Age and Saxon settlements at Springfield Lyons, Essex: an interim report', *Essex County Council Occasional Papers*, Vol 5, 1987.
22. Matthews, C. L., 'The Anglo-Saxon Cemetery at Marina Drive, Dunstable', *Bedfordshire Archaeological Journal*, 1962, pp. 93-105.
23. Williams, 1998, pp. 90-108.
24. Härke, Heinrich, 'Cemeteries as places of power', in De Jong, Mayke; Theuws, Frans with van Rhijn, Carine (eds.), *Topographies of Power in the Early Middle Ages*, Brill, Leiden, 2001, pp. 9-30.
25. Carver and Oswald, pp. 131-157.
26. Ibid.
27. www.arkeologigamlauppsala.se
28. Sturluson, Snorri, *Ynglinga Saga*, Midgard Books 1998, pp. 1-59.
29. www.arkeologigamlauppsala.se
30. Ibid.
31. Ibid.
32. Duncan, Conrad, 'Rare Viking boat burials unearthed in the first discovery of its kind in fifty years, archaeologists say', *The Independent*, 6 July 2019.
33. Klevnäs, Alison, 'Abandon Ship! Digging out the Dead from the Vendel Boat-Graves', *Norwegian Archaeological Review*, Vol 48, Issue 1, 2015, pp. 1-20.
34. Ibid.
35. Ibid.
36. Stolpe, Hjalmar; Arne, Ture, *Graffältet vid Vendel*, Stockholm, Kungliga Vitterhets-Historie-och Antikvitets Akademien 1912, p. 19.

37. Klevnäs, pp. 1-20.
38. Ibid.
39. Wikborg, Maja, 'The absence of human remains in Valsgärde cemetery. Natural process or ritual phenomena?', *Uppsala University Publications*, 2017, pp. 2-26.
40. Allmäea, Raili et al, 'The Salme I Ship Burial: An Osteological View of a Unique Burial in Northern Europe', *Interdisciplinaria Archaeologica*, Vol 2, 2011, pp. 109-124.
41. Harris, Oliver et al, 'The Viking boat burial on Ardnamurchan', www.eprints.gla.ac.uk, 2012.
42. www.nationaltrust.org.uk/sutton-hoo/features/the-royal-burial-mounds-at-sutton-hoo
43. Ibid.
44. https://en.m.wikipedia.org/wiki/Yucat%C3%A1n_Peninsula
45. Welsh, William, B. M., 'Classification and Analysis of Ancient Maya Burials and Burial Customs', PhD Thesis, University College London 1987, pp. 5-29.
46. Hooker, R., 'Native American Creation Stories', Washington State University, www.washington.edu
47. 'Exploring the Cave of the Crystal Maiden', www.discovermagazine.com, October 2014.
48. McVicker, Donald, 'Figurines are us? The Social Organization of Jaina Island, Campeche, Mexico', *Ancient Mesoamerica*, Vol 23, Issue 2, Cambridge University Press, 2012, pp. 211-234.
49. Welsh, 1987, pp. 5-29.
50. Cascone, Sarah, 'The Tomb of an Ancient Maya God-King Was Just Discovered in Guatemala', www.artnet.com, 21 September 2017.
51. Barrios, Ana Garcia, 'Mystery Queen in the Maya Tomb', www.nationalgeographic.com, 6 May 2017.
52. Connor, Steve, 'Mummies buried under a shanty town in Peru reveal secrets of the Incas' lost civilisation', *The Independent*, 18 April 2002.
53. 'Ancient Wari royal tomb unearthed in Peru', www.bbcnews.co.uk, 28 June 2013.
54. Dylan, 'Chauchilla Cemetery', www.atlasobscura/places/chauchilla_cemetery
55. Treeswithknees, 'Timbac Mummies of the Philippines', www.atlasobscura.com/places/timbac-mummies-of-the-philippines
56. Kabayan Mummy Caves, World Monuments Fund, www.wmf.org/project/kabayan-mummy-caves
57. Horne, Patrick; Ireland, Robert, 'Moss and a Guanche mummy: an unusual utilization', *The Bryologist*, Vol 94, Issue 4, 1991, p. 407.
58. www.en.wikipedia.org/Guanche-mummies
59. Ibid.

Notes and References

60. Morato, Luis, 'Guanche Mummy of Madrid', www.atlasobscura.com/places/guanche-mummy-madrid
61. Pinkstone, Joe, 'Two mummified babies discovered inside a cave on the volcanic island of Tenerife', *Mail Online*, 5 December 2018.
62. www.explore-gower.co.uk/paviland-cave-goat-s-hole-and-the-red-lady-of-paviland
63. Rosemarkie Caves Project, www.spanglefish.com/rosemarkiecavesproject
64. Connolly, Michael, 'Cloghermore Cave: The Lee Valhalla', *Archaeology Ireland*, Vol 14, 2000, pp. 16-19.
65. Knapp, Mary, F., 'Hawaiian Cave Burials', www.sevenponds.com, 13 March 2013.
66. Ibid.
67. Fullard-Leo, Betty, 'Sacred Burial Practices', www.coffeetimes.com, February 1998.
68. Apgar, Sally, 'Sacred Big Island Burial Cave Lies Open and Exposed', www.starbulletin.com, 26 August 2004.
69. Apgar, Sally; Vordino, Mary, 'Artefacts Trafficker Pleads Guilty as Part of a Plea Deal', *Honolulu Star Bulletin*, 25 March 2006.
70. Garside, Vicki, 'Toraja Death Rituals: Cave Burials, Effigies and the Walking Dead', www.maketimetoseetheworld.com
71. 'Mysteries of ancient caves in Mustang', www.trekkingmart.com, 19 February 2013.
72. Than, Ker, 'New Death Ritual Found in the Himalaya – 27 De-fleshed Humans' *National Geographic*, 1 March 2011.
73. Welsh, 1998, pp. 1-4.
74. 'Ancient Choctaw burial practice', www.choctawnation.com, 2012.
75. Boyce Mary, *Zoroastrians: Their Religious Beliefs and Practices*, Routledge, 1979, pp. 156-162.
76. Tait, Malcolm, 'The fate of India's vultures', *The Ecologist*, 10 January 2004.
77. Drigung Til Monastery, Tibet Travel and Tours, Tibet Vista, 2017.
78. www.culture-traditions/funerals/sky-burial
79. Ash, Niema, *Flight of the Wind Horse: A Journal into Tibet*, Rider, 1992, pp. 57-61.

Piety and Power

1. Da Silva, Bridgette, 'St Patrick and the Conversion to Christianity', www.strangehorizons.com, 27 July 2009.
2. Sanmark, Alexandra, 'Power and Conversion. A Comparative Study of Christianization in Scandinavia' *Occasional Papers in Archaeology*, The University of Uppsala, 2004, p. 555.

3. Jelling Project, www.jelling.natmus.dk, 2011.
4. Brusgaard, N. O., 'The Jelling Monument', Bachelor thesis, Leiden University, 2012, pp. 7-17.
5. Ibid.
6. Søvsø, Morten, Tidlig kristne begravelser ved Ribe Domkirke – Ansgars kirkegård? *Arkæologi i Slesvig/Archäologie in Schleswig*, Vol 13, 2010, pp. 147-64.
7. Bachelor 2012, pp. 7-17.
8. Bazaraitė, Eglė; Heitor, Teresa, 'Comparative Study of Christian and Pagan Burial Constructions', *Mokslas-Lietuvos Ateitis*, Vol 5, Issue 3, 2013, pp. 316-321.
9. Horkman, Cheri, 'Eklutna Cemetery and Spirit Houses', www.randomcurrents.com, 4 May 2017.
10. Wellcome Collection Online Photographic Library, www.wellcomeimages.org
11. Acquah, Francis, 'The Impact of African Traditional Religious Beliefs and Cultural Values on Christian Muslim Relations in Ghana from 1920 through the Present', PhD Thesis, University of Exeter, 2011, pp. 128-44.
12. St Catherine's Monastery, www.sinaimonastery.com
13. Ridler, Faith, 'With a population of just FOUR ... welcome to the tiny Welsh island believed to hide the graves of 20,000 saints', *Mail Online*, 4 January 2019.
14. Arnold, Catharine, *Necropolis – London and Its Dead*, Simon and Schuster, 2006, pp. 66-132.
15. Online catalogue of archaeology, buildings, industrial and maritime heritage in Wales, www.coflein.gov.uk
16. Iona Abbey, en.wikipedia.org/wiki/Iona_Abbey
17. Iona Abbey, www.scottishheritagehub.com/rarfa/cs9
18. Llandre Heritage, www.llandre.org.uk
19. Sayer, Duncan, 'Christian Burial Practice in the Early Middle Ages: Rethinking the Anglo-Saxon Funerary Sphere', *History Compass*, Vol 11, Issue 2, 2013, pp. 133-146.
20. Halsall, Guy, 'Social Change Around AD 600: An Austrian Perspective', in Carver, Martin (ed.), *The Age of Sutton Hoo,* Woodbridge: Boydell Press 1992, pp. 265-278.
21. Sayer, 2013, pp. 133-146.
22. Sanmark, p. 555.
23. Willsher, Betty, *Understanding Scottish Graveyards*, NMSE Publishing Ltd, 2015, p. 3.
24. Sayer, 2013, pp. 133-146.

Notes and References

25. Gordon, Stephen, 'The Walking Dead in Medieval England: Literary and Archaeological Perspectives', PhD Thesis, University of Manchester, 2013, pp. 77-80.
26. Sayer, 2013, pp. 133-146.
27. Hadley, Dawn, M., 'Burying the Socially and Physically Distinctive in Later Anglo-Saxon England', in Buckberry, Jo; Cherryson, Annia, (eds.), *Burial in Later Anglo-Saxon England c. 650-1100*, Oxford, 2010, pp. 103-15.
28. Sayer, 2013, pp. 133-146.
29. Willsher, p. 8.
30. Quinn, William A., *Chaucer's Dream Visions and Shorter Poems*, Routledge, 1999, p. 190.
31. en.m.wikipedia.org/Basilicaofsaintdenis
32. www.britishcadavers.co.uk
33. Roe, Helen M., 'Cadaver Effigial Monuments in Ireland', *Journal of the Royal Society of Antiquaries of Ireland*, 1969, pp. 1-19.
34. Scott, Leader, *Ghiberti and Donatello with Other Early Italian Sculptors* London: Sampson Low, Marston, Searle, and Rivington, 1882, pp. 27-50.
35. Monumental Brass Society, www.mbs-brasses.co.uk
36. Holmes, Mrs Basil [Isabella M.], *The London Burial Grounds: Notes on Their History from the Earliest Times to the Present Day*, London: T. Fisher Unwin, 1896, p. 42.
37. Lindsay, Suzanne, G., 'The Revolutionary Exhumations at St-Denis, 1793', in *Conversations: An Online Journal of the Center for the Study of Material and Visual Cultures of Religion*, 2014.
38. Dexeus, Ana, 'The bones of our ancestors. The end of burials in churches in the late 18th century', *Contributions to Science*, Vol 11, Issue 1, 2015, pp. 85-94.
39. Reed, David, 'The excavation of a cemetery and putative chapel site at Newhall Point, Balblair, Ross & Cromarty', *Proceedings of the Society of Antiquaries of Scotland*, Vol 125, 1995, pp. 779-791.
40. McKeggie, Lachlan, 'Kirkmichael, Balblair, Black Isle: Excavation and Watching Brief Report', Highland Archaeology Services Ltd, October 2017, pp. 1-57.
41. Ibid.
42. Herbert, Shiranikha, 'Letting sheep graze on consecrated ground is not disrespectful, diocesan Chancellor rules', www.churchtimes.co.uk, 15 February 2019.
43. www.llandre.org.uk
44. IBRA Bee Bole Register, www.beeboles.org.uk
45. Llantrithyd Place, Parks and Gardens, www.parksandgardens.org

46. Willsher, p. 4.
47. Old Jewish Cemetery, www.jewishmuseum.cz
48. Schuessler, Ryan, 'Pollution is destroying probably the oldest Jewish cemetery in the Western hemisphere', www.pri.org, 21 December 2016.
49. Alderney Road Cemetery, The London Parks and Gardens Trust www.londongardensonline.org.uk
50. Friends of the Penzance Jewish Cemetery, www.penzancejewishcemetery.org.uk
51. Swan, Caroline, 'The Hill of Bones: the story of Bunhill Fields', www.flickeringlamps.com, 25 June 2014.
52. Ibid.
53. Quakers in Britain, www.quaker.org.uk
54. The Pales Burial Ground, www.thepales.org.uk
55. The Gentle Author, 'Inside Spitalfields' Oldest Building', www.spitalfieldlife.com, 1 July 2015.
56. The Rothwell Charnel Chapel Project, www.rothwellcharnelchapel.group.shef.ac.uk
57. Ibid.
58. The Ossuary at St Leonard's Church, www.slhk.org/theossuary
59. www.rothwellcharnelchapel.group.shef.ac.uk
60. Sedlec Ossuary – The Church of Bones, www.sedlecossuary.com
61. Pilgrim, C, 'Melník Chapel of Bones', www.atlasobscura.com/places/melnik-chapel-bone
62. Skull Chapel, www.en.m/wiki/Skull_chapel, October 2015.
63. Our Lady of the Conception, www.rome.net/our-lady-conception-capuchins
64. Hallstatt Charnel House, www.atlasobscura.com/places/hallstatt-charnel-house
65. Black, Annetta, 'Capela de Ossos Bone Chapel', www.atlasobscura/places/capela-dos-ossos
66. Capela dos Ossos, www.en.wiki/Capela_dos_Ossos

The Deviant Ones
1. Geake, Helen, 'Burial Practice in Seventh- and Eighth-Century England,' in Carver, Martin (ed.), *The Age of Sutton Hoo*, p. 87.
2. Bodkin, Henry, 'Zombie invasion fears in medieval Yorkshire: Villagers mutilated to stop rise of the living dead', *The Telegraph*, 3 April 2017.
3. Gordon, 2013, pp. 101-130.
4. 'Burned with a stake through the heart: the medieval "vampire" burial', *The Telegraph*, 1 November 2012.

Notes and References

5. Bell, Michael, E., 'Vampires and Death in New England, 1784 to 1892', *Anthropology and Humanism*, Vol 31, Issue 2, 2006, pp. 124–140.
6. Betsinger, Tracy, K.; Scott, Amy, B., 'Governing from the Grave: Vampire Burials and Social Order in Post-Medieval Poland', *Cambridge Archaeological Journal*, Vol 24, Issue, 3, 2013, pp. 467-476.
7. Ibid.
8. ' "Vampire" skeletons found in Bulgaria near Black Sea', www.bbcnews.co.uk, 6 June 2012.
9. P, Sara, '4 Real Vampire Graveyards Discovered in Slavic Countries', www.slavorum.org
10. Whipps, Heather, 'Medieval Vampire Skull Found', www.livescience.com, 11 March 2009.
11. Pisa, Nick, '800-year-old Witch Burial Found in Italy', www.archaeologynewsnetwork.blogspot.com, 25 September 2011.
12. Lorenzi, Rossella, 'Skeleton of Possible "Witch Girl" Found', www.livescience.com, 6 October 2014.
13. Pisa, Nick, www.archaeologynewsnetwork.blogspot.com
14. Swan, Caroline, 'Buried under a boulder: the grave of the Lancashire "Witch"', www.flickeringlamps.com, 14 August 2015.
15. Hadley, 2010, pp, 101-113.
16. Buckberry, J. L.; Dawn, M. Hadley, 'An Anglo-Saxon Execution Cemetery at Walkington Wold, Yorkshire', *Oxford Journal of Archaeology*, Vol 26, Issue 3, 2007, pp. 309-329.
17. Reynolds, Andrew, *Anglo-Saxon Deviant Burial Customs*, Oxford University Press, 2009, pp. 10-26.
18. Mattison, Alyxandra, 'The Execution and Burial of Criminals in Early Medieval England, c. 850-1150', PhD Thesis, University of Sheffield, 2016, pp. 265-296.
19. Ibid, pp. 48-62.
20. Buckberry & Hadley, pp. 309-329.
21. Ibid.
22. Mattison, pp. 48-62.
23. Ibid.
24. Krakowka, Kathryn, 'Andover's outcast dead: Excavating an Anglo-Norman Cemetery', *Current Archaeology*, 5 April 2018.
25. Mattison, pp. 89-114.
26. Reynolds, pp. 4-35.
27. Mattison, pp. 135-142.
28. Krakowka, 2018.

29. Sherwin, Nyomi, 'Silent Neighbours: The BC Penitentiary and its Inhabitants', www.vancouvertraces.weebly.com
30. The Spike Island Project, www.ucc.ie
31. St Margaret Fyebridge, www.norwichmedievalchurches.org
32. Poore, Daniel, 'Excavations at Oxford Castle', www.oxoniensia.org, 2009.
33. Crone, Rosalind et al, *Guide to the Criminal Prisons of Nineteenth-Century England*, London Publishing Partnership 2018, pp. 21-71.
34. Oxford Castle & Prison, www.oxfordcastleandprison.co.uk
35. 'Gloucester prison closure: Criminals buried underneath', www.bbc.co.uk, 22 February 2013.
36. 'Calls for all Dorchester's Prison human remains to be exhumed', www.bbc.co.uk, 8 May 2017.
37. Berthoud, Peter, 'A Grim View Inside Newgate Prison in the 1890s', www.peterberthoud.co.uk, 29 May 2012.
38. 'A Peek Inside Wandsworth Prison', www.josefjakobs.org, 26 January 2015.
39. 'A Brief History', www.bodminjail.org
40. Pentonville Prison Cemetery, www.findagrave.com
41. Holloway Prison Burial Ground, The National Archives, Kew.
42. Rimmer Jayne, 'Analysing the Skeletons Excavated at the former Female Prison: An *Insight* Report', York Archaeological Trust, 2016, pp. 1-11.
43. Strangeways Prison, Manchester, www.capitalpunishmentuk.org
44. Crumlin Road Gaol Graveyard in Belfast, County Antrim, www.findagrave.com
45. Executions in Scottish Prisons www.capitalpunishmentuk.org
46. Crone et al, pp. 21-71.
47. Gonella, Paul, 'Uncovering the Secrets of Burrow (Rat) Island in Portsmouth Harbour', www.strongisland.co.uk, 3 May 2018.
48. Krakowka, Kathryn, 'Return to Rat Island', *Current Archaeology*, 2 May 2019.
49. 'The Pirate Cemetery of Ile Sainte-Marie', www.unusualtraveller.com, 3 June 2017.
50. www.en.m.wikipedia.org/AdamBaldridge
51. www.en.m.wikipedia.org/ThomasTew
52. 'The Pirate Cemetery of Ile Sainte-Marie'.
53. Sabur, Rozina, 'Pirate Graveyard in America', *The Telegraph*, 28 March 2018.
54. Steane, John, *The Archaeology of Medieval England and Wales*, Routledge, 2014, pp. 96.
55. Miller, Timothy, S; Nesbitt, John, W., 'Walking Corpses: Leprosy in Byzantium and the Medieval West', *The American Historical Review*, Vol 121, Issue 5, 2016, pp. 1728–1729.

Notes and References

56. Gilchrist, Roberta, 'Transforming medieval beliefs: the significance of bodily resurrection to medieval burial rituals', in Prusac, Marina; Hâkon, Roland; Brandt, J. Rasmus, (eds.), *Death and Changing Rituals: Function and meaning in ancient funerary practices*, Oxbow, 2014, pp. 1-21.
57. McCormish, J. M. et al, 'The Medieval Cemetery of St. Leonard's Leper Hospital at Midland Road, Peterborough', York Archaeological Trust, 2017, pp. 1-74.
58. Strochlic, Nina, 'Hawaii Still Has a Leprosy Colony with Six Patients', www.thedailybeast.com, 14 April 2017.
59. Warkentin, Elizabeth, 'The abandoned Greek island shrouded in mystery', www.bbc.com, 22 September 2017.
60. Robben Island www.robben-island.org.za
61. Crossbones, www.crossbones.org.uk
62. Crossbones Burial Ground Summary, www.museumoflondon.org.uk
63. www.crossbones.org.uk
64. Burchard of Worms, www.digihum.mcgill.ca
65. Hall, Denise, 'Saving Ireland's Forgotten Burial Sites', *Irish Examiner*, 29 May 2014.
66. Dutch Genealogy, www.dutchgenealogy.nl
67. Hereford Cathedral Church, www.research-information.bristol.ac.uk
68. Finlay, Nyree, 'Outside of life: traditions of infant burial in Ireland from cillin to cist', *World Archaeology*, Vol 31, Issue 3, 2010, pp. 407-422.
69. Boot Hill, https://tombstoneboothillgiftshop.com
70. www.en.m.wikipedia.org/Boothill_Graveyard
71. https://tombstoneboothillgiftshop.com

They Died in Heaps

1. Human Rights and Genocide, www.un.org
2. Hilts, Carly, 'The Kilkenny Workhouse mass burials', *Current Archaeology*, April 2013.
3. Devereux, Stephen, 'Famine in the Twentieth Century', *IDS Bulletin*, Vol 24, Issue 4, 1993, pp. 52-59.
4. Gray, Richard, 'The flu that swept the world', www.bbc.com, 28 October 2018.
5. Cholera Pits, www.canmore.org.uk
6. www.belfastcity.gov.uk/community/cemeteries/friarsbush.aspx
7. Cave, Damien, 'As Haitians Flee, The Dead go Uncounted', *The New York Times*, 2010.
8. Bedar, Gul, A., '"No hope" for those buried by mudslides, Afghanistan official says', *The New York Times*, 3 May 2014.

9. Hulme, Michala, 'Manchester's Forgotten Burial Sites', www.visitmanchester.com
10. Bannos, Pamela, 'Hidden Truths: Potter's Field', www.hiddentruths.northwest.edu, 2019.
11. Montanés, José, A., 'Staring Black Death in the face in Barcelona', www.elpais.com, 15 August 2014.
12. Boccaccio, Giovanni, *The Decameron*, Wordsworth, 2004, p. 321.
13. Ziegler, Philip, *The Black Death*, Sutton Publishing, 2003, pp. 53-163
14. Ibid.
15. Ibid.
16. Ibid.
17. Hawkins, Duncan, 'The Black Death and the new London Cemeteries of 1348', *Antiquity* Vol 64, Issue 244, 1990, pp. 637-642.
18. Dempsey, Andrew, 'DNA of Bacteria Responsible for London Great Plague of 1665 Identified for First Time', www.crossrail.co.uk, 8 September 2016.
19. en.wikipedia.org/wiki/Great_Plague_of_London
20. Poveglia Plague Island, www.atlasobscura.com/places/poveglia-plague-island
21. en.wikipedia.org/wiki/Great_Plague_of_Marseille
22. Aldersley, Miranda, 'Mass grave containing 1,800 soldiers who perished at the Battle of Stalingrad', *Mail Online*, 12 December 2018.
23. Fernández-Álvarez, J. P., 'Discovery of a mass grave from the Spanish Civil War', *Forensic Science International*, Vol 267, pp. 10-17.
24. 'Vietnam: Mass grave of war martyrs unearthed in Quang Ngai', Asia News Monitor, 2011.
25. Seidler, Christoph, 'Mass Grave Begins Revealing Soldiers' Secrets', www.spiegel.de, 27 April 2012.
25. Pittock, Murray, *Culloden: Great Battles*, Oxford University Press, 2016, pp. 58-98.
26. Battlefield Culloden MHG3047, www.her.highland.gov.uk
27. Lawson, Jim, 'Secret Jacobite Society Discovers Mass Grave', *Daily Express*, 14 April 2018.
28. Guillén Alejandra et al, 'How a decade of drug war turned Mexico into a burial ground', www.theintercept.com, 13 December 2018.
29. Ibid.
30. Ibid.
31. Ibid.
32. Ibid.
33. Office of the Special Adviser on the Prevention of Genocide (OSAPG), www.un.org

Notes and References

34. 'When Saddam gassed thousands of Kurds at Halabja', Fondation Institut Kurde de Paris, 16 March 2018.
35. Muhammad, Ako, 'Mass graves containing Kurds unearthed', *The Associated Press*, July 2011.
36. Salloum, Saad, 'Genocide still haunts Iraq's Yazidis', www.al.monitor.com, 2018.
37. 'UN verified 200 mass graves left by Islamic State in Iraq', *The Associated Press*, 6 November 2018.
38. 'More mass graves discovered from Rwanda's Genocide', www.voanews.com, 20 September 2018.
39. Ibid.
40. 'Rwanda: How the genocide happened', BBC News, 17 May 2011.
41. '4,000 Bodies Found in Rwanda', *The New York Times*, 22 September 1994.
42. 'UN Discovers Mass Grave in Rwanda', *The Associated Press*, 7 October 1994.
43. Neuffer, Elizabeth, 'Nieman Reports', www.niemanreports.org, April 2014.
44. Grant, Thomas, D., *Admission to the United Nations*, Martinus Nijhoff, 2009, p. 226.
45. Corder, Mike; Cohadzic, Amer, 'Srebrenica: 20 years after the genocide', *The Associated Press*, 9 July 2015.
46. Srebrenica – Holocaust and Genocide Studies, NIOD Institute, 2002.
47. Dayton Peace Accord on Bosnia, US State Department, 30 March 1996.
48. Nettelfield, Lara, J, 'Courting Democracy in Bosnia Herzegovina', *The Associated Press*, 17 May 2012.
49. List of people indicted in the International Criminal Tribune for the former Yugoslavia, en.wikipedia.org/wiki/List_of_people_indicted_in_the_International_Criminal_Tribunal_for_the_former_Yugoslavia

A Watery Grave

1. Young, C, 'Sir Francis Drake's body close to being found off Panama', www.bbc.co.uk, 25 October 2011.
2. Redmond, Jodee, 'Hawaii Burial Methods', www.dying.lovetoknow.com
3. Ernst, Douglas, 'WWII veteran given Viking funeral: Coastguard agreed to Norse send-off', *The Washington Times*, 2 October 2014.
4. Lunde, Paul; Stone, Caroline, E. M., *Ibn Fadlan and the Land of Darkness: Arab Travellers in the Far North*, Penguin Classics, 2011.
5. Lewis, Michael, *Napoleon and his British Captives*, Allen and Unwin, 1962, pp. 34-56.
6. Wiener, Robert, 'Israeli sailor, now of rockaway, recalls burying Eichmann at sea', www.njjewishnews.com, 18 April 2018.

7. Lewis, pp. 34-56
8. Pryor, Johnathan, 'Interment Without Earth: A Study of Sea Burials during the Age of Sail', *Archaeology of Death*, 2008.
9. Ibid.
10. Anonymous correspondence, www.merchant-navy.net, 2015.
11. Ibid.
12. 'Incredible photograph shows the mass burial of Titanic victims', www.express.co.uk, 12 September 2014.
13. www.funeralguide.co.uk, 8 July 2016.
14. 'Coffin requirements for burials at sea', Marine Management Organisation, www.gov.uk
15. Ibid.
16. Ibid.
17. 'Body of woman buried at sea found off Jersey coast', www.bbc.co.uk, 24 September 2013.
18. Department of the Environment and Energy, www.environment.gov.au
19. EPA's Code of Federal Regulations, Chapter 1, Section 229.1, www.epa.us
20. Hindu Funerals, Cremation and Varanasi, www.factsanddetails.com
21. Carey, John, *Eyewitness to History*, Harvard University Press, 1987.
22. Hindu Funerals, www.factsanddetails.com
23. Parth, M N., 'About 80 bodies found in India's Ganges River in apparent "burial"', *Los Angeles Times*, 9 Jan 2015.
24. Palus, Shannon, 'India once released 25,000 flesh-eating turtles into the Ganges', www.smithsonian.com, 19 November 2014.
25. Miller, Karyn, 'River Soar is new Ganges', *The Telegraph*, 10 October 2004.
26. Cee, Princess, 'Sunken Cemetery, Catarman, Philippines', www.atlasobscura.com
27. Kirkpatrick, Noel, 'The lost towns under Lake Murray', www.mnn.com, 10 November 2017.
28. 'Official apology over Tryweryn', www.bbc.co.uk, 19 October 2005.
29. www.kentuckylakehistory.wordpress.com, 9 December 2001.
30. Personal communication with Memorial Reefs International.
31. Official Neptune Memorial Reef website, www.nmreef.com
32. Black, Annetta, 'Ghost Fleet of Truk Lagoon', www.atlasobscura.com
33. Lamb, Kate, 'UK in talks with Indonesia over missing sunken WWII warships', www.theguardian.com, 7 March 2018.
34. Holmes, Oliver, 'Mystery wrecks of three Dutch WWII ships vanish from Java seabed', www.theguardian.com, 16 November 2016.

Notes and References

Boneyards of Steel

1. Brocklehurst, Steven, 'The day the German navy sank its own ships', BBC Scotland News, June 2019.
2. Chowdhury, Syed, T., 'Graveyard shift: Dismantling toxic ships in Bangladesh', *The Independent*, 26 July 2013.
3. Cloninger, B., 'Bay of Nouadhibou', www.atlasobscura.com/places/Nouadhibou 2016.
4. Inwood, Alex, 'Dubai's Supercar Graveyard', www.whichcar.au, June 2013.
5. D'mello, Chantelle, 'Massive car graveyard in Qatar', *Doha News*, December 2014.
6. Glon, Ronan, 'The real story behind the car graveyard in Chatillon graveyard', www.ranwhenparked.net, October 2015.
7. 'Mystery car graveyard discovered inside Welsh cave', Media Drum World, February 2016.
8. Earnhardt, Dale Jr, www.dalejr.com, March 2017.
9. Stewart, Harry, 'Welcome to Bolivia's Haunting Train Graveyard', www.theculturetrip.com, 31 July 2017.
10. Kautzor, Thomas, 'The Railways of Suriname', www.internationasteam.co.uk, September 2014.
11. Hirsch, A, 'Steam Engine Graveyard, East Germany', www.28dayslater.co.uk. September 2011.
12. Petrovski, Nikola, 'Red Star Train Graveyard', Abandoned Places, May 2017.
13. Davis-Monthan Air Force Base, www.dm.af.mil
14. Khoury, Albert, 'Elvis Presley's private jet just sold for well below its estimated auction price', www.digitaltrends.com, 27 May 2017.
15. 'Graveyards of Nigeria's Dead Airplanes', www.nairaland.com, 13 April 2017.
16. Kornev, Val, 'Deserted Airports', www.travel.com, 5 October 2018.
17. www.airplaneboneyards.com
18. Koleka, Benet, 'Albania's graveyard of MiGs to become NATO airbase', www.uk.reuters.com, October 2018.
19. Al Asaid Airfield, www.globalsecurity.org
20. www.airplaneboneyards.com
21. 'The great tank and truck graveyard of Asmara, Eritrea', www.artificalowl.net, November 2008.
22. 'Fort Knox Tank Graveyard', www.eerie-indiana.blogspot.com, 11 June 2013.
23. Lyons, Jeremy, 'Inside the Sierra Army Depot Graveyard', www.warhistoryonline.com, 17 October 2018.
24. Hall, John, 'Huge Abandoned Tank Graveyard in Ukraine', *Daily Mail*, 3 March 2014.

25. Private conversation with naval intelligence officer, February 2018.
26. Gordon, Michael, R., 'US and Russian Subs in Collision in Arctic Ocean near Murmansk', *The New York Times*, 23 March 1993.
27. Preuss, Simone, 'The Cold War Submarine Graveyard of Russia's Kola Peninsula', www.recyclenation.com, 7 September 2011.
28. Hughes, David, 'Nine nuclear submarines stored in Plymouth still contain radioactive fuel', *Plymouth Herald*, 3 April 2019.

The Return of the Cemetery
1. www.en.m.wikipedia.org/WadiasSalaam
2. 'Islamic State: The Pushback', *The Economist*, 21 March 2015.
3. Rutherford, Sarah, *The Victorian Cemetery*, Shire Publications, 2008, pp. 1-6.
4. Monk Travel, Park Street Cemetery, www.kolkatacitytours.com
5. Ghosh, Deepanjan, 'Agra's Roman Catholic Cemetery', www.doubledolphinblogspot.com, January 2018.
6. www.en.m.wikipedia.org/SaintLouisCemetery
7. www.theculturetrip.com/north-america/usa/louisiana/articles/a-guide-to-new-orleans-cemeteries/
8. Ibid.
9. Ibid.
10. Etlin, Richard, A., 'Père Lachaise and the garden cemetery', *The Journal of Garden History* Vol 4, Issue 3, 2012, pp. 211-222.
11. Paris, M., Pere-Lachaise cemetery, www.web.archive.org, April 2012.
12. Nunez, J., 'The public management of denominational spaces of the cemeteries of the City of Paris', *The Social Movement*, Vol 237, Issue 4, 2011.
13. Father-Lachaise Cemetery, www.ltotd.com, March 2005.
14. www.en.m.wikipedia.org/Pere-Lachaisecemetery
15. Rutherford, pp. 18-22
16. www.glasgownecropolis.org
17. Rutherford, pp. 10-11:
18. Holmes, Mrs Basil, p. 99
19. www.kensalgreencemetery.com
20. www.fownc.org
21. www.highgatecemetery.org
22. www.abneypark.org
23. www.fonc.org.uk
24. www.brompton-cemetery.org.uk
25. www.fothcp.org
26. Rutherford, pp. 27-31

Notes and References

27. Ibid.
28. Ibid.
29. Willsher, p. 12
30. Edwards, Amelia, B, *Pharaohs, Fellahs and Explorers*, Harper and Brothers, 1891, p. 159
31. Packer, John, A., 'Influences of Ancient Egypt on Architecture and Ornament in Scotland', PhD Thesis, University of Edinburgh, 2012, pp. 9-18.
32. Ibid.
33. Messinger, Paul, R., 'Papago Park pyramid: How the Phoenix landmark and tomb came to be', www.eu.azcentral.com, 11 October 2018.
34. 'Unbuilt London: The Pyramid of Death', www.ianvisits.co.uk, 6 August 2016.
35. www.bellefontainecemetery.org/historical-story/tate-mausoleum
36. Packer, pp. 18-19.
37. Soteriou, Helen, 'Inside Hyde Park's Secret Pet Cemetery', *The Telegraph*, August 2015.
38. Brack, Theodora, 'The Cat's Meow: Explore the Cimetière des Chiens, the World's Oldest Pet Cemetery', www.bonjourparis.com, 13 November 2015.
39. Hartsdale Pet Cemetery, www.petcem.com
40. www.musashinokk.co.jp/tomonokai

Lest We Forget

1. Freeman-Mitford, Algernon B., *Tales of Old Japan*, London: University of Michigan, 1871, pp. 10-32.
2. Summers, Julie, *British and Commonwealth War Cemeteries*, Shire Publications, 2010, p. 5.
3. HM Prison Dartmoor: American Prisoner of War Cemetery, www.historicengland.org.uk
4. Confederate Stockade Cemetery, Johnson's Island, Ohio, www.nps.gov
5. Apache Prisoner of War Cemetery, Fort Sill, Oklahoma Historical Society, www.okhistory.org
6. Laurent, Rosemary, 'St Helen's Honour's Boer War Prisoners', *History Today*, 10 October 1991.
7. Commonwealth War Graves Commission, www.cwgc.org
8. Ibid.
9. Kenyon, Frederic, 'The Kenyon Report', www.cwgc.org
10. www.cwgc.org
11. Ibid.
12. Butcher, Tim, 'Fury as Israelis damage war cemetery', *The Telegraph*, 13 November 2006.

13. www.cwgc.org
14. Legg, Joanna; Parker, Graham; Legg, David, The Great War 1914-18, www.greatwar.co.uk
15. www.ww1cemeteries.com
16. www.cwgc.org
17. Veterans Affairs Canada, www.veterans.gc.ca
18. www.cwgc.org
19. Ibid.
20. Ibid.
21. www.ww1cemeteries.com
22. www.ww2cemteries.com
23. Metz, Kaj, 'Commonwealth War Cemetery Delhi', www.tracesofwar.com
24. www.cwgc.org
25. Taylor, Ron, 'Roll of Honour, Britain At War: Sai Wan War Cemetery', www.rollofhonour.org.uk
26. www.ww1cemeteries.org
27. German Military Cemetery, www.historicengland.org.uk
28. American Battle Monuments Commission Brochure, www.abmc.gov
29. Personal communication with www.travelfranceonline.com, February 2018.
30. Douaumont Ossuary, www.verdun-douaumont.com
31. Qawasimi, Hanadi, 'Cemeteries of Numbers: Israel takes revenge on Palestinian corpses', *The New Arab*, 28 November 2018.
32. Ibid.
33. Breu, Philipp, 'The martyr's cemetery of Hezbollah in Beirut', www.philippbreu.com, 14 February 2016.

Thinking Outside the Box
1. Population Reference Bureau, www.prb.org
2. Biegelsen, Amy, 'America's Looming Burial Crisis', www.citylab.com, 31 October 2012.
3. New South Wales Government, www.industry.nsw.gov.au
4. Nuwer, Rachel, 'China's 3,000 Cemeteries Will Run Out of Space in Just Six Years', www.smithsonian.com, 10 October 2013.
5. McManus, John, 'The World is Running Out of Burial Space', www.bbc.co.uk, 13 March 2013.
6. Lewis, Leo, 'Corpse Hotel Caters to Japan's Waiting Dead', www.ft.com, 7 November 2018.
7. Janell, K., 'Unclaimed Burial Urns Pile Up in Japan', www.uk.mobile.reuters.com

Notes and References

8. McManus, www.bbc.co.uk.
9. Ibid.
10. Rosehill, Harry, 'London is Running Out of Burial Space – What Next?, www.Londonist.com, August 2018.
11. Mayor of London, www.london.gov.uk
12. www.catacombes.paris.fr
13. Ibid.
14. Hamza, Hani, *The Northern Cemetery of Cairo*, Cairo: The American University in Cairo Press, 2001, p. 27.
15. Jacobs, Harrison, 'Meet the Egyptian Families Who Live Among the Tombs in Cairo's Massive Cemetery', www.businessinsider.com, 19 November 2014.
16. www.jewishmuseum.cz
17. Burks, Gary, 'We're Running Out of Space to Bury Our Dead – It's Time to Reuse Graves', www.metro.co.uk, 3 July 2019.
18. Rudgard, Olivia, 'War graves lost as court gives council permission to bury civilians on top of World War I soldiers', *The Telegraph*, 10 March 2017.
19. www.southwarknews.co.uk, 5 October 2017.
20. Booth, Robert, 'Fears that graves are being dug up at a London cemetery to free burial space', *The Guardian*, 2 October 2018.
21. Booth, William, 'Israelis are running out of room to bury their dead', www.independent.co.uk, 21 May 2015.
22. Ghert-Zand, Renee, 'Underground cemetery project looks to the past for the graveyard of the future', www.timesofisrael.com, 11 November 2017.
23. 'Wiltshire's "Neolithic" long barrow burial chamber opens', www.bbc.co.uk, 20 September 2014.
24. www.sacredstones.co.uk
25. McManus, www.bbc.co.uk
26. Jozuka, Emiko, 'Death is a High-Tech Trip in Japan's Futuristic Cemeteries', www.vice.com, 2 March 2016.
27. www.securehaven.co.uk
28. Clemoes, Charlie, 'The San Cataldo Cemetery: Graveyard of Postmodern Architecture', www.failedarchitecture.com
29. www.dignitymemorial.com
30. www.memorialsantos.com.br
31. De Sousa, Ana, N., 'Death in the city: what happens when all our cemeteries are full?', www.theguardian.com, 21 May 2013.
32. 'Pressed For Space, Israel Building Cemetery Towers', *The Associated Press*, 17 October 2014.
33. www.lungyengroup.com.tw

34. Yates, Ronald, E., 'Over-crowded Japanese Facing a Grave Situation', www.chicagotribune.com, 14 May 1989.
35. Yoneda, Yuka, 'Vertical Cemetery's a Greenery Clad Final Resting Place for Mumbai', www.inhabitat.com, 28 August 2010.
36. Jones, Neil, R., *The Jameson Satellite*, Ace Books, 1967.
37. www.celestis.com
38. www.elysiumspace.com
39. Ibid.
40. www.celestis.com
41. www.acourseindying.com
42. www.natuurbegraafplaatshilligmeer.nl
43. www.joshuatreememorialpark.com
44. Cowling, Charles, 'Natural Burial – it's against nature!', www.goodfuneralguide.co.uk, September 2009.
45. www.naturaldeath.org.uk
46. Boret, Sebastien, 'An Anthropological Study of a Japanese Tree Burial: Environment, Kinship, and Death' in Suzuki, Hikaru, (ed.), *Death and Dying in Contemporary Japan*, Routledge, 2014, pp. 177-201.
47. www.capsulamundi.it
48. www.coeio.com
49. www.promessa.se
50. www.resomation.com
51. Lusher, Adam, 'It would be "wonderful" if people could have their dead bodies liquefied – if they wanted it, says death education expert,' *The Independent*, 18 December 2017.
52. www.heart-in-diamond.co.uk
53. www.cremationsolutions.com
54. Smith, Adam, 'AndVinyly will turn your cremated remains into a playable record', www.whathifi.com, 9 February 2017.
55. www.heavensabovefireworks.com
56. www.qpr.co.uk
57. www.cryonics.org

Select Bibliography

Acquah, Francis, 'The Impact of African Traditional Religious Beliefs and Cultural Values on Christian Muslim Relations in Ghana from 1920 through the Present', PhD Thesis, University of Exeter, 2011.

Arnold, Catharine, *Necropolis – London and Its Dead*, Simon and Schuster, 2006.

Barber, Paul, *Vampires, Burial, and Death: Folklore and Reality*, Yale University Press, 2008.

Beauchamp, Andree, 'The Black Death, Plague, and Mass Mortality', *Proceedings of the MASC*, Vol 30, 2012.

Bell, Michael, E., 'Vampires and Death in New England, 1784 to 1892', *Anthropology and Humanism*, Vol 31, Issue 2, 2006, pp. 124-140.

Betsinger, Tracy, K.; Scott, Amy, B., 'Governing from the Grave: Vampire Burials and Social Order in Post-Medieval Poland', *Cambridge Archaeological Journal*, Vol 24, Issue, 3, 2013, pp. 467-476.

Boddington, Andy, *Raunds Furnells: Anglo-Saxon Church and Churchyard*, English Heritage, 1996.

Boret, Sebastien, 'An Anthropological Study of a Japanese Tree Burial: Environment, Kinship, and Death' in Suzuki, Hikaru, (ed.), *Death and Dying in Contemporary Japan*, Routledge, 2014.

Buckberry, J. L.; Dawn, M. Hadley, 'An Anglo-Saxon Execution Cemetery at Walkington Wold, Yorkshire', *Oxford Journal of Archaeology*, Vol 26, Issue 3, 2007, pp. 309-329.

Carver, Martin, *Sutton Hoo: Burial Ground of Kings?* British Museum Press, 1998.

Crone, Rosalind et al, *Guide to the Criminal Prisons of Nineteenth-Century England*, London Publishing Partnership, 2018.

Dexeus, Ana, 'The bones of our ancestors. The end of burials in churches in the late 18th century', *Contributions to Science*, Vol 11, Issue 1, 2015, pp. 85-94.

Finlay, Nyree, 'Outside of life: traditions of infant burial in Ireland from cillin to cist', *World Archaeology*, Vol 31, Issue 3, 2010, pp. 407-422.

Geake, Helen, 'Burial Practice in Seventh – and Eighth-Century England,' in Carver, Martin, (ed.), *The Age of Sutton Hoo: The Seventh-Century in North-Western Europe*, Woodbridge, 1992.

Gilchrist, Roberta, 'Transforming medieval beliefs: the significance of bodily resurrection to medieval burial rituals', in Prusac, Marina; Hâkon, Roland; Brandt, J. Rasmus, (eds.), *Death and Changing Rituals: Function and meaning in ancient funerary practices*, Oxbow, 2014, pp. 379-96.

Gordon, Stephen, 'The Walking Dead in Medieval England: Literary and Archaeological Perspectives', PhD Thesis, University of Manchester, 2013.

Hadley, Dawn, M., 'Burying the Socially and Physically Distinctive in Later Anglo-Saxon England', in Buckberry, Jo; Cherryson, Annia. (eds.), *Burial in Later Anglo-Saxon England c. 650-1100*, Oxford, 2010, pp. 101-113.

Halsall, Guy., 'Social Change Around AD 600: An Austrian Perspective', in Carver, M (ed.), *The Age of Sutton Hoo*.

Hamza, Hani, *The Northern Cemetery of Cairo*, Cairo: The American University in Cairo Press, 2001.

Hawkins, Duncan, 'The Black Death and the new London Cemeteries of 1348', *Antiquity*, Vol 64, Issue 244, 1990, pp. 637-642.

Higham, Nicholas J.; Ryan, Martin J., *The Anglo-Saxon World*, New Haven: Yale University Press, 2013.

Hodgson, Jesslyn, E., 'Deviant Burials in Archaeology', *Anthropology Publications*, Vol 58, 2013.

Holmes, Mrs Basil [Isabella M.], *The London Burial Grounds: Notes on Their History from the Earliest Times to the Present Day*, London: T. Fisher Unwin, 1896.

Lucy, Sam, *The Anglo-Saxon Way of Death*, Stroud, 2000.

MacDonald, Michael; Murphy, Terence, R., *Sleepless Souls: Suicide in Early Modern England*, Oxford University Press, 1991, p. 383.

Mattison, Alyxandra, 'The Execution and Burial of Criminals in Early Medieval England, c. 850-1150', PhD Thesis, University of Sheffield, 2016.

Select Bibliography

McCormish, J. M.; Millward, G.; Boyle, A., 'The Medieval Cemetery of St. Leonard's Leper Hospital at Midland Road, Peterborough', York Archaeological Trust, 2017.

McKeggie, Lachlan, 'Kirkmichael, Balblair, Black Isle: Excavation and Watching Brief Report', Highland Archaeology Services Ltd, October 2017.

Freeman-Mitford, Algernon B., *Tales of Old Japan*, London: University of Michigan, 1871.

Murphy, Eileen, M., *Deviant Burial in the Archaeological Record*, Oxbow, Oxford, 2008.

Reed, David, 'The excavation of a cemetery and putative chapel site at Newhall Point, Balblair, Ross & Cromarty', *Proceedings of the Society of Antiquaries of Scotland*, Vol 125, 1995, pp. 779-791.

Reynolds, Andrew, *Anglo-Saxon Deviant Burial Customs*, Oxford University Press, 2009.

Rimmer, Jayne, 'Analysing the Skeletons Excavated at the former Female Prison: An *Insight* Report', York Archaeological Trust, 2016.

Rutherford, Sarah, *The Victorian Cemetery*, Shire Publications, 2008.

Sanmark, Alexandra, 'Power and Conversion. A Comparative Study of Christianization in Scandinavia', *Occasional Papers in Archaeology*, The University of Uppsala, 2004.

Sayer, Duncan, 'Christian Burial Practice in the Early Middle Ages: Rethinking the Anglo-Saxon Funerary Sphere', *History Compass*, Vol 11, Issue 2, 2013, pp. 133-146.

Sayer, Duncan, 'Laws, Funerals and Cemetery Organisation: The Seventh-Century Kentish Family', in Sayer, Duncan; Williams, Howard (eds.), *Mortuary Practice and Social Identities in the Middle Ages*, The Exeter University Press, 2009.

Steane, John, *The Archaeology of Medieval England and Wales*, Routledge, 2014.

Stolpe, Hjalmar; Arne, Ture, *Graffältet vid Vendel*, Stockholm, Kungliga Vitterhets-Historie-och Antikvitets Akademien, 1912.

Summers, Julie, *British and Commonwealth War Cemeteries*, Shire Publications, 2010.

Walsh, Martin, 'Throwing away the dead: communal sites for the disposal of corpses in pre-colonial south-west Tanzania', *Mvita: Bulletin of the*

Regional Centre for the Study of Archaeology in Eastern and Southern Africa, 1998, pp. 1-4.

Welsh, William, B. M., 'Classification and Analysis of Ancient Maya Burials and Burial Customs', PhD Thesis, University College London 1987.

Williams, Howard, *Death and Memory in Early Medieval Britain*, Cambridge University Press, 2006.

Williams, Howard, Mortuary practices in early Anglo-Saxon England, in Hamerow Helena; Hinton David A.; Crawford Sally, (eds.), *The Oxford Handbook of Anglo-Saxon Archaeology*, Oxford University Press, 2011.

Willsher, Betty, *Understanding Scottish Graveyards*, NMSE Publishing Ltd, 2015.

Ziegler, Philip, *The Black Death*, Sutton Publishing, 2003.